ONE HUNDRED DAYS

ONE HUNDRED DAYS

My Unexpected Journey
from Doctor to Patient

David Biro

PANTHEON BOOKS, NEW YORK

Grateful acknowledgment is made to the following for permission to reprint previously published material: *Harcourt, Inc.:* Excerpt from "East Coker" from FOUR QUARTETS by T. S. Eliot. Copyright © 1940 by T. S. Eliot and renewed 1968 by Esme Valerie Eliot. Reprinted by permission of Harcourt, Inc. • *Harvard University Press and the Trustees of Amherst College:* Poem #341 from THE POEMS OF EMILY DICKINSON, edited by Ralph W. Franklin (The Belknap Press of Harvard University Press, Cambridge, Mass.). Copyright © 1998 by the President and Fellows of Harvard College. Copyright © 1951, 1955, 1979 by the President and Fellows of Harvard College. Reprinted by permission of Harvard University Press and the Trustees of Amherst College. • *New Directions Publishing Corp.:* Excerpts from "The Injury" from COLLECTED POEMS 1939–1962, VOLUME II by William Carlos Williams. Copyright © 1953 by William Carlos Williams. Reprinted by permission of New Directions Publishing Corp. • *Ram's Horn Music:* Lyrics from "Shelter from the Storm" by Bob Dylan. Copyright © 1974, 1975 by Ram's Horn Music. All rights reserved. International copyright secured. Reprinted by permission.

LIBRARY OF CONGRESS CATALOGING-IN-PUBLICATION DATA
Biro, David, 1964–
One hundred days : my unexpected journey
from doctor to patient / David Biro.
p.   cm.
ISBN 0-375-40715-4
1. Biro, David, 1964—Health.   2. Paroxysmal nocturnal hemoglobinuria
(PNH)—Patients—New York (State)—New York—Biography.
3. Dermatologists—New York (State)—New York—Biography.
4. Bone marrow—Transplantation—Patients—New York
(State)—New York—Biography.   I. Title.
RC641.7.P37B55   2000
362.1'96151—dc21
[B]   99-34956   CIP

Random House Web Address: www.randomhouse.com

Book design by Trina Stahl Design
Printed in the United States of America
First Edition
2 4 6 8 9 7 5 3 1

For my family: Laszlo, Dolores,
Lisa, Debbie and Michele

And as always, for Daniella

When you hear hoofbeats, think horse—not zebra.

MEDICAL APHORISM

CONTENTS

PART ONE

ᮣᮝᮧ

Elusive Diagnosis

Illness is the night-side of life, a more onerous citizenship. Everyone who is born holds dual citizenship, in the kingdom of the well and in the kingdom of the sick. Although we prefer only to use the good passport, sooner or later each of us is obliged, at least for a spell, to identify ourselves as citizens of that other place.

SUSAN SONTAG, *Illness as Metaphor*

CHAPTER ONE

⛧

WEDNESDAY MORNING IN September. A brisk fall morning sends sunlight flickering through the blinds. I wake to the sweet stirrings of an old alarm clock. I am a doctor, thirty-one years old, just graduated from residency and the newest employee in my father's dermatology practice in Bay Ridge, Brooklyn. I awake, I'm not ashamed to say, with youthful vigor—life is good. My first stop is Downstate Medical School for a conference.

In the Outpatient Dermatology Clinic, patients wait in each examining room. They will be asked questions and examined by nearly thirty physicians. Later their cases will be discussed in the conference hall. The familiar faces of my residency are assembled outside the clinic. I am now an assistant professor. Dressed in a new suit, I am expected to answer rather than ask questions. The change in status is exhilarating.

There are several fascinating cases being presented today. One resident has brought in a young girl with ichthyosis, a condition named after the Greek word for fish; the girl's skin is covered with gray, adherent scales. Another patient with generalized blisters has pemphigus ("bubbles" in our Hellenized medical lingo). There is also an AIDS patient whose face is studded with numerous pimples that could easily be mistaken for acne— only he has a fungal infection called histoplasmosis that will inevitably kill him.

"David, come see my case," says an enthusiastic young resident. "It's an unknown. Tell me what you think." He refers to a patient who carries no diagnosis, a diagnostic dilemma that the department will attempt to solve collectively. As I look at the lesions on the elderly man's face, I suddenly feel a strange sensation sweep across my right eye. It's as if someone were shining a flashlight at me. It passes.

"Are you okay?" inquires the resident.

"Fine," I answer. "I just felt this weird . . . Nah, it's nothing."

Nothing. A minor disturbance, I decide, despite the fact that it continues to come and go all day. Still, it doesn't prevent me from contributing my opinion about the "unknown" case. Nor am I unable to perform my scheduled surgeries at the office later on in the afternoon. My vision remains intact, as we say in the medical profession.

On the way home that evening, I stop at my friend Tom's house. He is an ophthalmologist at a similarly early stage in his career. We play with Tom's two-month-old baby and debate which managed-care plans to join. As I am about to leave, Tom offers to examine my eyes. I resist. I'm a doctor, after all. Trained to detect signs and interpret symptoms in others, we doctors tend to dismiss our own complaints. I learned that from my father. Tom insists.

His office is in the basement of his house. I sit upright in the examining chair and read the letters on the wall, first covering my right eye, then my left. "Vision's twenty/thirty. Good. Now let's take a look inside." Tom swings around the crescent-shaped slit lamp into proper position. "Left eye looks fine." I hear his slow, heavy breathing; his face is less than an inch away from mine. "Right eye looks . . . Shit. There . . . there . . . there seems to be a problem."

A major one. The veins of my right eye are engorged and blood is spilling out into the space in front of the retina, signs of a blockage or clot in the central retinal vein. But thromboses—the medical term—don't usually happen in young, healthy adults. They occur in older patients who have abnormalities with their circulation.

Tom, who rarely loses his calm, is visibly nervous. He calls his mother, also an ophthalmologist. She is even more nervous. Tom phones the chairman of his department at Downstate Medical School. Dr. Wolintz thankfully defuses some of the alarm. He claims that, while uncommon, young people can develop thromboses like mine; he's seen it happen before. And unlike older patients, they tend to have a much better course. Nevertheless, he wants to see me tomorrow morning.

Should I be scared? I'm not sure. What do I know about the eye? I skipped that part of the body in medical school. And other than a fleeting, barely perceptible sensation, I feel great. I decide to be as confident as the expert and try to convey this to my wife, Daniella, when I tell her to cancel our dinner plans at the famous Bouley restaurant. We had waited two months for the reservation so that we could celebrate our fourth wedding anniversary in style. Tomorrow. September 14, 1995. A day of consequence. She agrees to cancel only if I promise a rain check. No problem.

The next morning, I am examined by Dr. Wolintz, who repeats the benign prognosis. There is no need for concern. Chances are, the condition will persist for several months and leave no permanent damage. It is also most likely an isolated problem; he doubts there is anything else wrong with me. To be sure, though, he sends me for a few blood tests. In rare cases, a thrombosis can be caused by a hereditary clotting disorder, an autoimmune disease (like lupus erythematosus), or even the dreaded scourge of the previous century, syphilis. I won't mention the last possibility to Daniella.

Before leaving, a host of residents are called in to see my case. They are told it is a classic that few will encounter a second time in their professional lives. One of them will undoubtedly be persuaded to present me at an ophthalmology conference. Now I am the curiosity on display.

AT LEAST I'M a relatively healthy curiosity. I go for the tests that afternoon, remaining confident they will turn out negative. A nuisance, that'll be the extent of it. Just as I had concluded in my own initial assessment. A little scary. Not the end of the world.

Thursday evenings at the office are busy sessions for me. I'm glad to be seeing patients. After my brief glimpse of patient-hood, I am unusually exuberant in my white coat.

"Those pimples are clearing up, Jenny. You're looking great. Keep up the good work."

"Warts are a funny business, Mrs. Jones. And little Michael seems to have particularly stubborn ones. Not to worry, we'll get 'em this time. Michael, a little freezing, that's all. Won't hurt a bit." I aim my liquid nitrogen gun at Michael's verucca and fire.

My next patient is Shoshanna Rubenstein, a twenty-three-year-old girl who has a severe form of alopecia areata, a mysterious disease that results in hair loss. Shoshanna has only a few clumps of hair remaining on her scalp, which she meticulously conceals with a wig. Ashamed, insecure and desperate, she wants eyebrows again; makeup isn't doing the trick. I want to help. Just as I'm about to inject the area with steroids, the nurse calls me to the phone.

"Dr. Biro?"

"Yes."

"This is Jody from Sherman Labs. Hope I'm not interrupting. Thought you might like to hear the results of your blood tests."

"Oh yeah. I completely forgot."

"Should I read the abnormal values first?"

The abnormal values?

"White count, 2.8. Hemoglobin, 10.3. Platelets, 47,000. The other tests are pending."

My insides drop, my entire body plummets downward. A sharp, rapidly expanding pain grips my spine, wraps around my throat and closes off the windpipe. For a second, I can't breathe. I need time to recover from the shock. Nothing makes sense. None of the values are normal. It's not possible. I feel fine. The needle-stick five years ago during my surgery rotation at Columbia flashes before my mind. Could it be AIDS? No, that's ridiculous. In fact, the whole thing is ridiculous. It must be a mistake. I gather myself and march back into the examining room, determined to go on seeing patients.

"Okay, Shoshanna. This won't hurt a bit." I pick up the syringe. Moving toward her eyebrows, my hand begins to shake. Maybe this isn't such a good idea after all. Embarrassed, I steady the syringe against my left hand and push the plunger forward, causing more discomfort than necessary. At that moment, I do not see Shoshanna. I am unaware of her pain. It's time to stop.

Fortunately, my father's associate is in the office and agrees to cover for me. I call home. My father takes the news with customary calm. He suggests we drive down to the local hospital and repeat the test. No use getting worked up unless we're sure of the facts.

The blood counts at Victory Memorial Hospital come back the same. There's definitely something wrong. We are sure now.

It's clear—relatively clear, although all this unexpected news is making thought increasingly difficult—that the most likely source of the problem is in the blood. My counts are blatantly abnormal. We drive back to the office and make calls, my father on one line, I on another. A friend from internship gives me the name of a hematologist at New York University. Dr. Raphael is not only an astute clinician, she assures me, he's also one of the nicest attendings on staff. Yes, I remember rounding with him when I was an intern at NYU a couple of years ago.

"Dr. Raphael," I say when the page operator finally connects me. "I hope I'm not bothering you." It is 9:45 P.M. "You probably don't remember me, but I have a problem and didn't know where else to turn."

"What's up?"

I tell him about my eye. I tell him about my blood tests.

There's a pause on the line.

Then he asks, "How have you been feeling lately?"

"Fine."

"Then there's only one way to find out what's going on. We have to do a bone marrow biopsy. How's first thing tomorrow morning? Can you be at my office at eight-thirty?"

"Of course. I really appreciate this, Dr. Raphael."

"That's quite all right. Just get a good night's rest. There's nothing we can do right now. We'll know soon enough."

Know what?

Do I want to know?

A good night's rest?

What will I tell Daniella?

Nothing yet. I am determined to hold my breath for the next twelve hours.

CHAPTER TWO

꩜

M Y WIFE AND I rent an apartment across the street from
NYU Medical Center. It was convenient for me during
internship. Now it's more so for Daniella. She manages the
commercial division at Giorgio Armani in the Flatiron district
of downtown New York. It's less than a mile away, so she walks
to and from work every day. Today she stands indecisively at the
door. My wife is never indecisive. "Shouldn't I come?" she asks.

"Nah," I answer. "It's nothing, just a few more stupid tests."

I lie. Another pearl acquired from Dad—and I suspect a
common trait among older and more paternalistically minded
physicians: Never share medical details and concerns with the
family, especially when those details are sketchy. Since they may
not understand, it will only create unnecessary panic.

I'm in the Medical Center at eight o'clock Friday morning,
waiting for an elevator to take me up to the ninth floor. Hematology and Oncology. It looks eerily familiar. Two years ago, I
was on the same floor with one of my best friends. Rema had
had stomach cancer and was there for a checkup. Diagnosed
when she was twenty-five years old and successfully treated by
surgery and chemotherapy, she was then in remission. But

Rema never believed it. She was terrified the cancer would come back. I tried to convince her otherwise. "You're nuts. Gastric carcinoma is a bad disease. If it was gonna come back, it would've come back already. You made it, Rema. It's over, I'm sure. Stop worrying."

I was wrong. The cancer returned on its five-year anniversary. I went to see her doctor when I found out. He was devastated. There were tears in his eyes—he too must have believed she was cured.

The months following Rema's relapse were hell. She died just last June. And as I sit here once again in the Hematology/Oncology waiting room, I am reminded of the many visits to her many hospital beds: NYU, Memorial Sloan-Kettering, and finally that rinky-dink hospital in Philadelphia, the only place that would take her. In no time, Rema went from being a spirited woman who once flaunted her beauty in television commercials to a swollen, deformed comatose body, the state she was in when I last saw her. My heart is pounding as I wait for the doctor, staring blindly at a *Sports Illustrated* magazine that somehow managed to slip into my hands.

"You can go in now," said the secretary. "Down the hall and to the—"

I bounce up and am halfway down the hall before she finishes her sentence.

"Sit down, David. Give me a minute and I'll be right with you." Dr. Raphael, sitting behind his desk, is writing frantically on a pad. He is a good-looking man, curly brown hair, dark complexion, gentle, well-proportioned features, in his late forties, early fifties. There are pictures of his wife and children on the walls, diplomas from Toronto. A Canadian. I trust the man at once.

"Okay," he says, clearing the papers from his desk. "Let's get a little history first."

I tell him exactly what has transpired over the preceding two days. I answer his questions. No, no other medical problems; no prior surgeries or hospitalizations; no family history of cancer or any other diseases. I gave up smoking last year. I exercise daily. I am the spitting image of Health. I am Salus, for Christ's sake, the fucking God of Health.

"Good. We'll go next door where I can examine you and take the biopsy."

He looks in my eyes. Listens to my heart and lungs, taps on my belly, surveys the skin over my legs and palpates my testicles. The exam takes less than five minutes. We both know it's a formality; the answer doesn't lie with these surface pokings and proddings. It is lodged deep inside my body, in the marrow.

The bone marrow. An organ famous for its depth, its centrality, its location at the very core of the body. One is chilled to the marrow, we say; one is wounded to the marrow, pierced to the marrow by love's caprice. More concretely and familiar to admirers of Italian cuisine, the marrow is also the substance one extracts from the veal shank in osso buco: fatty, succulent and delicious. But it is much more than an idea, a phrase or an Italian delicacy, as I will soon come to appreciate.

The marrow is a living tissue that fills the cavities of most of the bones in the body. While it contains a good deal of fat, the marrow's chief component is stem cells. These cells give rise to the entire panoply of our blood cells: red cells that provide oxygen, white cells that fight infection and platelets that stop bleeding. A problem with this organ, as you might imagine, would have far-reaching implications.

My blood counts are abnormal, yet they are not depressed

enough to cause symptoms. I am anemic (the red cells are low), but I'm not tired and haven't experienced shortness of breath. I am leukopenic (low white count), but I haven't had any more colds or other infections than would be expected. And I am severely thrombocytopenic (low platelets), but I haven't had bleeding problems or noticed any bruising. Evidently, the bone marrow has a large reserve before trouble begins.

"We know there's something wrong with your marrow," Dr. Raphael continues. "The only way to be more specific is to do a biopsy. So turn over on your right side, away from me, and let's get this show on the road." I try not to recall my own pitiful attempt at performing a bone marrow biopsy during internship. Despite excellent guidance from the hematology Fellow on call, I was too revolted to carry it through. The sound of grinding bone, mingled with my patient's screams, unnerved me. Please, I pray, let him be as gentle as he looks.

There is a splash of cool as he cleans the skin above my buttocks with Betadine; the marrow-rich pelvic bone is the preferred location for the procedure. "You'll feel a prick as I numb the area." He injects lidocaine to anesthetize the skin. He pushes deeper and deeper until the needle strikes bone. "Numbing the bone makes the biopsy less painful." Not that bad, so far.

"Now for the aspirate. You won't feel the needle, only when I draw back the fluid." He exchanges a small needle for a much larger one. The Illinois—the name of the infusion needle sounds more like a naval destroyer—slides in easily through skin. He has to force it into bone; it is starting to hurt. Then waves of pain as he sucks the marrow into the syringe. Brief sucks, a few seconds long, I jump with each one.

"Good. All we have left is the biopsy. I bet you'll remember this day. September fifteenth. Tax day." Tax day? I thought that happened in April. At the time, I wasn't aware of estimated taxes, so the comment didn't hit home. Not so with the Jamshidi needle. It is headed, all ten inches of shiny stainless steel, straight for my hip. He plunges it into bone. That awful grinding noise. A dull, burning pain. Even the memory hurts.

"Some people don't feel a thing. Others leap right off the table. You were somewhere in the middle." He is trying to be nice; I'm definitely more squeamish than most. After putting on a bandage, he sends me to the lab for blood tests and tells me to come back in two hours for the results.

Time passes quickly enough when I am doing—bloodletting, running from lab to lab, making telephone calls. It slows when the list of activities is exhausted. There is a complete stoppage as I take my seat in the waiting room again. Twenty minutes to go. My mind is racing. Thoughts are flying, one after another, mostly out of sequence.

Cancer. No one wants to utter the word. But it is there, a bold-lettered banner, streaking across the sky. That's the issue here. Leukemia or not? Images of Rema receiving chemotherapy float by. She is weak, unable to take my hand, unable to form a smile. How would I look bald? How would I look with cancer? Can this really be happening? To me?

The clock on the wall is a stagnant pond; algae is accumulating on the top curve. I follow the second hand. It is the only thing moving. I want to push it along.

And yet there is a pushing taking place that I'm not seeing. Because I'm a physician, Dr. Raphael has pushed aside his schedule. He runs the marrow aspirate to the lab himself and asks them to rush the staining process. He wants to assess the marrow and provide answers in two hours. Answers that an ordinary citizen could expect to wait several days before receiving.

Watching the clock go round. How horrible. And how lucky I am at the same time.

FINALLY, DR. RAPHAEL appears. I nervously follow him back to his office.

"I'll tell you the truth. I expected to find leukemia, but it's not there." Missing from the marrow sample are blast cells—large, immature, dark-staining monsters that are easily distinguished from normal white blood cells. Able to elude the normal differentiation process and grow autonomously, blasts signify cancer.

I breathe easier, recovering control over my body and its movements again. "So what is there?" I ask.

"The marrow is abnormal. The number of cells is reduced, especially the megakaryocyte line. But we already know that from your counts. We'll have to wait for the chromosomal analysis and some other tests I ordered."

"What are the possibilities?"

"There are a couple. Aplastic anemia. A viral infection. A myelodysplastic or preleukemic syndrome. But no use talking about it. Let's see what turns up. Main thing is that you don't have leukemia."

True.

"There's also something called PNH," he adds. "Paroxysmal nocturnal hemoglobinuria. Remember that from medical school?"

No.

"That would fit most closely with the findings. We'll see what the tests show."

Tests, waiting. More tests, more waiting. Names of diseases I've never heard of. Like the clot in my eye, this is not my field.

I know very little about myelodysplasia and PNH. I am moving into uncharted territory. I'm a patient now. How odd.

"I also scheduled an MRI for tomorrow. I want to make sure there's nothing in the orbit that caused the thrombosis. All right?"

"Fine."

Or so I think. On Saturday morning, accompanied by Daniella, I arrive at NYU's MRI center. After changing into a gown, I sit uneasily on the skinny table at the foot of the machine.

"Have you ever had an MRI?" asks the technician.

No.

He explains: You lie down, your head fits under the cage, the table slides into the machine, there are loud sounds, like a drum. It takes less than an hour.

"But why am I telling you this? You're a doc. You know all about it, right?"

I am surprised by how little I know.

"Let's do a trial run. Take this gadget. If you need to get out, push the button."

I lie down. A metal cage is secured over my head. The table creeps backward. Entering darkness. No way to move. The walls are closing in. I am trapped. I can't breathe. Shit. I'm screaming. Jamming the button. Help. Help. Help.

When I'm released and flapping my limbs again, the technician tries to reassure me. Relax, it happens. It can be scary in there. Nothing a little Valium won't take care of.

Is he kidding? All the Valium in the world wouldn't get me back into that contraption. I've always been anxious in small places, but this, this tiny sliver of airless space, goes way beyond small. They'd have to knock me out. Full-fledged general anesthesia. No degree of shame will make me waver in this decision.

"Give me a minute with my husband," says Daniella, standing over me while she waves away the tech. My wife is an imposing woman—almost six feet tall, slender and with a fierce, determined gaze. Though she's light-skinned, her long dark hair and Roman nose make her look Mediterranean, a strong-willed Italian diva. Gradually, the imperious expression with which she dispatched the tech yields to a smile as she folds up her limbs and crouches down beside me. "Come on, honey," she coaxes. "I'll stay with you."

Quickly realizing the effort is futile, she begins to laugh—at me, at her, at us, at the entire lunacy of it all. I can't help laughing with her. It was this fluid mix of strength and humor that attracted me to Daniella when she first appeared in my doorway seven years ago, a serendipitous gift from Roommate Finders. I was drawn to her instantly.

"I'll hold your hand." A last-ditch attempt. Daniella has become well acquainted with my phobias. She has talked me through tense situations before.

Not today. I'll take a CAT scan instead, even though it means more radiation and less sensitivity. Unbelievable, I want to scream. Doctors order MRIs by the thousands. And when they don't, patients demand them. Surely they have no idea how it feels—to be buried alive in a high-tech coffin.

CHAPTER THREE

N O RELEVANT INFORMATION is gleaned from the various and sundry tests performed over the next several days. CAT scan negative. A coagulation profile reveals no abnormalities. Thyroid function tests are within normal limits. Viral titers and hepatitis screen negative. The water-sucrose test for PNH negative. Chromosomal studies of the bone marrow do not show any genetic mutations.

"So where do we stand?" I ask Dr. Raphael on week two of my odyssey into the labyrinths of patienthood.

"Nothing solid turned up. That's good and bad. Basically it means we'll just have to wait and see. Look, you're fine right now. It's only the numbers that are screwy."

"It would be nice to know what's wrong."

"There's a department conference tomorrow. We'll be discussing your case. I'll let you know. By the way, how's the eye?"

"Annoying. I still get that weird sensation. Dr. Wolintz said it may last up to a year."

AFTER MY APPOINTMENT, I head for the medical school library to do some investigating of my own. I request the standard hematology text at the reference section and lug the ten-pounder to the nearest cubicle. We'll start with aplastic anemia, a disease of bone marrow failure; the marrow simply can't gen-erate enough blood cells to meet the body's needs. There is a list of causes: medications, environmental toxins, viruses. Bactrim is one of the drugs mentioned. I had taken it for a month about two years ago. Could that have damaged my marrow? Unlikely. The water in our apartment is filthy. I've rinsed under many a brown shower. Would that count for an environmental toxin? Nah. The book goes on to say that these types of aplastic ane-mia are generally short-lived; the marrow usually recovers over time.

My enthusiasm is also short-lived as I read on. It appears that these definitive cause-and-effect cases make up less than 5 percent of the total number. The most common cause of aplas-tic anemia is idiopathic. In plain language, that means there's no known cause. A lovely play of words reminiscent of Homer—I am no man, says Odysseus to the Cyclops. The cause is no cause, says medicine to itself. Wily doctors—when they're most clueless, they tack on the fancy Greek label "idiopathic." And medicine is filled with idiopathies. As you scan the literature, you will find that it heads the list of causes for just about every disease from hypertension to urticaria. We know next to noth-ing about everything (including etymology—*idio* comes from the Greek word that means "personal" or "your own"; idio-pathic disease should really refer to a personal disease or perhaps a disease as it plays out in the individual; instead, it refers to mystery diseases that affect the generic Everyman).

Fortunately, idiopathic aplastic anemia is not very common. PNH, on the other hand, as I discover in the next chapter, is in a class by itself. It's a perfect example of what doctors call a zebra ("When you hear hoofbeats," goes the aphorism, "think horse, not zebra."). Literally, less than one in a million people contracts this rare disease each year. The typical patient presents to his physician with a combination of bone marrow failure and blood clots. Often this is accompanied by a history of episodic dark-colored urine at night; hence the name paroxysmal nocturnal hemoglobinuria. Reading the chapter's concluding lines, I shudder: "PNH is a devastating disease. Over time, most patients succumb."

Succumb—what a dramatic word for a scientific text, a brutal euphemism. But I'm determined to ignore it. The water sucrose test, "the gold standard for diagnosing PNH," as it states on page 872, is negative in my case, and my urine, I swear, has always been a dashing yellow.

"WE THINK YOU have PNH," proclaims Dr. Raphael the day after the departmental conference. "That was the consensus. Nothing else fits."

"What about the tests? And the fact that there's never been a trace of blood in my urine?"

"It doesn't always happen. Besides, there's a new test for PNH. It's much more sensitive than the others."

He is referring to a highly sophisticated blood test developed a few years ago as researchers began to unravel the pathogenesis of the disease. PNH, we now know, is caused by a genetic mutation in bone marrow stem cells. (Why this happens, of course, is still up for grabs—another idiopathy for the books.) The mutation results in defective progeny spawned by the stem cell. Specifically, second- and third-generation cells, known as daughter cells, lack important protein markers carried on their surfaces. This presumably makes them more susceptible to hemolysis (red blood cell destruction) and the formation of thromboses (platelet aggregation). At the moment, my blood cells are being evaluated in NYU's hematology lab for the missing markers. Dr. Raphael promises to let me know the results as soon as they're back—day or night.

I pray the doctors are wrong. I want nothing to do with PNH and its succumbings. Of the possibilities, I am praying for the virus behind door number three. It seems like the best way out of this mess. As the textbook says, "Viral causes of marrow failure usually resolve spontaneously." Come on, virus.

ON SATURDAY, DANIELLA and I have breakfast at the Moonstruck Diner. I'm a big fan of their Popeye omelet (spinach, onions and swiss cheese). She loves the corn beef hash. "This is all going to turn out to be nothing," decides Daniella as she wipes her mouth with a napkin. She hasn't read the hematology textbook. I haven't filled her in on all the details. "A big misunderstanding. Look at you." I have just polished off my omelet and am reaching into Daniella's plate for her leftovers. "You can't possibly be sick."

After breakfast, Daniella goes to get her nails done and I walk home. A message is blinking on the answering machine.

"David, it's Bruce Raphael. I just spoke to Dr. Gates at the lab. The test came back negative. You don't have PNH! Enjoy your weekend."

The news leaves me swooning. It races through my veins like a tornado, gathering momentum. A winning lottery ticket worth millions wouldn't make me more ecstatic. I rush out of the apartment to track down my wife. Like a madman, I hurtle from one nail salon to the next. She is nowhere. I wait on the corner, peering up one street, down another. It's a beautiful fall

day and I am free, rescued from the throes of a savage killer. I
need to scream. I need to tell someone. Anyone.

There's a pay phone across the street. "Dad, Mom, I just got
the message. It's not PNH." My father, who like me was unfamiliar with the disease and just as scared, is relieved. So is my
mother. She's been talking to friends about my problem. Mrs.
Sclafani's son, she learned, also had a mysterious illness the doctors couldn't identify. He had fevers and lost forty pounds, then
miraculously made a full recovery despite a barrage of gloomy
prognoses. "You'll be like the Sclafani boy," she announces confidently.

After my parents, I call friends—Tom, Steven, Kenny, Ellen.
Whomever's phone number I can remember, until I see my wife
strolling down the street, nails glistening in the sun. A slow-
moving scene from a Zeffirelli movie—I sweep her off her feet
and sing sweet tidings in her ear.

CHAPTER FOUR

⚬

It's NOT PNH. Still, I have no diagnosis. The bad stuff has been ruled out, but nothing definite has been pinpointed. The plan is to wait and see, to be a patient patient. I am fine at the moment. Blood tests will be done every week to make sure the numbers aren't heading in the wrong direction.

Celebration gives way to uncertainty. I am a doctor, after all, New York City–born and –bred. Jewish to the angst-ridden marrow. I simply can't wait. I want answers. I demand answers. Dr. Raphael gives us the name of a specialist on marrow failure at Sloan-Kettering. I make some calls and get more names. By the end of the day, I have put together a directory of specialists from New York to Tokyo via Helsinki. My father suggests staying local for the time being. Appointments are scheduled on Monday and Wednesday with a few *machers* at Memorial Sloan-Kettering Cancer Center.

I'm not happy about visiting Sloan-Kettering. In my mind, it's one step away from the graveyard. Too many horror stories like my friend Rema's are associated with the place; they crowd my thoughts as I enter the outpatient wing on Sixty-seventh Street Monday morning. There is also the smell of hospital—

antiseptics and detergents trying to cover up the odors of the sick. I've never liked it as a doctor; it's even worse as a patient.

The waiting room for the Hematology Clinic is packed. Most patients are as hairless as Shoshanna, the young woman with alopecia areata I am treating. Some wear masks. There is one man with vague bluish marks over his face and scalp. As a skin doctor, I'm embarrassed to admit that I'm not sure what's wrong with him. I am sure, however, that he, along with the rest of the people in the room, is very sick. I am not comfortable. Neither is Daniella, nor are my parents, who insisted on coming with me.

We meet Dr. Hugo Castro-Malaspina for the first time. He fits into the solemn Sloan atmosphere well. Unlike Raphael at NYU, Castro has few jokes in his repertoire. Dark, medium height and build, with full beard, he is quiet and reserved—a man of few words, direct, to the point, a little too businesslike for my taste.

Dr. Castro has reviewed all the data and slides sent over from NYU. His assessment is far from encouraging. It looks like a case of aplastic anemia, moderate in severity. The marrow usually deteriorates over time. I will eventually require transfusions and perhaps immunosuppressive therapy. Fifty percent of patients go on to develop leukemia. The only cure is bone marrow transplantation. However, this has a 20-to-40 percent mortality. He wants all three of my sisters to be typed immediately. If we decide on transplantation, we need to know if there's a match.

I am not prepared for Sloan. Neither are Daniella and my parents. We are not prepared for such dire predictions, for those frigid, steely numbers. Statistics of death and dying. Are you kidding? Take a good look, pal, I'm healthier than you are. Why the gloom-and-doom speech? And all this gibberish about transplantation? And the outpouring of pity? I see it in Castro's eyes—bad luck for the young doctor, they seem to say, and it's only going to get worse. I thank him, vowing to stay as far away from Castro and his pitying eyes as possible. I'm in desperate need of a more positive forecast. My parents and Daniella, equally rattled, equally outraged, agree.

Having finished with doctor number two, we are certain that number three will have more pleasant things to say. A large man with red hair, rosy cheeks and an impish smile, Dr. Silver, chairman of Sloan's Hematology Department, swaggers into the examining room on Wednesday afternoon. He has an entourage of five Fellows in tow, de rigueur for a bigshot at a prestigious teaching institution. The crew barely squeezes into the room before Silver delivers his decree. There is a twinkle in his eyes, a grin swiftly spreading over his features: "We've made a diagnosis," he announces, then pauses for effect. "You have PNH."

Once again, the floor drops, my knees buckle, and only by grabbing onto the examining table do I prevent myself from falling. The doctor hasn't even introduced himself before flinging this ludicrous piece of information at me. It must be a mistake. I will correct him. Excuse me, Dr. Silver, you've got the wrong man. I have an ordinary case of aplastic anemia and had already been tested for—

"The test was repeated on Monday by Dr. Castro," he says, recognizing my confusion. "We have the world's expert in PNH right here, Lucento Lucenti. He has a more sensitive test than NYU. There's no doubt."

His grin would expand beyond the borders of his face if possible. This is a great day for the chief. A rare disease with an even rarer presentation (central retinal vein thrombosis) walks through his door. An excellent teaching case for the flock. Better yet, the case was missed by a downtown competitor. But here at superior Sloan, the riddle is solved in a flash. And to top it off, the leading expert in the field has just arrived from the Hammersmith Institute in London to set up a genetics department. Silver's grin, flushed with pride, serves up a rhetorical question: Are you impressed, my young friend, or what?

"I'm going to see if I can get Luigi Lucsanto to come down. Meanwhile, I'd like my Fellows to examine you. Do you mind?"

No, not at all. Poke and prod anywhere you want. Violate and pillage me if it will help. One doctor shines the ophthalmoscope into my eyes for ten minutes, then apologizes for his lack of skill. Another gropes at my neck to feel for lymph nodes. He mistakes my attempts to pull away for anxiety. "Don't worry so much. Luzziolo Lubiolo is the best. You're lucky he's here in New York. You're really lucky."

I am wondering about the phantom expert—Lucento Lucenti, Luigi Lucsanto, Luzziolo Lubiolo. Does such a person actually exist? And why all the confusion with his name?

I do not have to wonder long. After a thorough going over by the boys, a small man with an aquiline nose and warm brown eyes enters the room.

"You must be Dr. Biro," he says in a hearty Italian accent. "I am Lucio Luzzatto." At this point, Dr. Silver, still grinning, takes his leave, assuring me that I will be in better hands with the recent import from Europe.

"You seem nervous," says Luzzatto, looking directly into my eyes. He takes my hand in his. "Don't worry. PNH isn't necessarily so bad. I have many patients who are doing quite well. When I see you again, I'll bring an article. You will see."

He makes me feel good instantly. Castro, Silver and even Raphael begin to disintegrate in my mind. I have a diagnosis. I have a doctor. The world's leading expert, full of compassion, optimistic about my condition. He is my deus ex machina—the god in stories who rescues the hero just when you think it's all over. Maybe the hematology Fellow was right. Maybe I am lucky.

THE SPECTACLE OF MEDICINE

But to look in order to know, to show in order to teach, is not this a tacit form of violence, all the more abusive for its silence, upon a sick body that demands to be comforted, not displayed. Can pain be spectacle?

MICHEL FOUCAULT, *The Birth of the Clinic*

DOCTORS, AND I am no exception, love a good zebra. Not the ones with black stripes that roam the African bush. I'm talking about patients with rare, exotic diseases like PNH. We crowd around to see them, touch them, photograph them. We put them on display at conferences. We write their stories in journals. We do all this, I suspect, because they reawaken the spirit that first pushed us into medicine: a fascination with the human body, its incredible achievements and its terrifying failings.

In three quick months, I have not only relinquished my place in the safari of medicine but have become its object, its hunted. I've metamorphosed into a zebra on two unsettling occasions: first when my eye clot was discovered and second when the diagnosis of PNH was made. The fact is, I'm a lot more comfortable in my primary role as physician.

Medicine for me has always been a window onto the neglected world of the human body. Ordinarily, people don't take much note of their bodies. We work, we play, we sex—all of which ultimately depend on an accommodating body—but we do so unreflectively. A runner runs the marathon, he doesn't think about how the heart must pump or the cells must break down fat and sugar to fuel that furiously beating organ. Kasparov moves his bishop to pawn three, thinking two steps ahead and three steps back, but rarely about what makes all this thinking possible. Then again, if we were constantly thinking about such things, we wouldn't be able to run the race or make the move.

When the machine breaks down, however, and the body becomes ill, people in general and physicians in particular are forced to take a closer look. The heart of a man after a major heart attack doesn't work well anymore. You can see it in his legs, hear it in his lungs—fluid is accumulating in places where it shouldn't because the pump is failing. The man can hardly walk up a flight of stairs before losing his breath; the gossamer-like membrane of the lungs becomes clunky, unable to expand, with excess fluid. A woman with rheumatoid arthritis inevitably requires a knee replacement. The cartilage around the knee has been mutilated by her own immune system. For some reason, the body is attacking itself. There is a breach in its sacred code—it's no longer capable of distinguishing self from foe. A patient with AIDS has the opposite problem. A virus has caused a weakening of his immune system. The patient is no longer able to subdue minor organisms that a normal person routinely shrugs off. He gets white stuff called thrush on his tongue and a flaking of the face and scalp called seborrheic dermatitis.

Medicine, it could be said, operates for the most part in the reverse order. We first encounter and learn about the body in its defective or abnormal states. Disease is the key to knowledge. It provides important clues about how the body works in normal circumstances. We understand the heart better because we have seen heart-failure patients, the immune system because we have treated autoimmune diseases and AIDS. And this is doubly true for the zebras of medicine. Rare conditions like PNH not only add spice to our professional lives but are typically more illuminating than their more common counterparts.

A year before my own diagnosis, I presented a paper at a dermatology conference about a patient named José who had developed blisters in his eyes, mouth and throat. Over time, the blisters led to scarring and José's eyesight and breathing became compromised. I sent samples of tissue and blood to several researchers who studied cicatricial pemphigoid, as the disease category is known. They concluded that the patient didn't fit into the textbooks. He had antibodies to a protein no one ever heard of or knew existed. The protein (now called epiligrin), as it turns out, is essential to the integrity of the basement membrane of the skin. Without epiligrin, the skin doesn't hold together; it separates and forms blisters. We know this because some unlucky person contracted a "new" or hitherto unrecognized disease.

Illness opens a window. It allows us to see what takes place beneath the body's surface. From studies in both the clinic and the lab, physicians have begun to understand much of what they observe. Still a great deal remains mysterious, untapped, which only enhances our curiosity. The journey—encountering unusual cases, conferring with colleagues, engaging in research—is often as exciting as the destination.

Before I became sick, this is what the fascination of medicine meant to me. Since then, I confess, that meaning has broadened. Along with the shift in perspective, my story has been turned on its head. Like José, I am now a patient. *I* am the interesting case. What's going on in *my* body is fascinating. Illness is happening to me, not someone else in the next room. The comfort of remove has vanished.

I don't mean to suggest that physicians are entirely ignorant of how it feels to be a patient. After all, we deal with real people who are sick, who are dying, day after day. Pain, shame and fear are right before our eyes. We must have an inkling. Perhaps.

José and I were the same age when we first met. He was disfigured by the blisters and in pain. Chemotherapy wasn't working. I felt awful for him and wanted to help in any way possible. But this is more sympathy than empathy, where there is an exchange of seats, of points of view. I'm not making value judgments. The distance is important. If a doctor tried to put himself in every patient he saw, he'd be a lunatic by nightfall.

There is great sympathy, small empathy in medicine. At the same time, there's another emotion at play that is even more troubling. In the room with José, I felt terrible. Outside the room, I was excited, ecstatic. I had caught my first zebra. I wanted to show him to my colleagues, present him at a conference, write a paper about him. It was the case of the century.

I did not and do not miss the irony here. I was aware of the contradictory nature of my feelings. I felt guilty—being fascinated while José couldn't breathe. It was horrible, unfair. And it didn't help that knowledge was being gained, that studies on José's blood would lead to the identification of a new subtype of cicatricial pemphigoid, that this new subtype might respond differently to medication, and that, ultimately, José might make it easier for patients after him.

Now I was in José's chair. First at the ophthalmologist in

early September and later that month at Sloan-Kettering. I sat
meekly by as the doctors shuffled in and out, poking and prod-
ding, muttering under their breaths. I knew what they were
thinking, saw it in their eyes. I wanted to scream: Who the hell
do you think you're kidding with this pity routine? You'll be
chatting about my case at cocktail parties for the next decade.
Yes, I'm a zebra. So what? You don't have to dance in my face.

We doctors have an inkling. We're also aware that there's
something wrong about our divided and divisive feelings. But
medicine has always been a spectacle at the expense of sick people. For the person in the chair, the body everybody is gawking
at, the source of interest, it is downright degrading. This is the
other side—you might call it a subplot—of the fascination
story. And like the main plot, this side is also taught in medical
school. With much less fanfare, of course, but surely not to be
missed.

Any medical student who rotates through neurology will
tell you about Grand Rounds. Held in a large auditorium or
lecture hall, it features the patient du jour, wheeled out (neurology patients usually don't walk) to center stage after everyone
has taken their seats. The physician presenting the case stands at
a podium to the patient's right. The show begins.

After a brief history, the presenter will examine the patient.
The audience is encouraged to interrupt at any time. Mr. Jones,
can you lift your leg for us? Not really. (Of course he can't, the
man is paralyzed.) Can you wiggle your toe? (If there were any
movement, you'd need a magnifying glass to detect it.) That's
better. Now touch your finger to your nose. (The finger jerks
left, jerks right, then pirouettes into the left eye.) Obvious cere-
bellar dysfunction. Let us continue. . . .

Popcorn, anyone? Applause from the audience? Now tell
me—is this so different from parading the Elephant Man around

at the circus? Barnum & Bailey were always on the lookout for an exotic disease. Remember the Wolf Man (he had porphyria), Alligator Man (ichthyosis), the Siamese twins and the rest of the infamous zebras at the circus. On par with the clowns for entertainment value.

I'm exaggerating a little. There is a difference. At Grand Rounds, a patient is on display for a group of physicians, not the general public. The purpose is to instruct, not entertain. And in many cases, the patient benefits from the exchange of opinions.

But it's still a spectacle. A person who has already been stripped of citizenship in the normal, healthy world, is made to bare himself and his infirmity, to parade it in front of a group of strangers, to play the role of freak, and, in many cases, get nothing out of it. Of course, there is always the glimmer of hope that someone in the audience will have a brainstorm, a flash of medical insight. But the majority of neurology patients have conditions like multiple sclerosis and Lou Gehrig's disease, which we currently can't do much about. We wheel them around, talk about the case for hours, gawk, then watch them languish and die.

Unfortunately, the spectacle is necessary to medicine. There is no other way to teach and disseminate information as effectively. Surely, though, we can make it more dignified for patients. At the dermatology conferences at Downstate, patients wait in an examining room. Only one or two doctors are allowed to enter at a time. The relative privacy makes the experience less degrading. Yet even at Downstate, the spectacle is not free. There's a price to pay and the patient is footing the bill. As long as we understand that.

RESUMING MY ROLE as doctor, I try to remember this. But fresh as my experience with patienthood is, I forget. Last week, a patient came to the office with numerous lumps under his skin and on the surface of his eyes that had developed over a period of three weeks. I'd never seen anything so dramatic. I rushed for my camera and shot a roll of film. I had him come back the next day when my father was in. He shouldn't miss this impressive case.

It turned out my patient had leukemia, an extremely severe form. He will most likely need a bone marrow transplant. I am torn by conflicting feelings. By sympathy and fascination.

PART TWO

WAITING GAME

Viewed from a balcony, the whole thing would doubtless have been weirdly picturesque.

STEPHEN CRANE, "The Open Boat"

CHAPTER FIVE

⌒

THERE IS A positive side to having a diagnosis, even when it's a bad one. Although PNH scares me, there's an end to uncertainty. I know what's wrong. No more curve balls, or so I hope.

I am also relieved about the way things turned out. Not only do I have the world's expert in PNH as a doctor, but he happens to be Italian. A small detail, insignificant to most. Except me. I'm a sucker for anything and everything Italian. The first phrases issuing from the mouth of my new physician, accompanied by a Toscanini gesturing of his right hand, are like the sweet melodies of Italian opera. Pavarotti singing from *La Bohème*—*"Che gelida manina."* Tears well involuntarily at the corners of my eyes. I want to embrace him on the spot. Only with tremendous effort am I able to refrain.

There are reasons behind my passion for all things Italian. They start with my maternal grandfather. Although he was born and raised in Brooklyn, Poppy Jim's family came from a small town in the hills outside Naples. Traditions crossed the Atlantic with the Macchiarolis. Poppy was full of energy, of spirit. He loved to eat, joke and lavish attention on his children and grandchildren. Because I was the firstborn and only male in my family, I was his *preferito*. I helped him roll ravioli. I planted seeds in his vegetable garden on Fire Island. I cheered for his favorite baseball team. We talked loudly and laughed recklessly. Poppy died when I was fifteen. It was my first encounter with pain.

Along with Poppy Jim, there were many Italians in the neighborhood when I was growing up in Bay Ridge. This middle-class community in Brooklyn was a melting pot—Arabs, Jews, Scandinavians, Asians, Irish and Italians. While in the minority, Italians were the loudest and most visible. They had a passion for living that reminded me of Poppy Jim.

Nothing, however, prepared me for my first visit to Italy. I went to Rome during winter break of my sophomore year in college. The previous summer, I'd met an Italian girl while purportedly studying Spanish in Salamanca, Spain. Although my relationship with Barbara didn't last, I fell in love with Rome. Barbara took me all over the ancient city. I walked through the Forum piecing together stones in my mind and recalling Horace's odes and Catullus's *nugae*—"Give me a thousand kisses, my darling Lesbia, then a hundred more. . . ." I stuffed my face with bucatini, drank Frascati and afterward went to drool over Michelangelo's *Pietà* and Bernini's *Saint Theresa*. I wound around the city with the Tiber River and looked down upon its domes and rooftops from the Janiculum Hill. I was mesmerized, didn't want to leave. I felt at home in Rome.

All of which makes the total meltdown I experience in the presence of Lucio Luzzatto somewhat intelligible. What an incredible set of circumstances. Of all the doctors in New York City, in walks a gentleman from Genoa. He walks into *my* room, a room so acutely receptive to his charming accent. Why not a monk from Tibet or an Aussie from Down Under, or even a

Chechnyan on the run? Coincidence or plan? I'm still not ready to believe in God.

ONE WEEK AFTER meeting Dr. Luzzatto, we make a formal appointment. Sloan-Kettering seems less threatening this time. I am the only patient scheduled—it is Luzzatto's first clinic since arriving in New York.

"Well, Dr. Biro, how are you today?" asks Luzzatto with a warm smile. "You look quite well and that is the most important thing, you know, the clinical impression."

No disagreement there.

"I brought the article I promised. We'll have time to review it. First, I'd like to take a history and examine you."

Luzzatto is of the old, European school—slow, methodical and painstakingly thorough. I am with him for nearly two hours. Absolutely unheard of in a country of fast food and maybe even faster medicine. I still wonder whether he's a phantom of my imagination, of Sloan-Kettering's imagination. One thing is certain: He won't be a big hit with the HMOs.

"I looked over your tests and bone marrow slides," he says after completing his exam. "I'm very optimistic. PNH is a complex disease. There is a spectrum of severity. A few cases are bad, a few extremely benign and most fall somewhere in the middle. I have seen many patients improve spontaneously."

Lovely word, "spontaneously," especially sung softly in Italian undertones. Only I'm a little confused. What about the stuff I read in the textbook, the succumbings that are an integral part of PNH? What about Castro's dire predictions?

He senses my concern. "I have many patients with PNH who are doing fine. I even have a few in whom the disease just disappeared. PNH is not as bad as we used to think."

"What about me? Where do I fit in?"

"Difficult to say with certainty. There's a chance your blood counts may get better with time."

"Really?"

"Sure."

"Can you give me a number, a percent?" I'm pushing it. There's no way Luzzatto can provide me with statistics; there aren't enough patients with the disease.

He shrugs his shoulders. But unwilling to disappoint for long, he obliges with a smile: "Let us say fifty-fifty. But that's not what I want you to focus on. The point is, we don't know, and that's why we should remain calm and not do anything rash."

"Dr. Castro is typing my three sisters to see whether they match my bone marrow. He said I might need a transplant."

"It's important to know whether transplantation is an option. In my opinion, though, it would be your last option, the very last one. Bone marrow transplants, as I'm sure you're aware, have a very high mortality. People die from them. It's one thing to offer the procedure to a cancer patient that has failed every other type of treatment. But you're not in that position. In fact, you hardly have any symptoms. How could we seriously justify such a radical step at this time?"

I see his point.

"So for now," he continues, "I believe we do nothing. If you develop symptoms, then we talk about therapy. In that case, I would first try immunosuppresive medication, which is usually effective. But let's not worry about that now."

Although most cases of bone marrow failure are idiopathic, doctors have experimented with many drugs and found that corticosteroids and cyclosporine—medications that suppress the immune system—are often beneficial. This led to the hypothesis that marrow failure may be in part an autoimmune disease, one in which the immune system targets and destroys stem cells in the marrow. By curbing this misguided onslaught, immunosuppressive medication allows the marrow to recover.

"There's only one issue," he continues, "that I'm still undecided about. Because of your thrombocytopenia, I don't know whether we should anticoagulate you. I'm going to call some colleagues in London. For now, nothing."

Luzzatto is referring to a paradox of PNH. Patients like me can have thrombocytopenia (low platelets). This typically results in excessive bleeding (platelets enable blood to coagulate or clot; without them we would bleed to death). But not only haven't I had any bleeding episodes; even more bizarre, I had the very opposite, a blood clot in my eye. A clot and a platelet deficiency. It makes no sense, neither to me nor to the world expert, although he has his theories. If my platelet count were higher, he would certainly put me on medication to prevent clotting. But given my tenuous count, anticoagulation could be dangerous.

"One more thing. I want you to collect your urine." Dr. Luzzatto hands me a bag of twenty-five specimen containers. "For the next three days, take a sample every time you go to the bathroom." He is looking for traces of blood in my urine. "If you look hard enough, you always find some."

Not in my case, I'm sure. But for Lucio Luzzatto, I'll urinate in a test tube the rest of my life.

Walking out the door, I remember my dermatology boards. In the confusion of patienthood, I had forgotten to mention that in two weeks the national exam will be given in Chicago. Can I go?

"As long as the counts remain stable, I don't see why not," answers Luzzatto. "Have you been studying?"

I shrug. It hasn't been easy concentrating these days, especially with the periodic flashing in my right eye.

"Not really," I say. "I've had a few other things on my mind."

CHAPTER SIX

THIS WEEK IS Yom Kippur. An important holiday for Jews. The Day of Atonement, of reckoning. Even the nonobservant like me find themselves in temple. Especially during times of crisis.

My father and I leave for the Bay Ridge Synagogue Wednesday morning. I can tell he's upset; I see it in his walk. My father is a strong man, but his strength has always been subdued and gentle; his movements are decisively slow and fluid. Today he is jittery. There's an uncertain bounce each time he lifts his foot up off the ground, almost as if he were learning to walk again. He stutters more than usual. Although much of this can be attributed to a forty-year struggle to free his vocal cords from the heavy pull of Hungarian consonants, nerves exacerbate the problem. He is not comfortable in the position he finds himself in: a father unable to protect his child; a physician unable to fathom, much less treat, the strange disease that afflicts his patient-son.

My father will seek help in alternative corners today. He mentions he'll have a talk with his friend Saul Greenberg, the president of the Synagogue. He wants to make sure the rabbi includes me in the traditional prayer for the sick. A friend from residency had recently asked for my Hebrew name so that she could do the same at her shul.

Timing is critical. The Day of Atonement is also the day the Book of Life is sealed. If your name makes it into the Book, you're set for next year. Otherwise, start praying for the Messiah.

I'm happy that prayers will be said for me, even though I don't believe in God. A hedge, perhaps, in case I'm wrong. Besides, I believe in ritual. I'm sure my father feels the same. When his father died, he said the Yizkor (the prayer for the dead) on Yom Kippur. Every year on the anniversary of his father's death, my father attends shul and lights a candle at home. It is the only way to keep the dead alive. To keep the past alive. My father had always walked to temple with my grandfather on Yom Kippur, my grandfather with his father and so on. Ritual is a link to worlds that would otherwise be lost. I'm aware of this as my father hands me a yarmulke before entering the temple. I will continue the tradition as long as I live. So that my father always remains by my side.

Unversed in Hebrew, I follow the service in English translation. There are compelling stories and prayers, such as the Kol Nidre, that read like poetry. The voice of the cantor echoes mournfully across the room, which is filled to capacity on this holiest of days: children scampering up and down aisles, adults whispering back and forth, old men snoring, waking every so often to mumble a verse or two, then falling back asleep. I'm glad to be here. But I wonder, today more than ever, whether there is something behind the ritual, a higher being, a knowing God that decides who lives and who dies, that controls our destiny. In particular, my destiny. And if there is such a being, whether I should be doing more to influence Him, instead of relying on the prayer of a rabbi whom I've never met? I don't want to be forced into believing simply because a terrible thing has happened. Yet it's hard to dismiss the possibility of deliverance, the hope that someone could extricate me from this mess. I am not sick enough—at the moment—to play hypocrite.

The morning service brings up another unpleasant thought. On Yom Kippur, we ask forgiveness for the sins we've committed during the past year. There's a list that goes on for pages, sins that sound silly (bestowing wanton looks, appearing stiff-necked), and sins that seem unavoidable (lying, being haughty). I think about some of my own transgressions, about whether they might be connected with PNH. It's an unnerving conflation of entities, one that goes back to the beginnings of time. Illness as punishment. Because the Egyptians tormented the Jews, God rained down upon them a Pestilence, a series of plagues—"*Dawm, Tz'far-day-a, Kee-neem . . . ,*" we recount at the Passover Seder, dipping a finger into our glasses and dropping some wine onto our plates to commemorate each one, "Blood, frogs, vermin . . ." The notion is absurd, especially for nonbelievers. Still, it's difficult to resist the urge to find meaning. Why did I contract a rare, life-threatening disease? Could I have done something so wretched, so heinous, to deserve it? Or is it simply a senseless piece of bad luck? Life without meaning is not very comforting either.

I pray. I fast. I eat like a horse afterward. The shofar is blown the next day. Yom Kippur comes and goes. With it, the Book of Life. My name. Has it been inscribed?

NEW YEAR'S RESOLUTION: Shift focus away from PNH. To carry it out, I devote all free time to studying for the dermatol-

ogy boards. There are only two weeks left. Fortunately, I have
been reading and taking notes throughout residency, so it's not a
case of last-minute cramming. Pathology is creating some difficulty. Looking into the microscope hurts my right eye; the clot
has made it sensitive to bright light. I'll miss a few questions in
that section.

I also exercise my body. Convinced that my tight-fitting
goggles had something to do with the clot in my eye—a theory
supported by none of my doctors—I quit swimming and take
up running. Every day for no less than three miles, with push-
ups and sit-ups afterward. I must strengthen for whatever lies
ahead.

The following week, I visit the lab across the street from the
office.

"Hey, Doc, what can I do for you?"

I refer many patients to the lab and have spoken to the technician from Bangladesh on several occasions. "I need some
blood drawn."

"Sure thing."

Not so sure when he misses the large vein protruding from
my right arm. I try to hide my annoyance, he his embarrass-
ment, as a hematoma forms at the puncture site.

WHEN I RETURN to work, there's a message from Dr. Castro.
News, I presume, about the bone marrow test my sisters took
last week. I fumble dialing the numbers on the slip of paper. A
match would mean an escape route, a potential cure if the disease gets bad.

The matching process for organ transplantation involves the
examination of a blood sample for certain proteins called HLA
antigens. These proteins, situated on the outer surface of indi-

vidual cells, serve as I.D. tags or uniforms that enable cells to recognize each other as part of the same body, members of the same team. This is particularly important for T cells, a subset of white blood cells whose primary function is to patrol and search the body for intruders, be they microorganisms like bacteria and viruses, or foreign objects like a kidney from another person. When T cells spot kidney cells wearing different HLA markers on their coats, they launch an attack that can result in rejection of the graft. If, on the other hand, a transplanted kidney sports a similar uniform, one with matching HLA proteins, it is more likely that the host's T cells will befriend and tolerate their new neighbor.

There are three areas, or genetic loci, on one of our chromosomes that code for these critical HLA antigens. Every person inherits one gene from each parent at each locus, giving a total of six genes in all. For bone marrow transplants, it is almost always necessary for a donor to match a recipient at *all* six sites. And because these particular genes are full of polymorphisms— that is, because there are many subtle variations in these genes between different people—there is very little chance, one in a million in some cases, that an unrelated person would ever have the same HLA antigens. The odds are much more favorable for a sibling to match at all six sites—one in four to be exact, according to Dr. Castro.

Favorable but by no means a sure thing. Only three sisters, three attempts. It's a crapshoot, really, one slim go at the slot machine.

My sisters were aware of these odds when they converged on Sloan-Kettering last week. Much like certain cells in the human body rush to repair damage from an injury, they gathered to take the test of marrow. Each bared her arm without

question. Each yearned to be the donor. Each was terrified of
failing.

Dr. Castro finally answers the phone. He just received the
report from the lab. Lisa, my oldest sister, had gone first; she
matched at only three sites. Debbie, the second sister, followed
with four. Michele, the youngest, went last. And in that final
trepid pull of the lever, the third spin found purchase. Michele
matched on all six fronts. In the genetic lottery, she was my
jackpot.

"If you ever need a transplant," says Castro, "you've got one.
Congratulations."

My parents aren't surprised. "I knew it would be Michele,"
cheered my mother. "She looks the most like you." I don't
mention the fact that there is no connection between genes associated with physical appearance and HLA genes; it's only cellular appearance that matters here and fortunately Michele's
cells look a lot like mine. This degree of similarity, however, is
not essential for all types of transplantation. Solid organ transplants—such as kidney, liver and heart transplants—are routinely
performed with less than perfect matches, in many cases matching at only one or two HLA sites. The reasons for this are
largely practical. If patients had to wait for a matching sibling to
die before receiving a heart, there would be very few heart
transplants performed. Instead, the majority of solid organ
transplants utilize organs from cadavers of unrelated donors that
are HLA "compatible" rather than "identical." Although this
inevitably leads to a certain degree of graft rejection, it can usually be controlled with immunosuppressive medication.

Bone marrow transplantation, on the other hand, cannot
tolerate imperfection. This is less because of rejection of the
graft by the host than because of a far more serious problem:
rejection of the host by the graft. Graft versus host disease

(GVHD), as the condition is called, is unique to bone marrow transplantation because of the nature of the transplanted material. Unlike a liver or a heart, bone marrow is not an inert, powerless organ that can function as a relatively independent entity in another person's body. Instead, providing the raw materials for our immune systems, bone marrow plays a much more integrated and systemic role. Most importantly, it gives rise to those highly active, powerful and intelligent T cells that coordinate most immune responses. The T cells in inadequately matched donor (or graft) marrow will immediately recognize when they are placed in a strange and unfamiliar environment—the cells they encounter are wearing the wrong uniform; they have different HLA proteins. As a result, they will treat those cells as they would any threatening foreign virus or bacteria, by mounting a full-scale attack. And unlike the case of rejection of a transplanted heart by *host* T cells, here the assault is not limited to a single organ; *graft* T cells declare war on the entire body of the host, indiscriminately destroying anything and everything in their path. Complicating up to 60 percent of all transplants, GVHD is often debilitating and in many cases fatal.

It's not difficult to see that bone marrow transplantation is a far more risky and explosive undertaking than other types of transplantation. It involves dangerous rejection battles waged on two fronts instead of one: rejection of the graft by host T cells on the one hand, and rejection of the host by graft T cells on the other. A perfect match is theoretically supposed to limit the extent of the inevitable carnage. I am thankful that Michele's marrow qualifies for the coveted title. Even so, for now I'll stand by Luzzatto and remain as far from the fray as possible.

I SEE PATIENTS more confidently after the news. At 3 P.M., I call the lab for my blood results. Nothing yet. I call again at four. Still not ready. Can you put a rush on it please, I ask my Bengali friend. At five, I'm ready to start shooting. An apologetic voice at the other end promises a fax is on the way. I wait at the machine. There is a fist digging into my stomach as paper starts to feed out. I read each value as it appears. The numbers are the same as last week. I had hoped they would show some improvement. At least they didn't get worse. I fax the results to Luzzatto. Along with a brief note in Italian. To impress him. *Ci vediamo martedí prossima*—We'll see each other next Tuesday.

As patients come and go, I find that I've developed a new-found respect for blood tests. "Nice red count," I say to Phyllis Lepore, who is on Accutane for severe acne. "And that platelet count—360,000—absolutely phenomenal." She has no idea what the hullabaloo is about. Nonetheless, I'm envious of her. What I would do for those counts! I'm also envious of Joe Tremont, who follows Phyllis. Joe has acanthosis nigricans, a dark velvety rash in his armpits that is associated with obesity. Joe weighs close to three hundred pounds and has an offensive odor. That's okay, Joe, I'm still jealous. Jealous of your strapping good health. And that marrow of yours, full of vigor and churning out blood cells with panache. Not the slightest trace of PNH in those bones.

The following week, I'm back at Sloan, checking in at the front desk with a large shopping bag full of urine specimens. Where should I put them? I ask

"Why don't you take them with you," the receptionist says politely after peeking into the bag. "They'll be safer that way."

Fine. I put a lot of work into the project and wouldn't want to repeat it. Not easy waking up in the middle of the night and groggily trying to transfer the jet stream back and forth between container and toilet bowl.

Steven Fisch joins me in the waiting room. He is one of my closest friends. We went to college and medical school together. Our different personalities complement each other. Steven is straightlaced, reliable and has a sharp, scientific mind. I'm less conservative, more impulsive, which is why Steven has always felt the need to look out for me, like an older brother. I'm glad he is with me.

As a patient, I find that my mind loses its edge. Even worse, it seems to regress to an earlier developmental stage. I become blank in the presence of doctors, unable to remember what I wanted to ask or to respond coherently to what they have to say. Steven will do that for me today.

"*Buon giorno, buon giorno,* Dr. Biro, you look well, and that's the most important thing." Dr. Luzzatto always opens on a positive note. "I see you've brought me something," he says, looking at the shopping bag. "And this is . . . ?"

"Steven Fisch, my friend."

Luzzatto greets Steven warmly. Clean-shaven, the Italian sports a beige, woolen, cable-knit sweater. I picture him with a walking stick winding along the Alps at a brisk pace, inhaling fresh mountain air.

"Why don't you line up the cups in chronological order," says Luzzatto.

I try my best. Unfortunately, some of the cups aren't labeled. There are twenty-four in all. Different shades of yellow, a few colorless. None with any hint of brown or red. Dr. Luzzatto dips a small piece of paper into each cup. The chemical on the paper will turn blue if any trace of blood is present. No reaction.

"I'm surprised," says Luzzatto, shaking his head. "But it happens."

"Is there any chance that David doesn't really have PNH, Dr. Luzzatto?" my friend interjects. Go get 'em, Stevie. "There are some inconsistencies. And the percentage of normal cells on the test you did was close to ninety-five percent. I was under the impression that when symptoms of PNH appear, most of the cells should be abnormal." Excellent query, my friend.

Steven is referring to the special test performed in Dr. Luzzatto's lab. It revealed only a fraction of cells missing the surface markers (6 percent, to be exact) that characterize PNH. As a result, NYU's less sensitive test failed to make the diagnosis. Typically, this low burden of abnormal cells is not associated with complications of PNH like clotting.

"I understand your point," concedes Luzzatto. "There's some truth to it. Still, I have no doubt that David has the disease; marrow failure along with the positive PNH test, regardless of degree of positivity, is proof enough. I am not, however, a hundred percent sure that the retinal vein thrombosis was caused by PNH. Thromboses, as you say, do not occur this early in the course of disease. On the other hand, I am not comfortable with saying that two entities, the clot and PNH, each extremely uncommon in their own right, have absolutely nothing to do with each other. I am inclined to connect them."

Steven seems satisfied with the explanation. I have to agree; Luzzatto makes a good argument. Only I'm surprised—and will continue to be throughout my ordeal—at how indefinite things are in medicine. I thought having a diagnosis meant an end to uncertainty. I was mistaken.

On the other hand, there are some benefits to uncertainty; it opens a window of opportunity. Maybe the doctors are wrong and I don't have PNH. Maybe it's a virus after all. I will cling to any shred of hope.

My second visit with Luzzatto concludes with a physical examination and some further discussion. He is pleased that my counts are stable, convinced that no therapy is warranted at the moment and optimistic that my condition will improve in the future. "Get a blood test every week and come back in a month. Good luck on your exam."

Steven and I head down First Avenue and stop at the first bar we pass. We need to put things into perspective.

"You have to be happier now," says Steven.

"Thrilled."

"You know what I mean. You have a diagnosis. A great doctor. The counts have held their own. And there's still a good chance they could go up. Two weeks ago, we had a completely different view of PNH. Dr. Castro was talking bone marrow transplant, for godsakes." Steven is a master of rationalization. He could turn a locust storm into a positive experience. I've always loved him for that.

"You're right. I guess I feel a little better."

We order two pints of Bass. Steven attempts to bounce a coin into the mug. Like old times. Quarters at Doc Watson's Pub every Friday night of freshman year in college. Stumbling back to the Quadrangle, shitfaced.

"How is this possible, Steven? How could this happen to me?"

"*Only* to you, Biro. Only *you* could possibly come down with a disease like PNH." We start laughing, hesitantly at first and then uncontrollably.

It's true. I've always wanted to stand apart. The earring, the clogs, the ponytail, driving without a license, experimenting with drugs, pondering ancient Greek and Latin, composing poetry, chain-smoking in medical school. I was determined to be different—safely different though, pushing but never exceeding the boundaries of my middle-class existence. So it's only fitting that my first medical problem is neither pneumonia nor a broken leg, but an exceedingly rare malady named paroxysmal nocturnal hemoglobinuria. I can hardly pronounce the damn thing. What else is there to do but laugh?

We finish our beer in silence, watching the foam quietly dissolve at the bottom of our glasses.

CHAPTER SEVEN

⌐◡⌐

I AM ON American Airlines Flight 268 bound for O'Hare Airport in Chicago, frantically poring over my index cards that catalogue an endless series of skin diseases from acne vulgaris to pityriasis lichenoides et varioliformis acuta. Every twenty minutes, I make my way to the back of the cabin. I stretch, I jog in place, undaunted by looks of bewilderment from fellow passengers and stewardesses. I am ill, can't you see? Doctor's orders.

Luzzatto had warned me about sitting in the same position for too long. Immobility can lead to blood clots. There have been reports of deep venous thromboses of the lower extremities occurring after long flights. I won't let that happen. Upon returning to my seat, I massage the backs of my calves. Anything to keep the circulation flowing.

I continue the routine during the subsequent two days at the airport Holiday Inn where the dermatology boards have been given since their inception. My father was there thirty-five years ago on the same mission. Today, he is home worrying. Instead of quietly gloating over the fact that his son is following in his footsteps, he is sitting, wondering how everything could have gone so terribly wrong. When the test is over, I celebrate, at Dad's suggestion, with friends at Morton's Steakhouse. The porterhouse is better in Brooklyn. Nothing beats Peter Luger's.

WITH THE BOARDS behind me, life begins to assume its natural rhythm once again. An aspiring novelist, I write in the mornings and practice dermatology in the afternoon and evenings. Twice a week, I go to the medical school and teach residents; I'm in charge of the dermatology consultation service at Kings County Hospital, responsible for treating the skin conditions of inpatients. I exercise regularly. On the weekends, Daniella and I go out with friends. Afterward we make love. No mention is ever made of my illness. We ignore it. David looks fine, he is fine, and that's that. Only it's there, beneath the covers, under the sheets, silent, stealthy. It insinuates itself into a nervous glance, an awkward quiver, in the way we hold each other a little tighter, kiss a little harder.

THE MONTHS OF October and November move along peacefully. Weekly blood tests show no change. I continue to feel perfectly healthy. Every two or three weeks, my parents join me on my pilgrimage to the shrine of Luzzatto at Sloan-Kettering. On one occasion, we appear bearing gifts. Mom brings fresh mozzarella from the A&S Pork Store in Bay Ridge, Dad a vintage bottle of deep-bodied Barolo. We want to make sure Luzzatto has all the comforts of home while residing abroad; if that doesn't work and the need arises, I have no doubt the Biros would set up roadblocks to prevent our esteemed guest from leaving prematurely. Not necessary. Luzzatto is enjoying himself in the Big Apple.

The legato flow of time doesn't last long. Stabs of staccato intrude during the last week in November. For the first time, the counts change. As the paper rolls through the fax machine, I notice the number of red cells and platelets has dropped. Luzzatto tries to reassure. "Repeat the test next week. One test does not indicate a trend." We repeat. The numbers are even lower as the final month of 1995 gets under way. Luzzatto wants to see me immediately.

My parents accompany me to Sloan. Dr. Luzzatto is clearly concerned. He passes this on to my parents—my father paces up and down the small examining room; my mother repeatedly blinks her eye as if there were something in it. The latest platelet count, warns Luzzatto, is 18,000 (the normal range is between 250,000 and 400,000). I am moving into precarious waters. If the platelet count falls any lower, there could be bleeding, internal bleeding. Into my gut. Into my brain. Into other internal organs. There is no longer time to wait for things to improve. We must intervene.

Luzzatto lays out our options. Both hinge on the prevailing theory that most types of marrow failure, including aplastic anemia and PNH, are autoimmune diseases, like lupus erythematosus and rheumatoid arthritis. For unknown reasons, the body's immune system fails to recognize its own organs as self and begins to attack them. In my case, stem cells in the bone marrow are being targeted, leading to the fall in my blood counts.

There are two kinds of treatment used to thwart or suppress this misguided immunological assault. The more radical kind involves the infusion of antithymocyte globulin (ATG) into a vein. This substance is taken from the serum of a horse after it has been inoculated with T cells from a human thymus. The "vaccination" induces the horse to make immunoglobulins against the cells. When later administered to a human being, the horse immunoglobulins will seek out and destroy the patient's T cells. And since T cells orchestrate most immune responses, including self-destructive ones, this dampens and occasionally suspends those responses. As a result, many patients with marrow failure respond positively to ATG by a rise in their blood counts. There are potential problems however. Since the infusion of ATG is often associated with serious side effects, it requires hospitalization. Along with allergic reactions, patients can initially have transient drops in their blood counts which necessitate transfusions. And transfusions, if at all possible, should be avoided—apart from the transmission of infectious diseases like AIDS and hepatitis, they increase the complication rate of a subsequent bone marrow transplantation.

For these reasons, Luzzatto favors the more cautious type of immunotherapy. Cyclosporine is given in pill form. It too depresses T cells but not as dramatically as ATG, and side effects are rarely life-threatening. I am familiar with the medication because dermatologists use it in the treatment of severe forms of psoriasis. It can damage the kidneys, cause unpleasant sensations in the extremities and have adverse affects on one's appearance—flaring of acne, unwanted facial hair and overgrowth of the gums. I'd be a monster with a failing kidney and a thriving marrow. Lovely.

"Before we start, however, we must do another marrow biopsy. It's been almost three months since the first one. Can we do it today?" asks Dr. Luzzatto.

"Why? What will it show? How will it affect our decision about treatment?" I'm getting frustrated.

Dr. Luzzatto is quiet, more so than usual. He's upset that my condition has worsened and doesn't know what to say. He would like me to trust his judgment, to reserve my own. I will trust him. He takes my hand in his and says with emotion, "*Coraggio,* my friend." Courage. In no mood for the Illinois and Jamshidi needles being wedged into my pelvis, I am nevertheless so moved by my doctor's heartfelt feelings that I would do just about anything he requested at the moment—with the exception perhaps of an MRI.

"I'll be in touch," he says after the procedure. "We'll meet next week. In the meantime, you may want to discuss bone marrow transplantation with Dr. Castro. As we've always said, a transplant is the only cure for PNH. Right now I'm against it because there are safer alternatives. Okay?"

There are many things I'd rather do than meet with Dr. Castro again. But it's important to know all the options before making a decision. My father agrees.

SEVERAL DAYS LATER, I am sitting in Castro's office—alone this time, having convinced my parents and Daniella that the visit was only a formality. Nevertheless, I am prepared for Castro today, for the numbers and statistics he will hurl at me. Paper and pencil in hand, I am determined to take down every fact.

"Thanks for seeing me so soon. Dr. Luzzatto thought I should talk to you about the possibility of a transplant. Not right now, of course, but if things get worse."

"Yes, I spoke to Dr. Luzzatto. I agree that there's no rush at the moment. You can try cyclosporine first." Dr. Castro sounds less than enthusiastic.

"You don't think it'll work, do you?"

"It might."

"You think I should go for a transplant?" I ask.

No answer. I repeat the question.

"Look, David," says Castro finally, "a bone marrow transplant is a big decision. There are serious risks. You can't do something like that without believing in it. Yes, ultimately, I think it's your best option." Castro is different today, or perhaps I didn't read him accurately on the last visit. What I took for coolness now seems more like shyness. He finds it difficult to speak because he rarely has anything positive to say. So he holds back until he's forced. It's almost as if he were ashamed—to always be the disappointer—and would rather hide behind that Che Guevara beard of his. When words do emerge, however, they are sincere and sympathetic, qualities I didn't notice before.

"You're a young man," he continues in a subdued voice. "You have your whole life ahead of you. A transplant would mean a cure. I've seen bad things happen to patients with PNH. Plus, there's the threat of those bad things hanging over you at all times. You have to consider quality of life."

This line of reasoning strikes a chord. I'm naturally impatient and have zero tolerance for uncertainty. Quality of life isn't merely a consideration; it's just about everything.

"There are also several things in your favor that make you a good candidate for transplant: your age, health, and the fact that you've never had any transfusions. Although we went over the statistics before, I don't believe they apply to you. You have a better chance." A hint of a smile begins to appear over Castro's features.

"You said about seventy percent of patients survive a transplant. What would it be for me then? Eighty percent? Ninety?"

"It's hard to say. Most of our patients are sick at the time of transplant or have gone through several rounds of chemotherapy for leukemia. You're in a different situation."

"Over ninety percent?"

Unable to ignore my persistent and unrealistic requests for a definitive number, Castro accommodates. "I'd say between eighty and ninety percent."

That's not too bad.

"Why don't you think about it. There's no rush. I agree with Dr. Luzzatto. You can start on the cyclosporine and see

what happens. Call me if you have any more questions. Anytime."

I walk out of Sloan with a good feeling. Castro makes sense.
He is offering me a level of control over my illness. By choosing
the transplant, I could rid myself of PNH. No more worries.
Die or be cured. I like that scenario more than the one of me
treading a more cautious path—taking medication and always
fearing what will happen next.

I tell Daniella that the transplant option is starting to sound
more attractive.

"Have you lost your mind? That man is crazy." There's an
edge to Daniella's tone. It's the first time she has snapped since
my illness began. "Of course he wants you to have a transplant.
That's what he does. He runs the goddamn transplant service.
What else is he going to say?"

I'm surprised by the attack. Daniella has been so calm lately.
It almost seemed like she had gotten used to my being sick. Evidently not.

"But what about the quality of life?" I ask.

"There is no quality of life when you're dead." Daniella
doesn't mince words. "I was at the first meeting with Castro. I
heard him say twenty to forty percent of patients die."

"But I'm different. I'm healthier . . ."

"I don't believe that. Do what Dr. Luzzatto says. He's the
expert and he thinks the transplant is stupid."

I am starting to wonder whether Daniella's anger might be
misdirected. Maybe it's not Castro she's mad at but me. For
ruining her life. For ruining our life, when it had only just
begun.

Regardless, I know where she stands on the issue of transplantation. She's not alone either. This becomes clear as I delve
into the medical literature on the subject. Surprisingly, up to

this point I've made no serious effort to understand PNH and its treatments. After my encounter with the hematology text at the library, I thought it best to remain blissfully ignorant. I can no longer do that. My life is at stake.

The literature is less sanguine about bone marrow transplantation for marrow failure than Castro. Like Luzzatto, most doctors recommend a trial of immunotherapy, such as ATG or cyclosporine, at least initially. They do so because overall transplantation statistics are not as good as the numbers Castro quoted me. Some studies report mortality rates as high as 50 percent. In addition, there are the risks of long-term complications, including secondary cancers, sterility and thyroid disease. For these reasons, the general consensus is that bone marrow transplantation should be used only as a last resort. I can accept that. For now.

"You're right," I tell my wife. "We'll stick with Luzzatto for the time being and try cyclosporine. But if things get worse, I want the transplant."

"They won't. You're going to be fine." Daniella wants me to believe that she hasn't been rattled by the experience, that she's certain my illness will disappear as mysteriously as it came. It's the way she is and has always been. Daniella is self-reliance personified. At seventeen, she left the comforts of suburban New Jersey, rejected any assistance from her parents and took on New York City. She would make it on her own. A variety of jobs, night school and hard work later, she succeeded. And not only does she take care of herself, she does the same for all those she loves. "I promise, I won't let anything happen to you."

My wife seems so sure of herself. I can't help but wonder, though, whether deep down, she too has her doubts.

CHAPTER EIGHT

❧

T HIS WINTER IS turning out to be a nasty one. It is midway through December and we've already had three major
snowstorms. The last one has left my car buried in four feet of
snow. I consider waiting for the spring thaw, traveling by train in
the interim. The nebulous leitmotif of divine punishment drifts
by every now and then.

On the medical front, we await the results of a twenty-four-
hour urine test. The function of the kidney must be assessed
before starting cyclosporine. I am due back at Sloan the first
week of January. Until then, I am allowed to enjoy the holiday
season.

Daniella and I celebrate Christmas with her parents in
Westfield, New Jersey. I look forward to the holiday each year.
Outside, the air is bracing, the ground is covered with a light
frost. Inside, a fire flickers, yellow and warm, across the living
room. Daniella's father plays Frank Sinatra tunes, her mother
sips a glass of Pinot Grigio while stirring marinara sauce. Tara
and Matthew, Daniella's younger siblings, are home from Wash-
ington D.C. Everybody is in good spirits. A Christmas idyll—
though not without a confrontation or two as the festivities

proceed. The Vitales love a good fight and the decibel level always surpasses any records set the previous year.

This Christmas is different. For everyone. My illness has put a damper on things. Drinking a glass of wine, I wonder whether I'll be back next year. Something momentous is about to take place. A great obstacle in my path is threatening to stop the ticking of the clocks. I will either break on through or be broken.

As I sit alone in the living room before dinner, the revelation passes before me. No doubt it comes in the wake of change. I am experiencing symptoms for the first time since my diagnosis. Over the last two weeks, my energy level has waned. I'm beginning to feel weak, can no longer run in the mornings and am asleep by nine at night. This is surely the result of lower hemoglobin and red cell counts. Along with my platelets, they have fallen considerably.

"Come on, David, time for dinner," calls Daniella's mom. As I make my way to the table, it requires considerable effort to stall the closing of my eyelids; they're becoming heavier and heavier to support. I'm worried about the future. I try to hide it with a joke. Everybody is doing the same.

CHRISTMAS PASSES. THEN New Year's Eve, which we spend with friends at a trendy restaurant in Tribeca. More premonitions concealed behind nervous smiles.

We are now packing Daniella's bags. She is off to Italy on business tomorrow for the next two weeks. January and February are the biggest months of the year for her. Fashion shows in Milan are followed by market weeks in New York. Zipping up her garment bag, I can't help but reflect on the timing; it couldn't be worse. I don't say this. In fact, I don't reveal much— the results of the last blood count, for example, or my increasingly pessimistic outlook. I've tried to keep Daniella removed from the daily vicissitudes of my illness. I want to protect her until it becomes more clear how things will play out. I also want to protect myself; I'm afraid the tears and fears would be paralyzing if both of us began to panic.

To this point, there have been no scenes, only a healthy dose of denial on both sides. Daniella and I have carried on as if nothing were wrong, hardly ever uttering the smug trio of letters, PNH. We go to work each day, certain they will eventually dissolve in midair.

"Don't worry, honey," I tell my wife as she gets into a cab, "the cyclosporine will work." I almost believe it myself, saturated as I am in the charade.

Nevertheless, I'm on the phone with family and friends as soon as Daniella is gone. It's time, for me at least, to confront the crisis head on. I have to sort things out; they don't make sense. Luzzatto and Castro—superficial pleasantries and agreements notwithstanding—are on different poles of the universe. Luzzatto is offering me a few pills; Castro wants to replace my bone marrow. How can two doctors interpret the same facts so differently? It's beginning to sound like a political or economic debate. Either the economy is slowing down or it's growing— despite the same numbers on which to base conclusions, economists, like politicians and evidently doctors, never seem to agree. Why? Because facts aren't always facts. And even when they are, they're open to interpretation.

In my case, both doctors agree I have PNH. But what this really means is up for grabs. Luzzatto favors the Hollywood approach. The disease is bad but not that bad. There are frequently happy endings. Castro, on the other hand, reads more like Thomas Hardy. Nothing ever turns out well in his depressing tales.

Castro points to PNH patients who've had massive blood

clots in their livers and brains. He also believes that marrow failure, whether due to PNH or aplastic anemia, is a preleukemic
state; eventually a large percentage of such patients will develop
a form of leukemia. So it's better to eradicate the problem before it's too late.

Luzzatto, on the other hand, argues that these major life-
threatening clots are rare. He also disagrees with Castro's notion
of preleukemia. In fact, some doctors have hypothesized that
PNH might be protective, might actually decrease the risk of
leukemia in patients with marrow failure. Therefore, he prefers
a cautious approach.

Where does this leave me? Instinct puts me squarely in the
Castro camp. I'm a risk-taker. I'd rather drive aggressively and
dent a fender than sit in traffic for hours on end.

I'd like to believe this instinct is not simply reckless but calculated. I practice medicine the same way. Unlike many colleagues in dermatology, I am willing to prescribe methotrexate
and cyclosporine for treating psoriasis. Although these medications can have serious side effects, the rewards of clearing extensive forms of this disease are worth the risks—in my opinion.

I also feel relatively strong at the moment and this too
pushes me toward Castro. I'm convinced that I could withstand
the trauma of a bone marrow transplant and survive. Now. But
if my strength continues to deteriorate and the PNH progresses,
I will be at a disadvantage. So now seems like the perfect time if
a transplant is truly in my future.

On the other hand, Luzzatto has been my deus, my god. He
is the world's leading expert in PNH. And he cares about me.
How can I possibly reject his advice?

I speak to my father several times a day. I speak to friends in
medicine and friends outside of medicine. We survey the facts,

the *interpretations* of the facts. We go back and forth, up and down, sideways. No matter. There is always confusion. The only consensus is that a meeting with both doctors at the same time may perhaps clarify some of the issues. I could challenge Castro with Luzzatto's claims and Luzzatto with Castro's. How would they respond when they were sitting face-to-face with each other?

BOTH DOCTORS AGREE. A summit meeting is set for the second week of January. My father, who has been equally baffled by the conflicting opinions, and I arrive at the hospital early. We run into Dr. Araten, the hematology Fellow who works with Dr. Luzzatto. "It was a good idea to get them both together," he tells us. "First time I've seen it happen."

I am repeatedly struck by the uniqueness and privilege of my situation. Not everyone is treated the way I have been—a doctor, a young doctor, the son of a doctor. Most patients in fact can barely expect to get their physicians on the line for more than a minute at a time.

I inquire about the results of the bone marrow biopsy done by Luzzatto two weeks ago. He is evasive. "Dr. Luzzatto will discuss it with you, I have to run." I sense trouble.

We are escorted into a small room with a round table. Dr. Luzzatto and Dr. Castro are waiting. Dr. Luzzatto begins by summing up events of the preceding weeks and recommending a plan of action: Start cyclosporine immediately. "Don't you agree, Hugo?"

"Well, yes." Dr. Castro twists in his seat. I can see that my vision of a *Crossfire*-like debate is not likely to materialize. Neither seems ready to step on the other's toes. "Yes. I don't think it would hurt to try cyclosporine for a while."

"I've had success with it in the past," Luzzatto continues.

"Yes. It can certainly be effective in some cases," concurs Castro.

I'm starting to get annoyed. We're operating on the surface, the depth left untouched, unexplored. It's up to me to probe.

"Dr. Luzzatto, what about Dr. Castro's point about bone marrow failure being a preleukemic state?"

"That's controversial."

"And what about the fact that I'm healthy now, that I have a better chance of surviving a transplant sooner rather than later? I've never had any transfusions."

"This all must be considered. But . . ."

"And Dr. Castro's point about the special type of transplant they do here—the T cell–depleted type—which makes the procedure less risky?"

Dr. Luzzatto is fidgeting with a stack of papers. The conversation has deviated from his original plan. He'd rather be discussing other issues.

Recognizing Luzzatto's frustration, my father attempts to explain my interruptions. "I think David is just afraid of all the things that might go wrong. He doesn't want to live in fear. The idea that he can be cured is tempting." It is surprising how easily my father can articulate my feelings even though we've never actually discussed them. It's as if the familial lines of communication are open and active yet silent and unspoken, using a form of language different from the ordinary one.

Castro, who has been quiet during my outbursts, finally speaks: "This has to be your decision, David. You're a smart man. You have all the facts. You must decide. Dr. Luzzatto and I cannot do that for you."

He's right. Still I don't understand why we can't all agree.

And why Dr. Luzzatto can't see the appeal of the transplant. I turn to him and blurt out, like a child who can't fathom an unreasonable demand made by a parent: "But why? Why are you so against a transplant? Why don't you see the advantages?"

"Because," Luzzatto replies, placing his hand across my back, "I don't want you to die."

There is silence. A silent space in which to digest another shocker from Luzzatto. Like the earlier *coraggio* explosion, the utterance has swept across the room like a cyclone, leaving me paralyzed in its wake. It is so visceral, so heartfelt, so touching. This person next to me, whom I'd met only three months ago, is speaking to me like a father. I don't know how to respond.

At the same time, there is something strange about the communication. Doctors don't say things like that. There is a sense that Luzzatto has stepped over the boundaries of the doctor-patient relationship. He has dispensed with detachment, given away his feelings, embraced a patient. Overwhelmed, I forgive the transgression. From here on in, I will shut up. Let Luzzatto continue. Let him decide my fate.

Gathering himself, Luzzatto takes charge again. "The twenty-four-hour urine test showed that your renal function is normal. We'll start the cyclosporine at five milligrams per kilogram."

"Hugo, do you agree?"

"Yes."

"There is something else," says Luzzatto. "I didn't want to tell you," he continues after a pause. "I don't really think it's significant. I have an article here . . ." Dr. Luzzatto rustles through his pile uncomfortably.

"The marrow biopsy? Did something show up on the

biopsy?" I ask, recalling the evasiveness of the hematology Fellow earlier.

"I'm sorry, yes . . . it did reveal something, something unexpected. There was a chromosomal abnormality. Trisomy 6. I didn't want to tell you because I knew you'd worry. I don't believe you should."

Am I hearing right? Words are being tossed to and fro in a tempest. Sounds are being garbled, louder and louder, then fading to whispers. Everyone around me seems unreal.

"I don't believe it's significant," repeats Dr. Luzzatto, trying to penetrate my blank gaze. "I've done a literature search. I found a paper from Chicago. Two patients with PNH and trisomy 6, just like you."

Trisomy 6. Three copies of chromosome 6. I'm only supposed to have two. What hell did the mutant descend from? How did it slither and slime its way into my stem cells? And why now?

The shock is organic as well as psychological. My system has temporarily shut down, refusing to admit incoming signals or to send outgoing ones. Slowly, the haze lifts—words echoing off eardrums, materializing into phrases and sentences, begin to give off meanings.

"The two patients," says Luzzatto, waving the article in his right hand, "have been treated with cyclosporine for two years and are doing fine. I phoned the author of the paper. He's supposed to call me back."

Although I'm beginning to register and process information again, I cannot completely shrug off the shock-haze. As in the case of a person after a fainting episode, recovery is only partial at first; it takes time before one can launch back into the world of people and things. There is still a compelling push to the inside, an internal slowing down of time, a disturbing focus on the body's confusion.

I attempt to reach beyond myself. "Why now?" I ask. "All of a sudden. I don't understand."

"Actually, the trisomy was present in the first marrow biopsy at NYU. I spoke to the pathologist there yesterday. Of the twenty cells they looked at, one had the abnormality. Because of the low percentage, they didn't report it."

This can't be happening. It's absolutely absurd. "What is the percentage now?" I ask with trepidation.

"It has grown to thirty-two percent of the marrow cells tested. However, I don't believe it's significant. I would call it an accessory clone that should get smaller and perhaps disappear if we can strengthen the marrow. That's what happened to the two patients in the article. What do you think, Hugo?"

"I wasn't aware of these results before now. I'm not sure I agree with you. It is true that this particular abnormality is unusual, not the one you typically see in cases that transform into leukemia. But I have a patient with a trisomy 6 who's not doing so well."

Another curve ball. Another piece of information sent to muddy the waters. First PNH, now trisomy 6. And less consensus than ever. One doctor believes this, the other that, and I am left to ponder the universe from my tiny, insecure and woefully unintelligible vantage point.

"This doesn't change my mind," insists Luzzatto. "I believe we should still go forward with cyclosporine. Don't you agree, Hugo?"

"No, I would lean more toward the transplant now. But it's David who must decide."

I have lost my patience, cannot wait another second. For bits

and pieces of news that continue to arrive unexpected, unwel-
come. I'm sick of the lack of meaning.

"Give me a day," I say. "I'll have a decision tomorrow."

I ALREADY HAVE one. Only I'd rather not tell Dr. Luzzatto in
person. I don't want to disappoint him. He's been so kind.

Together my father and I drive home, solemnly, with few
words. I know the transplant is my only option. It is the obstacle that blocks my future.

I also realize that the decision must be made alone. Although I'm sure my father agrees, it's difficult for him to say so.
He doesn't want to take responsibility should something go
wrong. What would he tell my mother, my sisters, Daniella? No,
I have to make sure everybody knows this is my decision.

My father is a reserved man, a lot like Castro. He doesn't say
much. His emotion, always contained, smolders inside. But it is
present in the silence of his gaze. He knows what I will do, what
he would do. He wishes we could change places. That he were
not so helpless. It is shattering for him to see his son in this
predicament.

"David," he says, firmly grasping my shoulder in his right
hand, "you'll get through this."

The uncertainty makes me shudder. But my anxiety pales
before my father's. His face is ashen, his mouth twisted. He is
trying to speak. The words don't come.

It is almost more painful to watch someone suffer than to
suffer. I saw that when my friend Rema was sick. Her family
watched her die with unspeakable horror. Now it is my family's
turn.

NEMESIS

꧁

After Solon's departure, the weight of divine anger descended on Croesus, in all likelihood for thinking that he was the most blessed man in the world.

HERODOTUS, Histories

M Y LUCK HAD run out. That was clear to me sitting around the summit table with Drs. Luzzatto and Castro at Sloan-Kettering. Clear to my body, which was moving in two different directions at the same time. Contracting to a tiny fetal core one moment, fissuring into an infinite number of atoms the next. Tiny and divided, I was more vulnerable than I had ever been since my tenuous start in life thirty-one years ago. A tattered coat upon a stick, as Yeats once said. I had reached my nadir.

Not many people can imagine how it feels to find yourself in this position. Those who have encountered illness before, perhaps. But surely not a young, healthy person like myself. I was supposed to be immortal.

And yet I cannot say it was completely unexpected. For a

while prior to my illness, I had a sense, a premonition, that something bad was about to happen. My life was going too well; it was time for a setback of sorts.

It is true that such feelings after the fact are always suspect. Who didn't think Mike Tyson would lose his title or the Dow Jones would crash—after they happened? We are all soothsayers in retrospect. Still, there were reasons for my premonition.

Despite an aversion to religion and superstition, I am sympathetic to the Greek Goddess Nemesis, or at least the concept behind the deity. Nemesis, as I understand her, is what you might call the great Marxist equalizer. But instead of material wealth, she redistributes good fortune. The Greeks believed that there was only so much good fortune to go around and every man deserved his share. If one person somehow obtained too much, it meant that another received too little. Nemesis would be summoned to step in. She would redress the imbalance, typically by punishing the man who had exceeded his due.

I had a premonition that I was ripe for Nemesis. Too much good fortune. Too little mishap and hardship. I began to feel uncomfortable—sitting across from a friend who lost his father, a friend suffering from a chronic illness, a friend deserted by her husband. Everybody seemed to be involved with catastrophe, their own or that of someone close. Everybody but me. "Steven," I said one day, surveying the terrain of tragedy around me, "we're so lucky. Our families are healthy, we love our wives, we love what we do. . . ."

"Yeah, you're right," he interrupted. "Don't talk about it too much." Maybe Steven also feared Nemesis.

Besides too little of the bad, I was also benefiting from too much of the good. Not that I was willfully taking from others. I simply didn't believe that anyone deserved so much good fortune.

As the only son, I had been spoiled from the beginning. Expecting everything was practically genetic. But as I've grown older, these expectations have been tempered by the acquisition of common sense. I've come to understand my limitations. No longer aspiring to play football like John Elway, paint like Picasso or write like Joyce, I've become accustomed to the fact that I will move in more ordinary circles.

So why the premonition? When did I suspect Nemesis was eyeing my terrain? When I began to surpass the modest expectations that came with maturity.

The goddess likely first noticed me in the spring of 1986. Despite my distaste and neglect for the sciences during college, I'd been accepted to Columbia Medical School. She heard of me again the following year after I'd received a grant from Columbia to pursue an interdisciplinary project in medicine and literature. And she must have been tracking my nocturnal meanderings during those glorious days. For unclear reasons, I suddenly became more attractive to women and was dating at a furious pace. I'm convinced my new friend from Olympus was sitting on the train with me at six one morning when I exhaled the proud breath of a man after conquest—returning to school after spending the night with a girl I had had a crush on since college.

All a prelude. The real investigation began in 1989. Fearing medical school might have been a mistake, I applied for postgraduate work in English literature. Much to my astonishment, I was accepted at Oxford University. With scholarship to boot. They'd liked my preliminary work at Columbia on illness and literature and thought it could be extended into a doctoral dissertation. I took a leave of absence from medical school and moved to England. Nemesis pursued me across the British Isles.

Initially, there were problems. No one on the faculty was

eager to work with me. My project—the language of pain and suffering in literary and theoretical texts—was not traditional enough for the stodgy Brits. Until I met Terry Eagleton, perhaps the most famous of all the Oxford dons. Despite ripping apart my earlier work, he accepted me as his advisee.

With little background in philosophy or literary theory, I went to work with the discipline of a medical student. In two years, more than half the thesis was finished. I completed the rest back in the States during my internship and residency.

Nemesis was surely close by in the spring of 1993 when I returned to Oxford to sit for the viva voce, the final oral examination. My work was approved, a doctorate granted. Nemesis was whetting her stone.

I was married to Daniella in September 1991. We had fallen in love a year before my departure for England, after living together as roommates for several months. I cut short my stay there to be with her. After internship in internal medicine, I began a residency in dermatology at Downstate and unexpectedly received the highest scores in the country on my practice board exams. Dr. Shalita, the chairman of our department, chose me to be the chief resident. It was only a matter of time before the poisoning of my marrow.

After finishing residency, I joined my father's practice. While others scrambled to get a job, start a practice, I strolled into a fully established one. My father had a desk built for me opposite his and introduced me to his patients. He let me arrange my schedule so that I could write in the mornings and work in the afternoons. Twice a week I would go to Downstate and teach residents.

I was sailing on fantastic seas. A couple of years ago, I wasn't sure that medicine was the right profession for me. Now I loved it. Partly because I had combined it with my desire to write. I was almost finished with my first novel. My friend Ellen, an established writer and magazine editor, encouraged me.

Too good to be true, I knew it. I was beaming with success, in the office, at the writing table, home with Daniella. And all the while, unbeknownst to the beamer, my bone marrow was languishing. Stem cells were being targeted by an immune system as if they were a treacherous foreign invader. Struck down by antibodies and a host of cytokines, they produced less progeny. Gradually, blood counts began to fall. Silently. Insidiously.

Then on a fall day in September, a flashing sensation swept across the visual field of my right eye. A clot had formed in the major vein leading away from the fundus. Blood was backing up, like sewage in a clogged drain, and pouring across my retina. Not enough oxygen was getting through to the tissue, leading to the peculiar symptom. The goddess had revealed herself in the noise of a poisoned body. My roller-coaster ride along the slippery slopes of disease that would ultimately lead to the summit meeting at Sloan-Kettering had begun.

There is too much evil and tragedy in this world to pass through unscathed. It wouldn't be fair for only some to bear the brunt of suffering. Otherwise how could we communicate? With my father, for example, who was forced from his home in Hungary one innocent morning and shipped to a German concentration camp. With my unsuspecting friend Rema, who was informed one day that she had cancer, and five years later that it had recurred and would destroy her. With Rema's parents, who were forced to bury their thirty-year-old child. With my friend Tom who lost his father, Robert his brother, and Beth who contracted the disabling disease known as rheumatoid arthritis.

How can we talk to such people? What do we say? That we

understand what they're going through, how they feel? It is not possible. Writing my doctoral thesis on the rhetoric of pain, I was frequently asked how I'd chosen the morbid topic, whether I had had any personal experience. I would respond by mentioning the time I fell off a bicycle and bled into my elbow joint; that really hurt, I'd say, laying emphasis on the word "really." Beyond that, however, there was little experience with pain or injury. Still, the discrepancy didn't bother me. I could learn from others, what they had to say, what they thought. I was satisfied with the way my thesis turned out. It seemed I really knew my subject. *Really*.

It turns out, I had only learned something about language, about words, about the way we navigate difficult experience with words, approach them, wind around them, brush up against them, attempt to pin down their essence. I had learned everything in fact except the essence, the phenomenology of the experience. This is where my education stopped. Words are the wrong currency for the task. We cannot exchange pain for the way we talk about it. We always miss the pain we're trying to grasp.

PART THREE

᭒

PREPARATIONS

*When I become absorbed in my body, my eyes present me with no
more than the perceptible outer covering of things and other people,
things themselves take on an unreality, behavior degenerates into
the absurd, and the present itself, as in cases of false recognition,
loses its consistency and takes on an air of eternity.*

MAURICE MERLEAU-PONTY,
The Phenomenology of Perception

CHAPTER NINE

❧

I ARRIVE HOME AFTER the summit meeting with Dr. Castro and Dr. Luzzatto to an empty apartment. Daniella is in Italy. She will call any minute to find out the news. I am still shaken by the strange twists of my dream vision, a vision that continues to push me further from reality. There's a thick mist separating me from objects on the outside; I'm not sure about time, whether the sliver of light that slips through the blinds represents dusk or dawn; the noise on First Avenue below my second story window is muted; my movements, my thoughts excessively slow one moment, spinning out of control the next.

A ringing of the phone unsettles the mist.

"Honey? Is that you?" I ask hesitantly. There is a familiar delay as the connection is made across transatlantic wires.

"It's me. What happened today?"

"Nothing really." I lie, unable to tell her about my decision to go ahead with the transplant; she's 3,000 miles away, alone in an unfamiliar hotel room. "Everything's pretty much the same."

"Did you start the cyclosporine?"

"Tomorrow." On the other hand, I don't want to overwhelm her when she returns. Better to drop a few hints. "I've been thinking—I'd rather not stay with the cyclosporine for long. If it doesn't start working soon, I'm going for the transplant. So that I won't get too sick and then be in bad shape for it. Don't you agree?"

"Let's see what happens first. Stop being such a pessimist. What's the platelet count?"

"Same. Everything's the same. What's happening over there?"

Nothing is happening there except routine business matters. Daniella is exhausted. It's midnight in Milan. She is getting ready for bed. She sounds groggy, but there's also a tentativeness to her voice. Does she know what's really happening? I've long since become accustomed to Daniella's uncanny ability to look at me and read my thoughts, catch my lies. Is it possible that she can do the same over the phone? And if so, what is she thinking? That I'm making the right choice? I can't ask her these questions; I won't. I'm almost glad she's far away. Maybe Daniella feels the same. We are both trying to protect each other, both trying to protect ourselves.

Good night, honey. I love you. Click. Contact severed. Wires down. We sleep in separate beds tonight. Of all the terrifying nights to spend alone.

I desperately need to talk to someone, to tell them the truth, to drum up support for my decision. Tom and Steven are my closest friends. They are also doctors, they'll understand. Of course they'll meet me. We agree to go to Brew's for a burger at eight.

Although I'm afraid, it's a different fear than yesterday, the day before. There is still uncertainty, but the number of possible versions of the future has contracted. It has crystallized into two scenarios, clear and concise: life or death. A PNH palette of infinite colors and shades has been reduced to black and white, the sharp edge of a blade dividing them. But sharp as the blade feels against my skin, its uncertainty is easier to deal with than the earlier variety. I can pin it down and grasp it. The touching brings relief.

As I walk up Thirty-fourth Street, the mist begins to lift, my head begins to clear. With each step, my conviction grows stronger. In the cover of darkness, I manage a smile. I've made the right choice. Now to carry it through.

Steven and Tom are waiting for me at the restaurant. I update them on the day's events: the meeting with Castro and Luzzatto, the results of the bone marrow tests, the new chromosomal abnormality, the counts, each doctor's interpretation. I leave out my reaction. Let's see what they have to say first.

Not an easy task. A protracted series of "Wells . . ." and "Ums . . ." accompany seat twistings and turnings. Tom eventually completes a sentence. "Well . . . I think I know what you want."

"You've been moving towards the transplant since day one," agrees Steven. "I'm sure it's hard for you since Castro and Luzzatto don't see eye to eye. But at this point, considering your present counts, it seems like the right thing to do."

"Although I was leaning the other way before, I'm in favor of it now," says Tom. "There are too many things that can go wrong—another thrombosis, more serious than the first, a bleeding episode given the low platelet count, infections if your white count drops any further. What choice do you really have?"

None, I blurt out, none. It's too late for the damn cyclosporine. The counts are too low, the medication takes too long to work, and even if it does, I wouldn't be cured. PNH and all its complications would still be hanging over my head.

"There's also the issue of trisomy 6," adds Tom. "Wouldn't most hematologists consider it a myelodysplastic syndrome, or, at the very least, a preleukemic condition? I don't think you have an option here."

They are behind me. Thank God. Both Tom and Steven tend to be more conservative, less impulsive, than me. I wasn't sure they'd see things my way.

"You're young, you're healthy and strong as an ox," says Steven. "No one will recover from a bone marrow transplant faster."

"A rough couple of months and the nightmare will be over," assures Tom.

My father repeats the sentiments the following day. He supports my decision. He too is sure that I'll survive the transplant unscathed. No doubt whatsoever; I hear it in his steady, stutter-free voice.

I also talk to friends outside medicine. Neal, whom I've known since high school, gives the green light. So does my old college roommate Kenny. Someone at his brokerage firm had a transplant with Dr. Castro several years ago. "You'd never know the guy was sick. Besides, I have a good feeling about you—you're gonna make it." Ellen had a feeling too. It was corroborated by a psychic whom she happened to talk to after hearing my decision.

"Good news, David. You're going to make it. Mary T said so. She knew all about you. 'The man with the weird disease and the foreign doctor, right?' she asked. 'He will have a long life despite a serious setback.' That's what the woman said. I even asked her about the saying that only the good die young and told her that you were as good as they come. 'Not good enough,' she said with a wink, 'not quite good enough. Don't you worry, this man has plenty of life left in him.' Isn't that great?"

THE FOLLOWING MORNING, I call Luzzatto and inform him of my decision. He's surprised. He's also annoyed. "I'm sorry you feel that way. But it's your decision. You know what I think."

I don't understand. Luzzatto is acting as if I betrayed him. Not true, not fair. The choice, even if we assume that Luzzatto's assessment of my case is more accurate than Castro's, was a toss-up. No right or wrong. How could there be? No one agreed on the meaning of the facts, the significance of a cure. Intellectually, I could've gone either way. It boiled down to a matter of style. I opted for the radical approach, wanting closure and willing to die for it. Luzzatto disagreed. That doesn't explain why he couldn't empathize with me and accept my choice.

My situation, in fact, is by no means unique in the annals of medicine. Physicians are faced with irresolvable problems all the time. Medicine, even in the age of molecular biology and the Human Genome Project, no matter how much the lay public would like to believe otherwise, is still more art than science. And that's not surprising considering the complexity of the human body. We know a great many small details about a great many things and yet the big picture, the overall design and mechanism of the body and its diverse parts, continues to elude us. Simple metaphors, like the heart as pump or the brain as computer, helpful as they are to our understanding of how certain systems work, inevitably break down.

Dermatology is no exception. Many times, we are unable to give a rash a name. A skin biopsy is done and still the patient remains a diagnostic mystery. Eventually, such zebras find their

way to clinical conferences at teaching institutions like Downstate and Memorial Sloan-Kettering. And even when a diagnosis is made, we cannot always predict the course of a disease or
offer a satisfactory treatment. What causes eczema? asks a frustrated patient. What causes psoriasis? What do you mean there
is no cure? You are a dermatologist, aren't you?

Yes, I'm a dermatologist. And unlike my father and many
other older physicians, I was trained not to conceal anything
from my patients. If you don't know something, advised one of
my medical school professors, you must acknowledge that. If
there are several different therapeutic options (which usually
means there is no single good one), then you must discuss each
of them with your patient. My father cautions me about this
"modern approach." Patients don't want their doctors to be
unsure, he warns. They expect answers, they demand them. If
you offer them confusion instead, they will lose confidence.
And confidence is just as important as medication in the art of
healing.

My father is right, to a certain extent. Confidence is critical,
especially in ambiguous cases like mine. The indeterminacy of
medicine can be unsettling enough as a doctor. But as a patient,
one who recently sat by and watched two respected physicians
debate and ultimately disagree over the meaning of the data, it is
shocking, paralyzing.

And still, as a patient, I wanted the modern approach of
doctoring—to have the uncertainty of my situation acknowledged, to be offered every treatment option available and to be
actively involved in the decision-making process. Wasn't I enti-
tled? Why couldn't Luzzatto see that?

Though upset, I am unable to let go of my Italian savior.
"I'll still be your patient, right?" I ask him. "You'll follow me
through the transplant?"

"Of course I'll come and visit you. But from now on, Dr. Castro will be your doctor."

I feel like Luzzatto is betraying me and it hurts. Only I will not waver in my decision. There is too much at stake. I must be as focused as a marine. That's what Dr. Castro would want.

CASTRO CONFIRMS THIS when I meet with him the following day to discuss the specifics of the transplant.

"You're doing the right thing, David. But you must understand what you're in for and be prepared. This is a big decision. It's not going to be easy. You have to believe in what you're doing, no matter what. That is absolutely necessary if you intend to make it." Castro hints at a smile.

"I understand."

"I think you do. Now let's go over the procedure again in more detail."

We are in a consultation room that barely accommodates Castro's desk and the two chairs across from it. The walls are white and bare except for a small bookshelf containing a few reference books. There isn't the slightest shred of character, a diploma, for example, or a family picture. Only a glaring transience—doctors and patients alike pass through without leaving a trace.

Dr. Castro opens a drawer and takes out a few sheets of paper. He begins drawing and plotting, an activity I've become familiar with from our last meetings. I hope we're not going over statistics again.

"You'll be in the hospital for about eight weeks," he says, drawing a line across the top of the page. Below the line, he subdivides the time. "On the first day, the surgeon will insert a central line into your chest. The next eight days is the conditioning regimen: four days of TBI—which stands for 'total body irradiation'—and then four days of chemotherapy. That will wipe out your marrow and immune system so you'll be able to accept the new bone marrow. During this time, you can expect to have some nausea and vomiting."

I nod, familiar with the nausea and vomiting that follows chemotherapy. I've taken care of cancer patients during internship. And I watched Rema go through several cycles of the poison. It's surprising that the mere prospect, so terrifying and revolting, doesn't suffice.

"There will be a day of rest after the chemo. The transplant occurs on Day o. We'll harvest the marrow from your sister in the O.R. that morning. Then we'll separate out her T cells and by early evening her marrow will be injected into your central line."

Sounds like a military operation. Clean, methodical, precise. Almost easy. One step at a time. Day by day. And the next thing you know, my marrow is replaced with my sister Michele's. No problem.

"The two weeks after the transplant are the most difficult."

I knew there had to be a catch.

"That's the time of neutropenia—no white cells in the blood. As a result, there will be fevers and mucositis. The skin in your mouth and throughout your digestive tract becomes inflamed and then sloughs. You won't be able to eat so we'll need to feed you through a vein. You'll also be on a morphine drip for pain."

"You think I'll need it?"

"Everyone does. The mucositis is very painful. It will last about two weeks. As the white count starts to rise, the fevers and mucositis will resolve. When it reaches a safe level and you no longer require transfusions to maintain your red cell and platelet counts, we can discharge you from the hospital."

"I'll have to stay at home for a while, right?"

"A couple of months until your immune system recovers."

"Then I can go back to work?"

Dr. Castro laughs, a short dry laugh, well intentioned. "Yes, as long as there are no complications and your counts are stable."

"Complications like GVHD?" I ask. I know a little bit about graft versus host disease because it typically begins with skin lesions. GVHD occurs when T cells from the graft do not recognize host cells as self, as derived from the same body— since they don't wear the same uniform of surface markers— and mount an attack. This happens even in the case of a "perfect" match. Evidently, there are markers other than the six major HLA ones that are important immunologically but not accounted for in the matching process. In other words, there's no such thing as perfect unless your donor is an identical twin.

"Actually, the risk of developing GVHD is small in your case because we're doing a T cell–depleted transplant. The incidence is less than five percent."

This type of transplant, I learn, was pioneered at Sloan-Kettering. The concept is straightforward. T cells, a subset of white blood cells, are responsible for protecting the body against foreign invaders. A prerequisite for this duty is the T cells' ability to make subtle distinctions between the many different cells they encounter—between, for example, a healthy cell and an infected cell or tumor cell; between a cell from their own body and one from the body of another. They are able to do this by interacting with protein markers, like those encoded by the HLA genes, that sit on the outer surfaces of cells. Mature T cells are good at their job; they recognize a foreign human cell just as easily as they would a cell harboring a dangerous virus, like the measles or chickenpox virus. And so, when they find themselves

in unfamiliar territory—as graft T cells do when they are transplanted into another person's body—they become irate. This is
not their home. The cells they see are not like them but a dangerous enemy instead. They are compelled to go to war.

To circumvent medicine's version of the Problem of Other
Minds, researchers decided to remove mature T cells from
donor marrow before transplanting it. The remaining immature, or "mindless," T cells left in the graft are less skillful at dif-
ferentiating self from other. Allowed to develop in the host
marrow, they would learn over time to recognize only one
home, their new one. The technique worked. Risk of GVHD
dropped from 60 percent to 5 percent. And since GVHD con-
tributes significantly to the mortality of transplantation, it repre-
sented an important advance.

"T cell-depletion seems too good to be true. There must be
a downside," I comment.

"Only for patients with leukemia. They seem to need a
little GVHD. In those cases, donor T cells actually perform a
positive function. Although they attack and damage the skin
and liver of the host, they also track down any leftover cancer
cells that weren't killed by chemotherapy. But your PNH cells
aren't as resistant as leukemic cells. They should easily be destroyed by the conditioning regimen."

"Great."

"That doesn't mean the procedure is without risk. Although you probably won't get GVHD, you can still develop all
the other complications of bone marrow transplantation."

Dr. Castro refers to his graph and plots the various problems
that occur at different times along the way. During the first two
weeks after transplant when there are no neutrophils, I will be
susceptible to bacterial and fungal infections. There are power-

ful antibiotics to treat them if they develop. In the following months, we worry about opportunistic infections and cancer. I am like an AIDS patient, he says, with little immunity against organisms that don't bother healthy people—like cytomegalovirus (CMV), Epstein-Barr virus (EBV) and *Pneumocystis carinii*. Small numbers of these viruses and parasites inhabit the bodies of most people but are held in check by a vigilant immune system. When the immune system becomes compromised, as a result of the AIDS virus or the toxicity associated with a transplant conditioning regimen, these harmless bugs proliferate and wreak havoc. Fortunately, medication is available to treat the infections. And if that proves unsatisfactory, mature T cells from the donor could be injected to boost a patient's immunity.

"The first one hundred days constitute the critical period. That's when most complications occur. Once you pass that point, you should be okay."

One hundred days. Doesn't sound that long. In the scheme of things. I can do it.

"You'll be fine as long as you think positively. Don't underestimate that, David. I mean it."

I shake my head. I won't.

"Is there a possibility though," I ask, unable to cast aside every doubt, "that the transplant might not work?"

"None," answers Castro confidently. "As long as you survive the transplant, you will be cured. So far, we've had four patients with PNH that underwent bone marrow transplants. All of them are alive and well and have no trace of PNH in their new marrows."

"Let's do it then," I say. "As soon as possible. I don't want to think about it too long; I might change my mind. When can we schedule it?"

"Not so fast. There are several things we must do first—a few more tests and measurements for radiation. I also have to examine the donor. Then I'll go to the transplant committee and set up a date. I'll try to do whatever I can to speed up the process. In the meantime, have your sister call and make an appointment. And try to relax."

Dr. Castro also mentions that I will most likely be sterile after the radiation. "You should think about storing your sperm. There are a few places in the city. If you can't find one, give me a call."

The possibility of sterility hadn't crossed my mind. It sends a chill down my spine, so bleak-sounding and absolute. It will take some adjusting to. Practically speaking, however, there are ways around everything these days. I know plenty of people that have had fertility problems. They managed. So will I.

"Remember, think positively." Dr. Castro pats me on the back as I leave the office.

I like Castro more each time I see him. Initially, I was put off by his seriousness, his aloofness, his pessimistic outlook. That picture was myopic. Although he is definitely serious, Castro is neither aloof nor pessimistic. Just reserved and shy. And while he may not be as outwardly affectionate as Luzzatto, he cares deeply for his patients; it's obvious, less from his words and gestures, which are always muted, than from his actions. Above all, I am impressed by his strength and conviction. A small, quiet man, Castro believes in what he's doing.

CHAPTER TEN

✣

I AM ON A one-way road. No looking back except for two minor pauses. The first occurs when we question the choice of hospital. While second-guessing is a natural move for any family, it is inevitably carried to a higher pitch by a New York Jewish one. A cousin calls demanding that we cancel plans at Memorial immediately. Her best friend had a transplant last year and did all the research. "There's only one place in the world for a bone marrow transplant: Seattle. They've done more cases and more studies than any other center and have the best success rates. You'd have to be insane not to go!" A close friend of my father begs us to consult with big shots at the Mayo Clinic; he's working on the names and should have them momentarily. An uncle in Boston whispers—in this case a whisper is as effective as a shriek—the name Harvard into my father's ears. "You should at least *talk* to somebody at the Dana-Farber Cancer Institute." As if the mere idea of overlooking this most revered institution would be catastrophic.

My father and I respond by making calls, more with the intent to confirm rather than to change plans. There must be the appearance of pursuing all options, tirelessly. He calls someone at Harvard. He speaks to friends, friends of friends and friends of friends of friends in New York. I speak to a doctor at Johns Hopkins, a cousin of a colleague. Bottom line: Sloan-Kettering is a great hospital, Castro has an excellent reputation, and having a good support system in place is crucial to success. Furthermore, other centers haven't performed as many T cell–depleted transplants.

I am satisfied. I have come to believe in Castro and the concept of T cell-depletion. I also want to remain in New York. The thought of moving to Seattle for six months and leaving my family behind seems absurd. Already it has meant so much that my parents were with me for most of my doctor appointments at Sloan. And having them around at the hospital, along with Daniella and my sisters, will be even more important. Back on the road, looking straight away.

One final pause. Reading the brochure Castro handed me on my last visit (*Having a Bone Marrow Transplant: What to Expect*), I begin to tremble. "You will have a single room with a bathroom that will be your home for six to eight weeks. Although you won't be able to leave, people can come to visit. They must wear gowns, gloves and masks." The dreaded isolation factor. Up to this point, I had tried to play it down. Certainly, I knew there would be a barrier of sorts between myself and others. There had to be. Otherwise I would be exposed to infectious diseases that could overwhelm my weakened (in reality, nonexistent) immune system. But this was worse than I'd anticipated. Pain, mucositis, fever—they don't worry me half as much as the idea of being cooped up in a room for two months. I sleep with doors and windows open at all times, break into a sweat on elevators. I practically had a coronary attempting an MRI four months ago. Who am I kidding? There's no way I can go through with it.

I phone Castro. "I may not have mentioned this before, Dr. Castro, but I'm a bit claustrophobic. I may not be able to stay in a room for that long."

"Don't worry, David, everybody says that. They manage. There's no choice. We can't let an easily preventable infection ruin your transplant. Don't worry. You'll make it, I promise." Castro is reassuring. Even the cropped laugh that follows. It reads like the quick smile he makes in person: paternal, omniscient and confident enough to allow the entry of humor into what would otherwise be a brutal business. Everything will be all right, young man, trust me, I've been doing this for a million years—so the laugh seems to say.

I trust him. That doesn't mean there's no room for negotiation. "Any chance of getting out once in a while, just to stretch my legs a bit? That might help."

"We'll see. Don't think about it now. I'll have Dr. Passik come by after you're admitted to the hospital. There are medications and special therapies that can help the situation."

"He's a psychiatrist?"

Cropped laugh from Castro. "Stop worrying, David. One step at a time. Have you spoken to Pat yet?"

"Who?"

"Pat Walka. She makes sure everything is in place—insurance, tests, appointments—before admission. She'll be calling soon."

After I hang up with Castro, I phone Dr. Naftali Bechar. Naftali, who is now a hematology Fellow at Sloan-Kettering, did his internship at NYU with me. I saw him last month after an appointment with Luzzatto.

"What are you up to these days?" he had asked. "Visiting someone here?"

"Afraid not. I have a problem. PNH."

Shocked, he gave me his number, told me to call him any time. He'd just been appointed chief resident and knew everybody in the hospital. If there was anything he could do, I shouldn't hesitate to ask.

Now's the time, Naftali. I tell him I've decided to go ahead with a bone marrow transplant but am scared about being shut inside a room for so long. Any suggestions?

"Absolutely. We'll get you the best room in the house. With a big window and a good view. We'll also arrange for some diversions. TV with a VCR and an exercise bike. How does that sound?"

"Naftali, you're the best. Can you really get me a good room?"

"For you, my friend, the presidential suite."

"The bigger the better, okay?"

He promises. If Naftali were in front of me right now, I would embrace him like a long-lost brother. Fearful as I am about the future, I can't help but feel grateful for the special treatment I continue to receive from my medical colleagues.

ALL SET, I can now concentrate on the issue of fertility. I love kids and want to have some of my own one day. Dr. Debrovner, Daniella's gynecologist, is at his office. He is sorry to hear about my illness but assures me that he'll deliver my baby when it's all over. "Do you know what the conditioning regimen entails?" he asks.

"Chemo with Cytoxan and Thiotepa. And total body irradiation. They're also giving me an extra radiation boost to my testicles."

"Not much chance you'll have sperm after that. You'll have to begin storing it. How much time do you have?"

"Maybe two to three weeks."

"Start as soon as possible. You can give them a sample every other day as long as the sperm count is high enough. I would get as many samples in as you can. This way we have a few options when you're ready. Good luck."

Dr. Debrovner refers me to a colleague at Repro Lab. It turns out that the fertility clinic is three doors down from my apartment building. I throw on an overcoat and boots and trample through the dirty blanket of snow left on the ground from the last storm.

I'm buzzed into a small, uncluttered waiting room with a couch and an end table filled with magazines. On one of the walls there's a corkboard with ads for egg donors, surrogate mothers and counseling services. At the reception area, numerous photos of smiling babies are tacked to the wall. The receptionist hands me a folder and tells me to have a seat. I flip through the brochures, entering a new, and up to this time, unexplored world:

Repro Lab . . . semen cryopreservation for fertility and
cancer patients since 1989 . . . complete semen banking
services . . . semen analysis and storage . . . programs for
short and long term storage. . . .

The words conjure up a futuristic, brave-new-world-like vision—clean, cold and dispassionate. Until I get to the reprints of articles on leukemia and lymphoma patients. Repro Lab is not only for happy couples who need a little assistance in making babies. It's also for those hapless people who might never get the chance. One of the reprints states that cancer patients often don't possess viable sperm to store; their diseases and treatments may have rendered them sterile. A sperm analysis would reveal this. As I'm waiting, a man walks in and hands the receptionist a paper bag. He is bald and thin. "See ya in two days, Nell," he says, waving goodbye. I didn't detect the tragic side of Repro Lab when I first walked in. It's more obvious now, seeping from the immaculate, inconspicuous pores in the walls.

The receptionist asks whether I read through the information and have any questions. I explain my situation.

"Just fill out the paperwork then," she says. "You'll need a sperm analysis first. Then you can decide what plan you want to join. Why don't you follow me inside. Leave your coat and things in the closet."

"That's okay, I'll keep them."

After a few steps, Nell stops and turns around. She looks puzzled. "Sure you don't want to take off some of those things?"

"No thanks."

"Fine," she says, shaking her head, "whatever pleases you."

At the end of the hall, she opens a door to a small, closet-sized room with a narrow bench. She hands me a plastic container, motions me inside. "There are some magazines on the shelf if you want," she says. "Bring me the cup when you're done."

I'm stunned, unable to move. A second later, I start to laugh. The woman must take me for a madman—all bundled up in a heavy wool overcoat, a scarf wound tightly around my neck, ski gloves and hat. And I thought she was just giving me a grand tour of the facility.

"Sorry, but I live right up the block," I explain, grabbing the container. "I'll just take that home and come back when I finish. Okay?"

She giggles. "That's fine. Make sure you keep it warm and return within a half hour after you . . . you know . . ."

Back through soiled snow and freezing winds to a warm apartment. Now I can remove the arctic layerings. On the futon in the bedroom, with the container opened and close by, I imagine a steamy encounter and masturbate. Approaching orgasm, I reach for the cup and direct the flow of semen inside. It comes in spurts. When it's over, there's barely more than a tablespoon at the bottom. Horrified, I meticulously push in any remnants of the viscous fluid stuck to the sides. Is that all? Could there be something wrong with me? Could my sperm be damaged, as in the case of the leukemia patients I read about? Would there be enough normal ones to fertilize an egg?

After putting the cup in a bag, I rush back to the lab. Nell removes the cup and leaves it on the counter while she fills out some forms. Embarrassed, I gaze at my pitiful sample, naked and puny—sitting quietly on the counter as a curious customer in the waiting room peruses its contents.

"The doctor will call you with the results," says Nell.

Later that day, Dr. Marks phones me at the office. "The count is good, seventy thousand, and so is the motility, two out of three. We also did a freeze-thaw test, which didn't reduce the numbers much. That translates into about two attempts per container." Like Debrovner, Marks suggests that I wait a day between samples and collect as many as possible before admission to the hospital.

What a relief. My semen is up to snuff. Not stellar but adequate, the normal range being between 40,000 and 160,000. Sperm counts in general, for reasons unknown, have been declining over recent years and mine is no exception. The quality of the sperm is also assessed in the analysis; individual sperm are inspected under a microscope and rated on how fast they move and buck their tails. Mine get a score of 2 on a scale of 1 to 3+. I wonder if there's anything I can do to juice them up a bit. Finally, sperm should be resistant to freezing. That is, when thawed, both measures should remain approximately the same, which they did in my case.

And I was worried about the inadequacy of my seed. No doubt now that there's an army of little Davids and Daniellas swimming around that precious tablespoon of nectar. Save your energy, rascals. Rest up. You'll have plenty of work to do someday when you awake. A wistful final farewell before my sperm are immobilized in Repro Lab's deep freeze, set at −196 degrees centigrade.

I am now comfortably installed in two banks, Chase for checking and Repro for sperm storage. I choose the five-year plan with unlimited samples, costing roughly $1,600. When the time expires, the contract can be extended. Every other day I head for the bank to make a deposit. No longer ashamed, I proudly hold forth my samples to Nell, who whisks them away to the back for cryopreservation. Daniella, who has been gone now for a week, is oblivious to the wanderlust of my sperm in her absence. She will be reassured to learn that our future offspring are peacefully resting at the bottom of a giant freezer.

CHAPTER ELEVEN

〜∞〜

P AT WALKA CALLS the following day. She has good news. The transplant committee met yesterday and put me on the schedule for the first week in February, two weeks away.

"Dr. Castro wanted to get you in as quickly as possible, especially since you're a doctor—it usually takes longer."

"That's great—if I have too much time to think about it, I might change my mind."

"You won't, I promise. We have plenty to do before admission."

We meet in the waiting area of the outpatient building at Sloan-Kettering on January 18. Pat has a folder in one hand and a cup of coffee in the other. She insists on getting a cup for me. In her early thirties, casually dressed and animated, Pat easily slips into conversation, a useful quality for this pivotal player on the transplant team. Her role is to prepare patients—medically, financially and emotionally. It's obvious that Pat enjoys what she does and is good at it.

She asks how I'm dealing with my decision, whether I'm scared or depressed. A little of both, I reply. "But more than either, I feel numb—as if this isn't really happening or happening in a dream. As if I'm moving along on one of those electric walkways they have at airports."

"Everybody is different," she says. "As long as you think positively, that's the most important thing."

I ask how others manage. Babies and children, she replies, do best because they're fearless and don't know any better; being sick is perceived as natural, not abnormal or deviant. In these settings, she has to make sure the parents are coping effectively. Men in general are more difficult. They typically play a macho role, hiding their fears and dismissing her efforts to help. The most challenging cases, however, are young mothers who will be separated from their children. Plans must be arranged for their care. The children need to be prepared for life without their mothers.

I wonder whether arrangements are made in case the change is permanent rather than temporary. We talk, as I do at home with Daniella and my parents, about separations and interruptions. On the surface, everyone exudes confidence. But underneath, apart from the euphemistic words and gestures, lies the very real possibility of death. What happens if I don't survive? Nothing to me—personally that is, since I'll be enveloped in a blanket of insensibility. It's Daniella and my family, waking to the horror of loss, that will suffer great pain. I hadn't thought about this scenario before. It makes me cringe.

And yet at least Daniella is a mature, self-sufficient person. What about a child in the same position, a child who is left behind by a mother she depends on. What happens to that child if her mother dies? And how must that mother feel when this possibility crosses her mind? I feel sick thinking about it.

"I don't envy your job," I tell Pat. She disagrees. Actually, in many ways, it's inspiring, she says—to see how courageously people respond to a crisis and are able to endure so much; to watch families gather around and support a loved one. And there's nothing like seeing someone pull through. It almost makes up for those who don't do as well.

Pat asks about my family, whether they'll be able to spend time with me during the transplant. I'm close to my parents and three sisters, I explain. They've been incredibly supportive since all this started and promise to visit me in the hospital every day. I'm also hoping Daniella will be able to sleep in my room.

"It shouldn't be a problem if she stayed over a few nights."

"She'll want to be there the entire time."

"It's a long and tiring ordeal. She'll need her rest. Talk to Dr. Castro, he'll tell you. It looks like you won't be needing the social worker. I'll give her your name anyway. Now, let's go over your schedule."

Pat hands me a white card that folds in half. On the front, the name of the hospital is written in fancy lettering below the Sloan logo; inside there's a list of appointments. It looks like an invitation to a ball or timetable of events at a spa. Today we call on the radiation oncologist, who will take some measurements and a few X-rays. Tomorrow I'm booked at the dentist. He will make sure there's no gum disease or tooth decay that might act up during the days of neutropenia, a low neutrophil count. Next week I'm down for an echocardiogram to evaluate my heart. Since the chemotherapy can be toxic to the heart, it's important to know if there are any baseline abnormalities. Finally, I have a date with the surgeon who will insert a Broviac catheter into one of the large veins in my chest. Having three ports, the catheter makes it possible to funnel several different medications into my circulation at the same time.

Pat drops me off at Radiation Oncology. She'll make a few

phone calls to my insurance carrier while I'm there. Phoenix Life must approve the procedure before the hospital can officially schedule a date.

I am introduced to Dr. Martins, one of the Fellows in the department. He goes over the treatment schedule and some of its potential complications: sterility, cataracts, thyroid dysfunction and secondary cancers. Before signing the consent form, I ask for statistics on the incidence of these complications. I'm most concerned with the risk of developing cancer. He can't give me specific numbers but will ask the attending physician. Never mind. Why would I want to know anyway? It wouldn't change my mind at this point. I sign on the dotted line.

Next comes simulation planning. In my case, the strategy is not very intricate. Total body irradiation is a lot less selective than radiation for cancer, where the objective is to deliver a blow to the tumor while sparing surrounding healthy tissue. They will be much more generous with me; I will simply be plopped down in front of the machine so that my *total body* can be radiated, Hiroshima–style. This is the only way to wipe out the entire bone marrow. Since the marrow resides in bones and since bones occupy just about every square inch of body surface area, nothing can be spared. "Can you at least put shields over my eyes so we can skip the risk of cataracts?" Sorry, but you're forgetting about orbital bone. We need to hit that too.

The chest, because it houses the lungs, which can be irreversibly damaged by treatment, is the only area considered sacred. However, it also contains the marrow-rich rib cage. The technicians take several X rays and then mark my upper body with pinpoint tattoos. This will enable them to position a lead shield over my chest so that radiation exposure is maximized to the ribs and minimized to lung tissue.

The following day, I visit with the dentist, who takes a series of films. No cavities, he assures me, my wisdom teeth are inactive and there are no potential sources of infection in the immediate future. He warns me that my mouth will be dry after the transplant. Radiation damages the salivary glands. It takes six to twelve months for them to recover. The next week a cardiologist informs me that my heart is in excellent shape and should tolerate chemotherapy well. I meet the cocky surgeon last. He talks to me for less than five minutes, delivers his brief assessment into a small recording device he carries in his right hand, and then flies out of my room.

"Is he always like that?" I ask Pat afterward.

"Surgeons tend to be stingy with bedside manner. He's not a bad guy when you get to know him."

Pat raises another issue. Daniella's company is changing our health insurance policy, effective February 1, four days before my scheduled admission to the hospital. The new insurer, New York Life, refuses to approve the transplant. They're throwing out terms like "preexisting illness" and "uncovered procedure." She's pretty sure they'll agree, but they need a push. She wants someone from Daniella's office to get on the phone.

"I haven't told Daniella yet."

Pat looks perplexed.

Embarrassed, I try to explain. "She's been in Italy on an extended business trip. I just can't tell her over the phone. She'll be back in a few days. I'll tell her then."

IN THE MEANTIME, I'm as busy as Pat anticipated. Besides the daily visits to Sloan-Kettering, I continue seeing patients at the office in Bay Ridge. Every morning, I exercise. Too weak to run anymore, I ride a stationary bicycle, then do push-ups and sit-ups. It's as though I'm training for a marathon. I *am* training for a marathon.

Whatever free time remains, I work on my novel. I want to finish it before the transplant. Ellen, my friend and editor, thinks it's almost ready, but there's no point in rushing. I could work on it in the hospital or during my convalescence. Not good enough. I've invested too much not to see it through. And what if I don't return? No, I must hand it off before leaving. Ellen promises to help.

My schedule is packed with one activity after another. Doctors appointments, trips to the sperm bank, exercise, office hours and writing in between. I manage it in businesslike fashion, unreflectively and with little emotion. Despite falling blood counts and the increasing languor I feel as a result, this spirit carries me through each day. At night when I finally roll into bed, I have no energy to arrange the pillows beneath my head. Feeling the weight of gravity bearing down upon my body, I sink into my futon mattress and fall asleep.

CHAPTER TWELVE

⚓

D ANIELLA ARRIVES AT Kennedy Airport on Saturday morning. Always happy to see her after a business trip, today I'm ecstatic. I need her to be with me right now, physically and emotionally. I'm also nervous about how she will respond to my unilateral decision.

After embracing and kissing, more embracing and kissing, then hauling her luggage to the car, I break the news: "I didn't want to tell you when you were gone—the counts went down. There were chromosomal abnormalities on the marrow test. There wasn't enough time to see whether cyclosporine would work. I decided to go ahead with the transplant. Enough is enough. I want it to end."

Daniella is not surprised. She had suspected that I was leaving out a few details in our phone conversations. She asks whether Luzzatto is behind the decision. No, but it doesn't matter; it's the right decision. How about your father? she asks. He's for it. When will it be done? A week from Monday.

Silence—I watch the groove over Daniella's brow deepen, the right side of her upper lip twitch.

"You're sure about this?" she says finally.

"Yes."

"You won't die on me, right?"

"No."

"Okay. Then let's do it."

Daniella adapts quickly to change and maintains her res-olutely positive outlook. I doubt the impressive show of strength is insincere.

I tell her about Repro Lab and my efforts to preserve my sperm. By the end of the week, I'll have given them seven sam-ples. That translates into fourteen attempts at whatever method we choose—insemination, IVF, GIFT or any other imaginative technique they've invented by the time we're ready. Dr. De-brovner doesn't think there should be a problem.

She asks whether she can stay with me in the hospital. Yes, I talked to Castro. As long as she wears a mask and gloves. I'll be there for about eight weeks. She'll try to rearrange her schedule, postpone her upcoming business trips. What about your family? They'll be around as much as they can. She raises her eyebrows. There has always been some friction between Daniella and my family, as there seems to be with spouses and in-laws every-where; it comes with the territory, I guess. But until now, it has been limited to minor squabbles about when to schedule birth-day parties or where to make dinner reservations. I just hope this extended period of forced proximity doesn't generate more serious conflicts.

In any case, Daniella has joined me on the direct line to bone marrow transplantation. From now on, we will travel to-gether. Returning home, we make a list of items I might need in the hospital: posters, music, fan, phone, pajamas, slippers. Daniella divides up the work. She also assures me that someone at Giorgio Armani will harass the insurance company. Swift,

methodical and fastidious, Daniella assumes control of the preparation process as I imagine she manages her division at work.
She even finds time for some humor, like yesterday when she
presented me with a pile of my favorite, old ripped T-shirts and
begged me not to take them. "Honey, give me a break. I'm in
the fashion industry," she teased. "I can't have you running
around the hospital in rags." Only on rare occasions does the
slightest hint of fear slip past her confident gaze, and Daniella,
recovering instantly, brushes it off and proceeds to the next task.

During the following week, I rummage through old photographs and select pictures of Daniella and me, my family,
friends, babies of friends. I take down my favorite posters and
maps of Italy from the walls. Daniella buys a phone with an answering machine. I purchase a small stereo from the Wiz. She
buys several packages of T-shirts in a variety of styles and colors.
In addition to the essentials, she picks up a few scented candles
and herbal sprays; lavender is healing, she's been told, eucalyptus
soothing.

Family and friends clamor to help. Michele brings a fan,
Debbie some movies for the VHS player and Lisa a hand massager. Packages arrive every day. Steven decides that tapes of
Hemingway, reading his short stories, will cheer me up. Howie
disagrees; he is convinced that only Bob Dylan can get me
through the bad times and sends a duffel bag filled with cassettes
and a Walkman. Beth finds the perfect bathrobe, David Rothenberg a Woody Allen anthology. I may have to hire a U-Haul to
transport all my belongings to Sloan-Kettering unless cuts are
made.

BY FRIDAY, FEBRUARY 2, three days before admission, prepa-
rations are complete. I'm ready to go. After the morning session

in the office, my father sits down with me in his study. "Every-thing set?" he asks.

"Just about."

My father tells me not to worry about the office. His part-ner and he worked out a new schedule; they divided up my hours.

"Are you sure?" I ask.

"Absolutely sure."

"Well, I won't be gone for long. I'll be back as soon as they let me."

"I know you will." My father is as confident as Daniella. Still, he wants to offer more. Despite his quiet and restrained ex-terior, I can see that. I want to assure him that his strength and love are more than enough.

"What's a couple of months in the big picture," I say non-chalantly. "Besides, I'm going to write a book in the meantime. About my transplant—about how I survived it." I smile.

My father tells me that Mom called Castro in a panic yes-terday. She'd had a bad dream the night before, imagined that the blood tests were botched up, that Michele wasn't the real match. She wanted the girls to be tested again. Castro reassured her. They don't make mistakes like that at Sloan-Kettering. Michele is the one.

"Let's hope," I say. We laugh together.

Later on, after my last appointment, my father long gone, I sit at my desk and survey the room. My father built this office eight years ago and made his study the centerpiece. On one side is a long, curved mahogany desk. On the other a conference table. Across from the desk, where I'm now sitting, there used to be a couch. Floor-to-ceiling bookshelves cover the walls. They are filled with medical texts and journals. A few months ago, the carpenter was called back. A desk was needed for Dr. Biro, Jr. The carpenter suggested removing the couch and replacing it with a desk, custom-built to fit the space.

It turned out a little smaller than I would've liked. I'm a slob and require excessive physical space to fashion order from the chaos of my mental life. My father said we could swap in a year or two; he'd take the smaller desk.

Sitting in front of its freshly finished surface on this ominous Friday evening, I can't help but slump a little. Only six months ago, I'd finished residency and joined my father in practice. It was his dream. He worked hard to make it happen: building the practice, enlarging it, moving from a smaller office to a larger one, forever praising the virtues of his profession. All for my benefit. And I responded like any spoiled child might, with militant resistance: At college, I bivouacked in the Classics Department, far away from the rattle and smut of the organic chemistry lab. When in Rome, I posted a letter detailing my plans to move to Italy and teach Latin. At Oxford, with just one year left to complete medical school, I informed my father of my decision not to return to Columbia. Instead, I would stay in England and become a professor of literature.

The rebellion ceased shortly after this last foray. I woke one morning to an altered landscape. No longer believing that academia, especially the humanities, would satisfy me, I felt compelled to do something more practical. Returning to medical school, I discovered a new respect for medicine, both as an intellectual pursuit and as an emotionally gratifying one. I enjoyed internship in medicine, dermatology residency even more. And when I finished, my father was waiting with open arms to receive his prodigal son. It was nice to spend time with him, discuss interesting cases, share a mutual passion. It was perfect.

Until PNH. I sit up and look around, trying to impress the features of my father's study into memory, wondering whether I'll ever be back. I start to cry. The tears are for my father.

DANIELLA AND I spend the weekend packing and purchasing a few last-minute items. Saturday evening, friends take us to dinner at Da Umberto. I order the *osso buco* and meticulously extract every morsel of fatty marrow from the succulent veal shank. On Sunday morning, we visit a spa for aromatherapy, a massage with essential plant oils. It's my first time. As Arturo, a short, dark, muscular man, rubs oil over the surface of my body, Eastern music softly pulsing against the walls of the darkened room, he whispers the beneficent healing properties of the treatment: lavender soothes the digestive system and enhances circulation. What about the bone marrow? I'd like to ask. I leave feeling so light and relaxed that I might have been persuaded to have back to back bone marrow transplantations—as long as Arturo could be called in periodically to revive me.

Daniella plans a movie for later in the evening. Midway through the generic action-thriller, the screen begins to empty of familiar characters, chase scenes and explosions; images of myself, my thoughts and fears materialize in their place, gradually taking over. My heart pounds, the sounds reaching my ears become garbled, an invisible weight pressing down upon my chest, heavier and heavier, until it is difficult to breathe. I lean back, close my eyes and take deep breaths. Some of the intensity passes but the terror remains. Suddenly, the reality of tomorrow strikes, strikes violently. I have, in fact, been gliding along on an electric walkway, not thinking, simply moving. Now I understand why. The reality is overwhelming, disabling. I want to stop it, to wedge a clog into the mechanism, to run backward, away from this nightmare. Next to me sits Daniella. What is she thinking? Does she sense my fear? I don't understand how she remains so calm. But I am thankful—as she squeezes my hand firmly, bringing me back, propelling me forward, always forward.

My heart is still pounding when we return home. I take a Valium, held in reserve for times like this. Better for Daniella not to see me so upset. I also need sleep. The alarm is set for five-thirty. My bags are out in the foyer. Once again the utter exhaustion of my body, with its falling red count, comes to the rescue. I don't have the energy to panic. There is only sleep.

DAVID AND GOLIATH

※

David triumphed over the Philistine with a sling and a stone; without a sword in his hand he struck down the Philistine and killed him.

1 Samuel 17:50

THIS IS NOT the first time my life has been on the line. Apparently, I am a veteran when it comes to potentially fatal illnesses, so my mother reminds me. The story has been told many times over the years, at birthdays, Passover seders and various other family functions. It has reached epic proportions. And if not for the prominent scar that traverses the inner aspect of my left ankle, the story would be more myth than reality. But Mom can always point to the hollowed curve in my leg for verification.

Now in 1996, she needs more proof. She hasn't slept in weeks, pacing empty hallways until daybreak, trying to make sense of fact and fiction. Despite the dizzying list of questions she poses each morning, she receives few answers. In part because there often aren't any. In part because, like Daniella, she is the wife of a doctor, and as such must be zealously guarded against the terrifying mysteries of medicine, informed of only sanitized bits and pieces of information at appropriate moments. And yet one thing is desperately clear: Her child is in trouble, her boy, her only son. She wants to help, to reassure him. She needs to find something tangible to grab on to.

In the attic, she recovers an artifact central to the myth: a small faded, yellowing card, that had at one time accompanied a flower arrangement. On it is written, in my father's illegible scrawl, a message he sent to my mother from Maimonides Hospital in Brooklyn thirty-one years ago:

> David will beat Goliath
> Love, Les

The story is told in the following way (I can vouch for none of its accuracy). I was born in 1964, five pounds and two months premature, with hyaline membrane disease. The same disease the Kennedy boy had, my mother never fails to point out. At the time, few hospitals in the country were able to treat the often-fatal condition. My lungs, incompletely developed, were unable to expand adequately. I required hyperbaric oxygen to breathe and was fed through a vein in my foot; hence the scar.

The doctors predicted a fifty-fifty chance for survival. They gave my father two options: Leave me at Maimonides and pray that the lungs matured spontaneously before I died; or transfer me to Columbia-Presbyterian, where they were better equipped and more experienced at dealing with the disease. Complicating matters further, the doctors weren't sure, considering my precarious state, that I would make the ambulance ride to northern Manhattan.

Not a pleasant or easy dilemma to be faced with on the happy occasion of your first child's birth. But my father made a decision. They would stay at Maimonides and sweat it out. And like all his decisions, he stood by it adamantly and was sure of the outcome. That was when he sent the note and flowers to my mother who was home recuperating from her difficult labor.

And lo and behold, the gods looked down kindly on the Biro family and, in particular, tiny David, who was struggling against all odds with a mighty Goliath. With strong hands and outstretched arms, they gave David enough strength to overcome his adversary. Three miraculous weeks later, David was back home enjoying the fruits of his victory. The story's finale is usually followed by amens, smiles and toasts for continued health and happiness.

My mother is clinging to the story again on the eve of her son's bone marrow transplant. She wants a sequel. If he could beat Goliath once, there's no reason to doubt that he can do it a second time. She clutches the faded, yellowing card, proof of the miracle.

PART FOUR

ROOM WITH A VIEW

From this hospital bed
I can hear an engine
breathing—somewhere
in the night . . .

WILLIAM CARLOS WILLIAMS,
"The Injury"

CHAPTER THIRTEEN

✥

S TARTLED BY THE loud buzzing of my alarm clock, I spring to attention at 5:30 A.M. on February 5, 1996. An alert sleepwalker, I move quickly to the bathroom, undress and turn on the shower faucets. The warm water feels good against my skin. Today I'm not bothered by the brown sediment curling around and into the drain. Or the water stains on the ceiling, the slow dehiscence of tile around the soap dish. I've grown attached to my shower. *My shower.*

Dressed and ready, I return to the bedroom to say goodbye to Daniella. Two eyes flashing in the darkness, the only sign that her splayed, motionless body beneath the covers is awake. I kiss her through a film of tears that collect at the corners of her lips.

"Don't worry," she says, leaping from the covers to embrace, "everything will be fine." She tries to wipe away the moisture—involuntary, regrettable—but it continues to accumulate. "Let me come with you, David, please let me come."

"No, it's silly. I'm going straight to the O.R. for the catheter placement; you won't be allowed in. Don't cry, honey, everything will be fine. You just said that. You believe it, don't you?"

"Yes."

"I do too. I'll call in the afternoon, after the surgery. I promise."

I throw on my coat and grab the bags in the foyer—a suitcase, duffel bag and computer. My keys will remain on the demilune table beneath the mirror; I won't be needing them.

The air is frigid and still beneath the cover of a steel-gray sky. It is perhaps the only week during this snowy winter that the ground lies bare. I hail a cab, easy this time of day, and am soon ensconced in the back seat, clutching my luggage. I'm off.

To the Mediterranean? To a dermatology conference in Old San Juan or some other tropical clime, trying to escape the blistery cold of New York? So it feels, this routine of early waking, bathing and hauling of luggage; this hailing of cabs in the wee hours.

"Airport, sir?" asks the driver complicitly.

"No thanks," I reply. "Not today. Memorial Sloan-Kettering Hospital. York Avenue between Sixty-seventh and Sixty-eighth Streets." Though not bound for a holiday by the sea, I am still heading into unfamiliar territory and, like any traveler, anxious about what to expect. But the element that distinguishes this excursion from previous ones is my desire to see it end—as soon as possible. It's the end point, not the journey, that propels me forward.

My father and sister Michele are waiting for me in Hospital Admissions. The room is packed with families like mine, bundled up in outerwear and surrounded by luggage. We could be sitting in an airline terminal, listening for our gate announcement before boarding the plane. Everyone is jittery. We talk in fragments. Michele squirms in her seat. I may need to be restrained to stay in mine. All I want is to be whisked to the O.R., done with surgery and installed in my room, the one my friend Naftali Bechar, chief resident at the hospital, has selected for me.

"I guess this is where I'll be coming next week, right?" asks Michele, in a hollow, halting voice. Since her older brother and father have been momentarily incapacitated by fear, the responsibility of breaking the silence has fallen on her shoulders. Little Michele, the baby of the family, called upon to save the day. This particular one. And then again in another week when she is scheduled to return for a bone marrow aspiration. They'll suck marrow out of her and dump it back into me. A simple rerouting of vital fluids. A temporary shifting of the plumbing lines—to flush out my stagnant, diseased organ; to fill it with new blood, new life.

Is she nervous about the upcoming procedure? She'll be put to sleep and jabbed numerous times with a large-bore needle. There will be considerable pain afterward. Yes, she must be. But I suspect she's even more concerned about the possible dissolution of her family.

My name is finally called.

"David Biro?" asks the clerk at the desk.

"Yes."

"You completed the preadmission testing?"

"Yes." Pat Walka had arranged for the blood work, chest X ray and anesthesiology consult to be done last Thursday. I had also filled out a form giving Daniella authority to make medical decisions in the event that I become "incompetent." The memory sends my left eyelid into spasm. I press down on it with my fingertips, embarrassed.

"Then you're all set. Sign the consent first. Josie will take you to the second floor. You can change in the dressing room." She motions to a room behind her.

I slip off my jeans and sweatshirt, put on a white gown. Josie drops my clothing into a plastic bag and places it on the bottom of a gurney. She asks me to lie down. I prefer to sit. We roll to the second floor, my father following along on one side of the gurney, Michele on the other. There a nurse examines me and takes vital signs: blood pressure, pulse, respiratory rate and temperature. Everything is in order; I am cleared for surgery.

While waiting for transport, I observe the traffic of gurneys being wheeled into and out of the second floor. Patients must pass through this toll area before proceeding to the operating rooms. Like me, they come with family. And like me, their anxiety is visible in every gesture, it spills from every pore. But my surgery, I rationalize, will be an easy one: Dr. Kent will insert a Broviac catheter into a large vein in my chest. Others will have more involved and far riskier procedures, to remove deadly cancers that fill their intestines and lungs. Memorial Sloan-Kettering Cancer Center is a chilling place—what happens to people here, what is done to them. I can't help but shake.

An elderly woman in an arm cast identifies herself as the hospital chaplain. After a joke about her recent accident, she asks us to join her in prayer. Before I can interrupt her unintelligible mumblings and let her know my feelings about God, she is finished. Smiling, she moves on to the next gurney.

I am rolling again, this time on my back, waving goodbye to my father and Michele. They will take my bags up to the room and meet me there later. Shivering in a skimpy gown, cold and scared, I wrap myself in the blanket. We pass through empty corridors, stark white walls, antiseptic smells. Electronic doors open magically to allow us entry. When we reach our destination—O.R. 6—the transporter deposits me in the middle of the room.

There is commotion all around me as nurses in scrubs scramble to set up surgical trays and equipment. Ignored, I gaze at the spotless white tiles on the walls, the umbrella-like lights hanging from the ceiling. I haven't been in an operating room since medical school. I hated holding retractors for arrogant surgeons. The procedures were long and monotonous with one or two exceptions—the aortic aneurysm repair, for example, on the old Italian man pushing ninety. After removing the damaged part of the aorta, the body's largest artery, the vascular surgeon was unable to sew on the graft; the adjacent "healthy" tissue was friable and would disintegrate with each stitching attempt. Other surgeons were called in to help. Endless units of blood were pumped in to match the patient's steady losses. Six hours later, the team gave up. The old man left the O.R. in a plastic bag. Why am I reviving this memory now?

"Mr. Biro, how are you this morning?" A cheerful Dr. Kent is smiling down at me from an artificial sky. "We're just about to transfuse two units of platelets before we start, so you won't bleed during the surgery. I hear there was some difficulty obtaining them." He laughs.

"Yes, there was. But they are from one of my friends, right?" I ask nervously.

He nods.

Good. When Dr. Castro informed me I needed platelets from donors outside the family, I called Kenny and Steven. Unfortunately, Kenny passed out at the sight of the needle and not enough platelets could be extracted from Steven's blood. A second team, headed by Tom and David Rothenberg, was recruited. I'm relieved they were successful.

The anesthesiologist introduces herself. She inserts a catheter into a vein in my right hand. Before letting the platelets run, she will inject some medicine. It will make me drowsy, she warns. I feel a tingle and a swish move rapidly up my arm as she presses down on the syringe. The overhead umbrellas begin to collapse inward, their lights dimming—dimming into darkness.

I AWAKE FOR the second time today in an unfamiliar place. Groggy, I sit up to have a look. To my right are several gurneys lined up in a row; each contains a sleeping or sedated patient. We are just outside the operating rooms, waiting to be taken upstairs to our rooms. I reach under the covers and feel the large bandage covering the right side of my chest. No pain.

Time passes and I am rolling again, up and down corridors, in and out of elevators. We stop outside a room on the sixth floor, room 622. Michele is waiting there for me.

"How do you feel?" she asks.

"A little woozy but other than that, okay." Gradually emerging from the anesthetic haze, I inspect my new home. It's a smallish rectangle, about nine feet wide and twelve feet long. There's a large window on one side. Facing west, it looks out onto the apartment buildings and skyscrapers of midtown Manhattan. On the other side is a bathroom; the shower is clean, the toilet surrounded by steel bars for handicapped patients. A formidable, mechanized bed sits in the middle of the room. On the wall across from it hangs a TV.

"It's not that bad, is it?" I ask Michele. She is sitting quietly in the corner, not sure what to say, how to react. "Are you staying?"

Yes, she nods, she would like to stay.

"Don't you have class?" Michele, who finished college last year, is currently enrolled at Columbia's School of Occupational Therapy.

Yes and no, she smiles wryly. Michele has olive skin and a long, narrow face with prominent cheekbones that she inherited from my father's mother. I see myself in that face and yet hardly recognize the person behind it. I left home for college when Michele was eleven, then she did the same when I was in medical school, and suddenly, after years of separation, we find ourselves reunited in a hospital room, preparing to shift marrow. It's a strange twist of fate that neither of us knows quite how to handle.

"Then help me fix up the place," I say. It's easier sometimes to do than to think.

Michele is happy to help. Just like she is happy to share her marrow. We don't talk about her generosity. We don't mention the miracle of her perfect match. Or the lurid details of her upcoming surgery: general anesthesia, needle thrusts to the pelvis, soreness for weeks after. It's all understood tacitly, a matter of family. Were the situation reversed, I would do the same; anyone in my family would do the same.

"Should I hook up the stereo?" asks Michele.

"Sure. Put it on the windowsill."

Together we work to make the empty white space more homey. I unpack my clothes, mostly boxer shorts and T-shirts, and put them in the drawers. Michele assembles the ministereo. I attach the corkboard to the wall opposite my bed and begin arranging my photographs. There are pictures of Daniella and me, from our honeymoon in Baja, Mexico, and our most recent trip to Rome. Pictures of my parents and sisters. There's a great shot of Kenny's daughter, Molly, with chocolate smeared over her face. We fill the walls with family and friends.

Next to the pictures I put up a map of Italy. I also have some reproductions of famous paintings. We'll save the gloomy

Munch and de Chirico for another day. Matisse's bathers evoke happier times. I am especially struck by Ghirlandaio's close-up of Teodoro Sassetti, a beautiful young Renaissance boy. Looking into his father's eyes, he dreams of a future, full of possibility and hope.

My sister is impressed by the collection. "Great idea," she applauds. "I have a few pictures from Fire Island you might like too." Michele brightens at the prospect of being able to do something for me, something that, however small, is thoroughly concrete. "I'll bring them tomorrow."

Dr. Passik is also impressed. He introduces himself after helping me tape the last print to the wall. Dr. Castro had asked him to stop by. He's the psychiatrist on the transplant service.

"I was worried about being confined to a room for so long," I explain. "But I don't think it'll be a problem. The room doesn't feel that small."

"That's wonderful," says Dr. Passik. "I'll come by tomorrow anyway and we'll talk. There are some relaxation techniques I'd like to show you. You might enjoy them."

I raise my eyebrows as the doctor leaves, never a firm believer in shrinks or psychotherapy. Michele appears to have similar feelings.

Our next visitor is Dana, my nurse for the day. Naftali, she says, prepared her for my arrival. "I hear you and Dr. Bechar trained together at NYU. That's where I went to nursing school. Dr. Bechar wanted you in this room because it's closest to the nursing station—so we never forget about you." She giggles.

Dana is young. She has warm, round features, speaks with a nasal tone and smiles a lot. I like her immediately. "Is this your sister?" she asks when Michele returns from the bathroom. "You guys look alike."

"Yes and she's also my donor." Or should I say "the Donor," which is how my doctors refer to Michele. And how is the Donor doing today? they ask. Just fine, I reply.

"That's nice," says Dana smiling. She asks me to lie down on the bed. After removing the surgical dressing, she gently taps the skin around the wound. "Does it hurt?"

"No."

"The anesthesia hasn't worn off yet. When it does, ring me and I'll bring some Percocet." She places a transparent bandage over the skin where the catheter exits my body. Branching off into three separate tubings, the catheter hangs down over my chest like an eccentric piece of jewelry. Dana warns me to be careful with my new pendant. An abrupt tug could easily disengage the delicate connection. She's seen it happen before. Big mess. She giggles.

Michele leaves the room with Dana. She's meeting my mother for lunch and will be back in an hour. I don't mind; I'm tired and would like to rest.

I PLAY WITH the buttons on my control panel, moving the bed into a variety of positions—an acrobat, this mechanical monstrosity. With the head raised, the middle section lowered and feet level, I take in my new surroundings. After a hectic week of preparation—numerous tests, insurance crises, purchasings and packings, room reservations, sessions at the office, and the completion of a draft of my first novel—I finally made it to the hospital. Nothing more to do except wait. For the next eight weeks I'll be lying passively on this bed. Things will be done to me. Dangerous things. Obscene things.

I recall a conversation with Pat Walka. As expediter for the bone marrow transplant service, she is charged with preparing four new patients for admission to the hospital each week. This week being no exception, there must be another three patients somewhere on the floor just like me. And just like me they have recently returned from the O.R. and are settling into their rooms.

I wonder about my new colleagues—where they are, what they look like, how old they might be. I am tempted to pay them a visit. To trade war stories, share concerns, urge them into battle collectively. Until I remember Castro and his statistics. Twenty to 40 percent of patients will not survive the procedure. According to these numbers, at least one of our group, the class of February 5, 1996, will not see the new year. One out of four. One out of four of us will die.

How can I communicate with people in this setting, in Memorial Sloan-Kettering's version of Russian roulette?

I decide not to leave my room.

CHAPTER FOURTEEN

❧

A KNOCK AT THE door. It goes unheard. I am lying on my
bed staring at the ceiling and the pictured walls, the Manhattan skyline through the window. I feel surprisingly calm.
Everything is running smoothly. I slept through the first night at
the hospital without interruption, without Daniella by my side.
This morning, I had my first radiation treatment—no more violent than a whisper of air tickling the hair on my arms. A moment ago, I stopped pedaling on the exercise bike brought in for
me at the request of Dr. Naftali Bechar; nonstop, for thirty minutes, I worked up a nice sweat. All told, it hasn't been that bad.

A second knock at the door, this time accompanied by a
small head poking hesitantly through a small opening.

"Can I come in? It's me, Ellen."

The familiar voice of my friend interrupts my interior meanderings.

"Ellen," I shout, recognizing her face in the doorway.
"What are you afraid of? Come on in."

"I wasn't sure if you wanted visitors."

"Are you kidding? I'm happy to see you."

"You alone?" she asks. "Where's Daniella?"

"At the Asia Society. They're getting ready for the Armani

show tonight. She's been there since yesterday morning and won't be back until late tonight. It worked out perfectly."

Ellen looks perplexed. "What do you mean? Don't you want her to be here?"

"No. Not now. Nothing's happening right now. She'll be here enough in the next two months."

I'm glad Daniella is working, her mind preoccupied with business matters. This ludicrous timing of events—January and February being her company's busiest time of year—will hopefully allow her to ease into the hospital experience more gradually; it'll give her less time to think about it.

"Besides," I tell Ellen, "I don't want her to see me go down for radiation. She'd get upset. It's quite barbaric. Now you, on the other hand, my good friend Ellen, because you're so damn stoic, are invited to attend the next session—that is, if you'll be around at one."

Ellen isn't going anywhere.

"Then it's a date. Don't be afraid. Doesn't hurt at all. It's just the setup that's a little scary. Reminds me of a medieval torture chamber."

Ellen can hardly wait. She asks about the triple-pronged tubing hanging from my chest.

"My Gucci necklace." The radiation and chemotherapy, I explain, will destroy the lining of my digestive tract, from mouth to anus. I won't be able to swallow. Everything—food, fluids and medicine—will have to go directly into my veins through the catheter. "For the next few days, though, it's useless—a mere ornament." I laugh, twirling the plastic tubing around my wrist.

"You're in a good mood," remarks Ellen.

"Would you rather have me sobbing?"

"No, of course not. And I have some news that will make you even happier. Marshall and Will read your novel. They liked it a lot. I think it's time to let Julie have a look."

"They really liked it?" I ask, incredulous. Marshall, a close friend of Ellen's, is a journalist; Will, Ellen's husband, an editor at *Rolling Stone*.

"Yes, they really liked it."

"Then what are we waiting for? Let's get it to Julie."

Julie, another friend of Ellen's, is also a literary agent. An agent that Ellen believes may want to represent me. My own agent. I'm beaming again.

Dr. James Young notices this when he enters the room. "You look very happy today," he says smiling. "We missed you this morning. The team usually rounds at seven. You were down at radiation. How'd it go?"

"Fine."

"Good. I'm Dr. Young," he says, reaching over to shake my hand. "I'll be on service this month and will come by every morning with the team to check on you. If you need me for anything else, just ask one of the nurses to page me. See you tomorrow."

Ellen is confused. She thought Castro was my doctor. He is, I explain, but since he's not on the transplant service this month, he won't be overseeing my day-to-day management. Dr. Young will do that.

I was equally confused and upset upon learning of the last-minute switch. After finally getting used to Castro, growing to like and trust the man, he deserts me and in walks a stranger, with a completely new face, a new personality, that has been entrusted—by whom?—with the task of leading me through the most perilous journey of my life.

"I didn't have a choice, Ellen. That's the way it is here. The doctors rotate every month. Castro was on service in January."

"That's so not fair," says Ellen. "But Dr. Young seems nice."

"Yeah," I reply casually.

When I first discovered that my fate depended on the whims of an arbitrary transplant schedule, I immediately and very uncasually phoned Naftali. Who was on in February? I asked nervously. Who would take care of me? Naftali's research pointed to Dr. James Young. So what's he like? Some of the residents think he's a bit cold, admits Naftali. But that's just his way. He's a WASP from Alabama; it takes him a while to warm up. Don't expect hugs and kisses when you first meet. But he's an excellent doctor, a stickler for detail; nothing gets by him. He'd be my number-one choice if I were in your shoes. I thanked Naftali for the background check and felt relieved. Relieved but also astonished—that I, as a patient, would actively have to seek out this information, that my doctors never fully explained the vagaries of their hospital rotation, never apologized or tried to reassure me. Aren't they aware of how important the bond between a physician and a patient is? It's that issue of pathos again—doctors, myself included, often display a lot more sympathy than empathy.

AT ONE O'CLOCK, Vincenzo appears. He will come three times a day for the next four days to escort me to and from the radiation department. We met earlier this morning—a lean face, a bulbous nose, wedged in the doorway, roaring with heavy Italian accent: "My friend, we go." And we went, Vincenzo whistling as he pushed me along in a wheelchair.

I know the routine the second time around and climb into the wheelchair without a fuss.

"We go, eh, my friend?" booms the merry shepherd.

"Yes, we go." I wink at Ellen as we begin our tortuous journey through a maze of faceless corridors. Ellen asks why I can't walk down myself.

"No walk," booms my cicerone. "He rides. The rules. Right, my friend?"

Right. I had made a similar request earlier, which Vincenzo denied. He was adamant. The hospital had rules and he was there to enforce them. "Sit back," he said. "And enjoy."

I'm glad to have company and go out of my way to make Ellen laugh. While Vincenzo whistles, I sit back in my throne like a king, demanding some grapes and a fan. Ellen is amazed to see me so relaxed. "You're not nervous?" she asks.

"Not really. The radiation takes ten minutes and doesn't hurt in the least. I swear."

I'm not lying. It feels like nothing happens in that gloomy, underworld chamber.

Vincenzo deposits me in the holding area outside the Radiation Oncology Department. He picks up another patient who has been waiting there—an older woman wearing a turban. I recognize her from the morning commute.

Three nurses work the radiation machine. They are all young and attractive, particularly the head nurse. She is Daniella's height, wears tight-fitting jeans and sports a coy British accent.

"So, how are we doing after the first treatment, Mr. Biro?" she asks cheerfully. "Not too bad, I presume. Two more sessions and we'll be through for the day."

I rise from the wheelchair, feeling shleppy in my bathrobe and slippers, and hand the nurse my wedding ring and glasses— no metal objects allowed in the radiation chamber.

The room is dark. At one end there is a large, beige cylindrical machine, the size and shape of an airplane engine. At the other, opposite the sleek engine, is a makeshift structure that could be used for a gymnastic routine; it has two handlebars, placed at waist height, and an old bicycle seat angled slightly below the horizontal. "This is where I go," I tell Ellen, sliding into position. Standing on tiptoe, I grip the handles with my arms extended at the elbows. The nurse straps me into a heavy canvas vest and then secures the vest to the apparatus. "I'm not supposed to move, only my toes and head." I swing my head around and laugh. Ellen attempts a return smile without success.

"Did you bring any music?" asks the svelte nurse.

"I left my Bob Dylan cassette on the table, *Blood on the Tracks*. It's my favorite. You like Dylan?"

"Sure," she replies, inserting the tape into a recorder on the floor beside me. "Feel okay?"

"Never better," I say nonchalantly, following her blurry form exit the room. I take a deep breath.

The door closes, slowly and methodically; it is wired electronically to a control panel outside. A video monitor and microphone ensure that the nurses can see and hear me during the treatment.

"Ready in there?" asks the nurse over the intercom, interrupting Dylan. "Remember—three sessions, each four minutes, with a short pause in between. Any problems, give a holler. Here we go."

Vertically taut and immobile, I stand facing the radiation engine fifteen feet away. A red grid suddenly appears on its face. I trace the laser-generated map back to myself, where it is lighting up my body like an airfield. A loud alarm sounds. The green light above the machine turns off, the adjacent red one turns on.

A second later the alarm stops and I feel a sudden rush of air sweep across the surface of my body. I feel it passing over the small hairs on my cheeks and ears, then the taller ones on my arms and legs. The hair sways slightly in the monotonous wind.

There is no pain or discomfort. No sign of damage to my skin. I take a whiff; no smell either. And yet the artificial breeze carries destruction—"a lethal dose of radiation" were the exact words one of my doctors used. I'm very much aware of this at the moment and it terrifies me. Alone in the dark room, bound securely to the apparatus, I stare at the engine and the bright red light above it—glassless, semi-naked and defenseless against the invisible rays that are harming me, outside and inside, my skin, my face, my eyes, my heart, my lungs, my liver, my spleen. I am powerless to stop it, this torture, this violation. I am crying, crying along with Dylan:

> 'Twas in another lifetime, one of toil and blood
> When blackness was a virtue and the road was full of mud
> I came in from the wilderness, a creature void of form
> Come in, she said, I'll give you, shelter from the storm

I scream the lyrics, desperately trying to shut down the machine, the one I control, the mental one—pretending I'm somewhere else, surrounded by friends, far away from this nightmare. The nurse asks how I'm doing over the intercom. She tells me the first session is almost over. Ellen praises my operatic voice.

"I forgot you could hear me." Imagining my dissonant broadcast, I manage a smile. "Show's over."

The alarm rings, red light off, green back on. The machine shuts down. I can relax, feel safe again.

"Second session," calls the nurse. "Ready?"

"Ready."

Alarm buzzing. Green off. Red on. Rush of air. I feel the urge to urinate. I tell the nurse. I tell her not to worry though, I'll hold it in. I wiggle my toes, grip the bars harder. It gives me something to do. But the urge to urinate is getting stronger; it takes considerable effort to control. And though the breeze is still blowing, moisture begins to collect on my forehead.

"How we doing?" calls the nurse. "Tell us if you want to stop."

"I'm okay," I say, holding on to the bars, holding on to myself—holding everything in, tight, tighter, so that I'm getting hotter and drops of sweat are running down my face. I am dizzy, my vision is blurry. It is becoming blurrier. I feel nauseous. I want to vomit. I'm holding everything in, tight, tighter—until the tension finally cracks and the entire world is sucked up into a vacuum and there is blankness. . . .

I AM HANGING from the apparatus, a tangle of straps supporting the full weight of my body, dragging downward. A trio of nurses hover over me, trying to release me, set me down. Although I see them, understand their movements, I cannot halt my groundward fall. I cannot help them lift me. I cannot speak. I'm a zombie in a shock world, mouth agape, watching a film in slow motion. I feel my body hanging limply in their grasp as they finally unhook me and lay me down on the floor. My attempts at speech eventually materialize into stuttered garble, then a phrase. "I'm sorry, so sorry."

"Don't be sorry," says the head nurse. "Everything's just fine. You fainted. Happens all the time. You were trying to be strong. If you feel that way again, you have to let us know. Okay?"

The nurse hands me a plastic container to urinate in and turns the other way. She asks if I need some time before starting again. No, I reply, I want to get it over with. I want to get the hell out of here.

She hooks me back to the apparatus. I purse my lips and stare defiantly into the eyes of the radiation engine. I will not let it get the better of me a second time. Rage, rage—I think of another Dylan—against the dying of the light.

The nurses are encouraging on the way out. They promise it won't happen again. Ellen is beside herself; she has no idea what to say. I am back in the wheelchair, feeling queasy, my head throbbing. Vincenzo is at the helm. He is whistling. I am silent.

CHAPTER FIFTEEN

❧

T HE FAINT DURING my second radiation treatment draws
a line of demarcation on the Kettering clocks. Time before and time after. There is no bridge across the divide, no possibility of retracing my steps.

The changes are apparent as soon as I return to the room.
My mother and Lisa are waiting with pinched expressions. Ellen
mumbles the details of my collapse. Still in a haze, I interrupt
with my own explanation. It was nothing, a matter of not having eaten, being dehydrated, maybe even anemia. Can't you see,
they're filling me up with red cells as we speak. It won't happen
again.

Dr. Young, paged by the radiation nurses, appears with the
team and confirms my theory. Morning blood tests did in fact
show that my red count had dropped precipitously. The hemoglobin level was 6, the normal being around 12. Two units of
blood were ordered. Dr. Young says I will feel better after the
transfusion.

Worried and upset, my mother ignores my rambling ex-
cuses. Lisa refuses my repeated requests for privacy. Together
they make up a schedule. From now on, I will be accompanied
to and from radiation. A member of the family will always be

on hand to break any future fall, to provide moral support. I am given no choice in the matter.

Daniella arrives later in the afternoon. She has been working feverishly and hasn't slept in over forty-eight hours. Exhausted and labile, she finds me sitting sullenly on a chair, staring out the window.

"My God, David, you look so pale. What have they done to you?" she asks, rushing over, tears streaming down the sides of her face. Daniella no longer pretends to be in control. "What have they done?"

"Nothing, I'm fine." I try to look relaxed. "Bad headache. That's all."

"I'm calling work. I want to be with you."

"No, absolutely not. You'll come in the evenings, you'll sleep here. That's enough. Besides, someone will be around every minute of the day. Lisa has taken care of that."

"I want to be with you."

"No." I won't budge. I won't allow Daniella to see me in that degrading position—strapped into the apparatus, facing the radiation engine. I know how much it would upset her, weaken her. That would make it worse for me.

Changes on the outside—this tidal wave of family, nurses and doctors sweeping over me—are accompanied by internal ones. Fear has assumed a physical dimension. I replay the scene in the radiation chamber over and over again and shudder each time. For a few interminable seconds, I was in limbo between mindfulness and nothingness. I could see and hear the nurses around me, feel their breathing. Yet I was miles away—utterly remote. I could not move, I could not cry for help.

For the first time in my life, I imagined what it might be like to die. Before this, illness and mortality were abstractions that flitted past consciousness. I was never *really* sick. Tired perhaps in January when the counts were at their lowest, but never sick, never threatened bodily, beyond the tests, beyond the slips of papers with their abnormal values. I'm sure that's what troubled Dr. Luzzatto most. Relatively asymptomatic and healthy, at least in a clinical sense, I opted for a transplant that would surely make me sick, sick enough to die. Most patients are terminal when they make that choice; they have suffered; they understand the risks involved.

Awaking from the fainting spell, I find myself in a new reality, far less abstract than the old one, much more tenuous, and without the possibility of escape. I can no longer pretend, look the other way. My body won't allow it. Its injured surfaces are speaking, warning me. I'm terrified of going back down to radiation. I'm scared about what might happen next. Castro's statistics flood my thoughts. The future is no longer a given. Each time its uncertainty is acknowledged, my heart speeds up, my breathing rhythm stutters, I gasp for air. Sudden attacks of panic.

I am grateful to Dana, my perceptive nurse. She brings Ativan to pacify me. Dr. Passik comes by later to help train my mind to relax itself. He heard about the earlier incident.

"I was anemic," I explain. "They gave me a transfusion. Everything's fine now. But I'm glad you're here anyway. Some of your relaxation techniques may come in handy at home. I'm as stressed out as the next guy."

And I am playing games with a psychiatrist. He must see right through me.

Dr. Passik dims the lights and asks me to get comfortable on the bed. We will tape the session so that I can replay it when I'm alone. Take a deep breath through your nose, he says into the recorder. Then slowly exhale through your mouth. Concentrate on the breath as it moves into and out of your body. Picture yourself on the beach in Fire Island, where you love to spend the summer. You are resting, the sun is shining, the water rolling in and rolling out. Like your breathing. The cool, fresh air sweeping into your nose and slowly passing out through your mouth . . .

I THANK DR. PASSIK when the session is over, still doubtful about its value, but willing to try anything. Orpheus picks me up at 5 P.M. for the third and final radiation treatment of the day. After a struggle, Daniella and my mother agree to leave the hospital for dinner. Lisa will accompany me on the descent into Hades. It goes without a hitch this time. The nurses dance around me, coax a smile from my lips, congratulate me on completing the first day. "Brilliant. Absolutely brilliant," says the Brit, waving goodbye.

I almost believe her, so relieved that 25 percent of the treatment is over. I revive more back at the room. My entire family is there. Michele, Debbie, her husband Anthony, Lisa and her husband Michael, Daniella, my father and mother. A train of sympathetic voices and gestures, my family crowds around my bed and encircles me, providing me in effect with another layer of skin, a second coat of protection, that insulates me and keeps all the evil hospital humors away. They make me feel safe.

My mother and Lisa arrange the vapid Kettering spread of withered greens, congealed chicken chow mein, brittle rice and rubbery Jell-O. I consume every last morsel. Friends arrive and squeeze their way into the crowded room. They bring books, sweets and other gifts. Wendy, Kenny's wife, hands me a container of chocolate cookies that Molly, her three-year-old daughter, baked. So she says.

FINALLY, THE ROOM empties out and Daniella and I are left alone. Although we are both exhausted, I persuade her to take a stroll on the floor. Pretty soon, the door will be closed and this small luxury will no longer be allowed. We walk by the nursing station. Interns and residents are writing notes in the charts. I recognize the nurse who took care of me last night.

"That's the one I told you about," I nudge Daniella, pointing to the tall blond with icy green eyes. "She was rude, bursting in every hour, no apologies. I don't like her."

Daniella hopes there will be someone nicer tonight. We walk past open doors. Patients are lying on their beds, IV poles hovering over their heads like trees with twisted branches. The rooms for transplant patients are easy to identify. Like mine, they have cleaning areas out front with sinks, bactericidal soaps and paper towels. There are boxes of gloves, gowns and masks. On each door hangs a white piece of paper. The patient's name, medical record number, age, donor and CMV status are written at the top. Below is a detailed schedule for the coming weeks. I look at them as I pass. They are all the same. Day −10, or ten days before the transplant, Broviac placement. Day −9 to day −6, Total Body Irradiation. Days −5 and −4, Thiotepa, followed by two days of Cytoxan. Day −1, rest day. Day 0, BMT (Bone Marrow Transplant). Day +1, TPN (Total Parenteral Nutrition). Days +5 to +13, Steroids and ATG (Antithymocyte Globulin). Then a week of Aerosolized Pentamidine. Blank spaces occupy Days 26 to 44. Seven weeks in all.

Completing the circle, I am back at my room, standing in front of the calendar on my door:

> David Biro; medical record number—35-36-25;
> donor—sister; age—31; CMV status—positive.

I touch the paper, as if the touching might make it seem more real. It's only Tuesday, Day −9. Many more days lie ahead.

The tattered blue leather chair next to my bed folds out. One of the nurses supplies Daniella with sheets. She lies down, fully extending her long limbs; her feet drape over the edge— Daniella is almost six feet tall. I ask whether she'll be comfortable, whether we should try to arrange for something better. No, she's fine. I reach out and grab her hand. Clasped, our hands hang tautly between beds. I'm glad Daniella is with me. Nighttime has always been a source of trouble for me. My first night passed smoothly enough. The nurse had given me Percocet for the pain from my newly placed catheter; I fell asleep immediately. Tonight is different. In the darkened room, with Daniella beside me, motionless as a corpse, my mind begins to race, over territory covered and territory yet to be covered. I can't stop it.

Years ago I suffered from insomnia. No matter how tired I was, when the lights went down, my mind took off, soaring through consciousness like Brancusi's bird in flight. I would stay awake for hours, thinking, remembering, worrying—flexing the mental musculature, admiring its breadth and depth. Medical internship cured my problem. Exhausted by the rigorous schedule, I would collapse into deep sleep before my brain could get started.

Recalling my trips to radiation, obsessing over small details—the ritornello of the tune Vincenzo whistles, the stitching pattern on the white blanket he wraps around my legs, the color of the tag on the back pocket of the head nurse's jeans, red or orange—I realize a relapse of my condition is in progress. I try my breathing exercises, inhaling through the nose, exhaling through the mouth, imagining the beach on Fire Island, the waves, rolling in and rolling out. I am on the verge of relaxation when a sandy-footed Vincenzo materializes from the void and pulls up alongside my towel. He is followed by the British nurse, clad in skimpy bikini, motioning to the dunes behind her, where the radiation apparatus and its monstrous engine are waiting.

The spectral intrusions hardly matter. Every four hours, the night nurse tramps in and sticks a thermometer under my tongue, inflates a blood pressure cuff around my arm and grabs my wrist to take the pulse. It's Irene again, the roughhouser, so different from Dana, who never misses an opportunity to comfort. Hopefully, the nurses here are more like her. Otherwise I may never sleep a wink at Sloan-Kettering.

CHAPTER SIXTEEN

꩜

THE NEXT THREE days pass without incident. I am settling into a routine. At six each morning, the night nurse takes the final vital sign readings of her shift. I get up soon after, the room still occupied by the dark winter sky moving silently past the window, past Daniella, my faithful vigil, huddled on the pullout chair. I begin a workout designed by the physical therapist for patients with low platelet counts—stretching and leg lifts on the bed, squats and push-ups against the wall. Then I sit down and prepare my "bicycle," a metal bar that attaches to the front legs of the chair on one end and has a set of pedals on the other. I cycle for thirty minutes.

Daniella wakes to the screeching sounds of my racer; its aging joints are coated with a rusty veneer. She changes in the bathroom down the hall—an outrage, she decides, that would be condemned by any sane city inspector. "How can they tolerate such filth? In a hospital? In a hospital with sick people?" She leaves midway into my workout, with a kiss and praise for my stamina. Between 7 and 7:30 A.M., the team arrives. It features a battery of hematology Fellows, residents, interns and medical students. An invading army, they enter and surround me as I pedal a last imaginary lap, pushing a little harder for effect. Dr.

Young, a short, thin man with hair parted to the side, brings up the rear. He is a well-mannered southerner who ushers others through doors before he himself enters.

Maneuvering to the front of his regiment, Dr. Young greets me and then asks the usual questions—"How did you sleep? How do you feel? Pain? Nausea or vomiting? Diarrhea?"

Just tired, I reply. "It's not easy sleeping here. Besides the noise of intercoms and medicine carts, the nurse wakes me every four hours."

"You'll get used to it," says Dr. Young with a smile. "Besides, this is the easy part. The real stuff begins next week."

I can hardly wait.

The doctors take turns peering into my mouth, listening to my lungs, rapping on my belly. When they leave, I shower, careful to protect my pendulous catheter, presently unencumbered by connections to IV medications. I shave with an electric razor my mother brought. No blades are permitted; they can cause bleeding in thrombocytopenic (platelet deficient) patients. Scrubbed and buffed, I ring for the nurse. Dana and Mary are my favorites. Fresh out of nursing school, sympathetic and pampering, they make me feel good at the start of each day. Dana is animated and jovial. Mary is more reserved; there is a transparent kindness and serenity about her, which I've always associated with deeply religious people. In real life, I'm usually wary of such people, but here I find comfort in Mary's spiritual embrace. Every morning, they come to clean my wound, the site where the catheter exits the skin. After putting on sterile gloves, they wash with Betadine, apply Bacitracin and place a clear dressing over the wound. This must be done meticulously to prevent infection. "You're all set," says Dana with a giggle, Mary with a beatific smile.

Michele and Lisa, the early shift on the Biro family schedule, arrive before eight. Naturally gregarious, they have befriended the entire nursing staff, bringing coffee one day, donuts the next. They also have ulterior motives—they want to make sure their brother is well treated.

A punctual knock on the door at eight o'clock is followed by the yodeling of my friendly shepherd Vincenzo. "Eh, Mista Beero, gooda morning, I come for you. We go, eh?"

Fond as I've become of the Italian, I'm never excited about the tortuous descent into the Kettering underworld. My resistance to the wheelchair, however, has completely dissolved. I am now grateful for the chauffeur service. Each successive radiation treatment has left me weaker. I don't admit this to my sisters, as our convoy passes down and around monotonous white corridors, the weight of my body, requiring a little more effort to sustain each day, mercifully supported by the soft, cushioned seat of my humiliating vehicle.

I arrive at the holding area where an older woman, who has just finished her treatment, is waiting to be taken back to her room. Her ghostly white complexion matches the color of the turban she wears on her head. She is hunched over a plastic basin. Periodically, her body stiffens and coils about itself in spasm until her mouth opens to emit a dry heave; she is never able to expel the poison satisfactorily. I want to say something but can never find the right words. My mother, with me in the afternoons, is more successful in her attempts to console.

I am followed on the radiation schedule by a Hispanic man about my age. Emaciated, pale and hairless, he appears even sicker than the old woman. "I'm okay," he initially tells me, then later admits to being nauseated. "Tired too; I sleep all the time." Both patients have probably been through several cycles of chemotherapy. Like most transplant patients—I am an exception—they have some form of leukemia. For any hope of long-term survival, their cancers must be in remission prior to transplantation. My colleagues have been to battle before; traces of their aggressive treatment regimens are evident over their frail, weary bodies.

The sight of the woman before, the man after, is disheartening. I feel terrible for them, for their suffering, for the fact that they are always alone. No one accompanies them down to Radiation, no one is around to hold their hands, tell them jokes. What must they think when they see me and my entourage? Me, who compared to them physically, might seem ready to compete in the Olympics—if only the Special Olympics? I'm embarrassed, embarrassed because I am so different.

Yet in the same terrifying instant, I am the same. I see my face in their faces, my body in their bodies. Here at Sloan-Kettering for identical reasons, we have become one. And though we may not have started at the same point, I will soon catch up. Perhaps this upsets me most—not pity for them but fear for myself.

My response, instinctual and selfish, is to further distance myself from them, making it impossible that I do not come out on top. In a perverse sense, this *is* a competition and the prize is survival. I am stronger and less diseased, I rationalize. Clearly, my chances are better. Clearly, if someone had to die, one of the four members of the class of February 5, 1996, it would be one of them and not me. These thoughts, passing through my mind, as I watch them shudder and heave, leave me cold and speechless. Initially embarrassed that my colleagues should see me so "healthy," so well attended, I am now thoroughly mortified that they might somehow discover my monstrous assessment of our situation. Apart from basic pleasantries, I decide to keep to myself.

THE RADIATION TREATMENTS continue. The trio of genial nurses chatter encouragement as they strap me into the apparatus. The door closes automatically. Green light turns to red, the alarm sounds. I feel the hairs rise on my arms with every blast of gamma air, the swish of my gown against my legs. Four minutes. Pause. Another four. Pause. A final four. It seems that I cling to the bars for hours, gritting my teeth, glaring defiantly at the radiation engine. Along with the nurses, Lisa, Michele, Debbie, my mother, my father, and Daniella, disregarding my objections, watch on closed-circuit television. They cheer me on. "Two minutes to go—you can do it."

On Thursday morning, the nurses hang a lung shield in front of the apparatus. Its horizontal metal strips are aligned with my ribs, a design that allows the radiation beam to penetrate marrow-containing bone without affecting intervening lung parenchyma. On Friday morning, I am the proud recipient of an extra dose of radiation to my testicles. I had argued unsuccessfully with Dr. Castro earlier about the necessity of the "testicular boost." The rationale for cancer patients is clear: the boost eliminates rogue leukemic cells that conceal themselves in the testes and thereby evade chemotherapy. "But I don't have cancer, right?"

Yes and no. According to Dr. Castro, my chromosomal abnormality makes me more like a cancer patient than a routine case of PNH or aplastic anemia. Besides, I would be bombarded with so much radiation as it was. Would a few extra rads really make much difference? And explanations notwithstanding, I have no choice. Since bone marrow transplantation is a relatively new procedure, the first one performed only thirty years ago, there is still no standardized approach. Hematologists in transplant centers all over the world are still experimenting with and trying to optimize the technique. Therefore, every patient, including me, must be enrolled in a scientific study. And if the protocol for a particular study says boost to the testes, then boost it is. And so it was.

After my three sessions on the apparatus, the nurses set up a table directly beneath the radiation engine. As I lie down, they direct the beam at my groin. Trying to squeeze some humor from an uncomfortable situation, the sexy British nurse does her best John Wayne imitation: "Okay kid, drop the drawers." She places a lead shield with a small hole over my genitals. With a string around the base of my scrotum, she lifts my testicles through the hole; my penis, thankfully crushed under the shield, will be spared. The nurses leave the room and after the familiar light-alarm sequence, the magnificent radiation engine thrusts its gamma rays at my defenseless testicles, scarcely protected by the shriveled sac in which they are encased. No pain. Simply shock, shock at what is being done to me.

MORNING SESSIONS AT Radiation Oncology are followed by a barrage of phone calls back at the room. Lisa set up the telephone and answering machine on Tuesday. Since then, the line hasn't stopped ringing. Calls from family and friends. Colleagues from the Dermatology Department at Downstate send their wishes. There are even calls from long-lost high school friends. Most spectacular, however, is communication with Steven. An associate at an investment banking firm, where he went to work after leaving his medical residency—a radical and highly unexpected move for my supposedly steadfast friend— Steven travels all over the country and world to merge, form and consolidate pharmaceutical and health care companies. He phones from 3,000 feet in the air, flying to Los Angeles. Static and the screeching of metal accompany his call from the Amtrak Metroliner en route to Philly. "I'm in Rome now, Davie old boy," comes his delayed voice over the receiver. "How do you feel? Shall I smuggle in some bucatini, some tartufi, for that discriminating palate of yours?"

If only the midday platter of rubbish brought in by the nurse could be exchanged for a hearty Italian *pranzo*. Nevertheless, I finish every last morsel. After lunch, I'm back at Radiation with my mother and Debbie. Later on, friends stop by before the official quarantine begins. Howie and David, ambassadors from the world of high finance, are dressed immaculately in tailored gray suits and polished shoes. They seem out of place in a hospital room where I roam about in T-shirts and boxers. To lighten the incongruity, they doff ties and slouch down in their seats.

Ellen appears on Friday, shortly after my testicular boost, breathless. She brings news from Julie, the literary agent. Julie loved my novel and wants to represent me. "Happy now?" asks Ellen with a smile. Ellen also hands me a fictional press release of my novel-to-be, replete with praise from faux critics and photos of a future book-signing at my neighborhood bookstore. I do not question the sincerity of Julie's note or Ellen's efforts, whether boosting my spirits may have played a small role in their motives. I'm in need of a good boosting at the moment, a more nourishing variety than the earlier one to my testes.

Vincenzo collects me at 5:30 P.M. for the final session of the day. On Friday evening, the British nurse congratulates me. "You're finished, all done. You were brilliant. We'll miss you. Come back and visit." Thanks, but there's no way I'll return to the radiation chamber, even for tea and biscuits with the lovely Englishwoman.

More visitors in the evening: Tom and Marissa, Neal and Anna, Kenny and Wendy, Pam and Rich, Ellen and Will, Scott and Galit, Eric and Chia, Allison, Rhonda, Beth, Lani. I preside over guests in the tiny room, cluttered with paintings, maps and photographs, like a Royal at Court. Though tired and nervous about the future, I am happy in the presence of others, unable to imagine anything going wrong with so many well-wishers around. I find myself joking as if I were at a party.

Daniella finishes work at 8 P.M. and rushes over to the hospital. She is upset by the hordes of people gathered in my room and spilling out into the hall. Daniella is a private person. She prefers not to share her feelings with others and finds all the affirmation and support she needs in one person, her husband. Besides, she tells me, she hasn't seen me all day and wants to spend time with me alone. She would rather have people come earlier and be gone by the time she arrived.

"But my friends may not be able to come earlier," I object. "And my family wants to stay as long as possible."

"They have plenty of time during the day," she insists. "By the time I get here, you're exhausted and ready for bed. That's not fair, I'm getting cheated."

I understand how Daniella feels. I only hope she doesn't antagonize people, especially my family. They go about things so differently. Whereas Daniella retreats inwardly in these situations, my family becomes more expansive. Where Daniella becomes silent, they cannot stop talking. If it were up to my family, they would send for some cots, commandeer the hallways and never leave the hospital.

EVENTUALLY, DANIELLA AND I are by ourselves. She is right. Four days of radiation have taken their toll. No longer called on to prepare my face in front of others, I feel every atom of energy slipping away. But I'm hopeful. Daniella is at my side, no more gamma rays, and week one on the transplant calendar is over. I'm ready for the chemo.

CHAPTER SEVENTEEN

✦

M Y BROVIAC CATHETER, uncapped since its placement five days ago, will no longer be mistaken for decoration. On Saturday, February 10, it assumes its preordained role as direct conduit into my circulatory system. With her characteristic wide-eyed smile, Dana barges into the room, juggling four IV bags under her arms. "Today's the day, kiddo. We're gonna hook you up to the pole. Sorry," she adds wistfully.

"What's on the menu?"

"Let's see, what do we have here? There's Bactrim, acyclovir, Zofran and a bag of normal saline. You know what they're for, right?"

I nod. The Bactrim and acyclovir are given prophylactically to prevent infection when the white cell count plummets, specifically infection with *Pneumocystis carinii,* herpes simplex and herpes zoster. These organisms are present in most of our bodies in an inactive or dormant state; immunosuppression releases them from hibernation, allowing them to proliferate unchecked. Zofran is a powerful antiemetic that works to alleviate nausea associated with chemotherapy. Normal saline is simply salt water used to hydrate patients in case they are unable to drink enough fluids.

"Did they get blood from you today?" asks Dana.

"No, not yet."

With an empty syringe, Dana withdraws blood from the middle port of my catheter and fills four test tubes: a purple top for cell counts, a green top for chemistry, and two red tops for a type and cross so that matching blood products could be prepared.

"A lot easier than sticking you in the arm, don't you think?"

I think. I detest blood-drawing: the shiny, oversized needle that cuts through skin, occasionally piercing both sides of an elusive vein; the stinging sensation when blood is sucked into the Vacutainer; the purple swelling that follows. This is much simpler. And painless. "Help yourself," I say magnanimously. "It's on the house."

When the IV bags are secured to the pole, I excuse myself to go to the bathroom.

"Be careful," warns Dana, "not to pull out your catheter."

I realize immediately this won't be easy. I'm connected by numerous tubings to a pole. Where I go, it goes, and when the distance between us increases beyond arm's length, I feel a tugging at my chest. I am a dog with an inanimate object for a master. Pushing the pole along, I lift it across the bathroom threshold and shut the door. It stands quietly by as I urinate. My new friend, so quickly have we become intimate.

It will also accompany me in the shower. I learn to maneuver my soap hand nimbly around and in between tubing while I pirouette to avoid tangling. I drag my pole-master-friend around during exercises and make sure it is resting comfortably when I begin pedaling. I am enslaved and accommodate; there's no choice.

Dana returns with another IV bag for the pole: Thiotepa, the first chemotherapeutic agent. Daniella and I watch intently

as Dana opens the valve and lets the harmless-looking yellow
fluid flow into the largest port of my catheter. Harmless but
deadly. Ordinarily, there is a limit to the amount of poison that
a patient can tolerate; if the dosing is too high, the bone marrow would be irreversibly damaged, leading to the cessation of
blood cell production and certain death. In the setting of transplantation, however, lethal amounts can be administered because
donor stem cells will "rescue" the obliterated marrow. This in
fact is the rationale for transplanting cancer patients, those with
ovarian and breast cancer for example, that have failed standard
chemotherapy regimens; megadoses of the very same agents
with which they were previously treated will theoretically be
more effective at destroying their tumors. But unlike me, these
patients will typically have their *own* marrow (as long as it is
healthy and disease-free) harvested and then returned back to
them, a procedure known as *autologous* bone marrow transplantation, as opposed to the *allogeneic* variety, in which the stem
cells come from the marrow of *another*.

After five uneventful minutes of following the fluid flow
into my body, Daniella and I relax a little. The poison does its
work silently. I feel nothing. We both laugh nervously.

So goes Round One of chemotherapy. It is followed by
transfusions, a unit of red cells and two of platelets; my counts
have dropped again. According to Dr. Young, I will need blood
products every day. "You should arrange to have family and
friends donate at the Blood Bank; you're going to go through a
lot of blood in the next few weeks."

As soon as she hears, Lisa draws up a schedule, the fifth one
thus far. A fund-raiser and party-planner for a charitable foun-
dation, Lisa has always been very organized. She's also fiercely
protective of me. The sister I am closest to, Lisa was devastated

to learn that she wouldn't be my donor. She felt guilty, she wanted to be the one, she wanted to make the sacrifice.

Instead, she will direct her energy into mobilizing the family. From now on, someone will appear at the Blood Bank every morning. The more stalwart will donate platelets, a task that involves hooking up an IV circuit to both arms with a filtering machine in between. It can take up to two hours to collect a sufficient amount of platelets from the circulating blood. Lisa's name appears on the schedule more than any other.

During transfusions, I usually nap. Premedication with Benedryl, an antihistamine that prevents allergic reactions to the foreign blood products, puts me to sleep.

Saturday churns along. When I wake, we take a stroll around the floor: Daniella, myself and the pole. Daniella's parents come by in the afternoon. Her mother is a nurse on a cancer ward and is familiar with my treatment. I tell her that my head, especially the area in front of my ears, is throbbing. It makes it difficult to hear. A common side effect of chemotherapy, she assures me. "Just feel lucky you don't have much nausea." They stay with me when Daniella goes home to shower.

My parents arrive later. My father, visibly upset, inquires about my earache. "When I remembered that streptomycin can cause deafness," he admits, "I got scared." So scared, in fact, that he tracked down Dr. Young, who at the time was relaxing at home, to voice his concern. But David hasn't received any antibiotics, replied Dr. Young. The pain is from the Thiotepa. It'll resolve in a few days.

"Dad," I ask, trying not to laugh, "what were you thinking? Streptomycin hasn't been used in the last forty years." It is strange to see my father, usually so calm, rattled.

"I wanted to make sure," he says, stuttering.

In the evening, I complain of heartburn. A nurse brings antacid. I fall asleep to the antics of Peter Sellers in *The Pink Panther*. Comedies had been ordered for this very purpose. Norman Cousins claimed they cured him of ankylosing spondylitis, another fatal zebra in medicine, when his doctors stood by helplessly. Who knows? A little Vitamin C, a healthy dose of humor and the body will take care of the rest.

Soporific tranquillity gives way, at some point before midnight vitals, to unease. I see myself swaying on waters that a moment ago appeared soothing. My head is spinning. I wake to find it's no dream; I'm going to vomit. Jumping out of bed, I stagger to the bathroom, forgetting my tangled web of attachments. The tubing jerks, sending my IV pole crashing to the floor. Daniella wakes and rushes to my aid. While I throw up my dinner in and around the toilet bowl, she picks up the pole and IV bags and moves them closer to me. Barely finished heaving, I feel a sudden urge to defecate. No time to clean the mess before a watery trail exits the other end of my body. The stench of the room is making me even sicker. I'm too weak to feel embarrassed, to order Daniella out of my cesspool. She wouldn't listen anyway.

MY MOOD SWINGS from high to low, involuntarily and with unaccustomed alacrity. It parallels my physical state. There are times like Saturday night when I feel miserable; all I want to do is crawl into a hole and disappear. Then unexpectedly, the following morning, I wake refreshed, ready to exercise and knock another day off the transplant calendar.

After my second dose of Thiotepa on Sunday, I realize my ear doesn't bother me anymore. Excited, I convey the news to Daniella. She has just returned with breakfast and the *New York*

Times. I ask her to pull the Real Estate section; we might as well start looking for apartments again. Our plan to move stalled at the advent of PNH. Now that I would soon be cured, the process should be resumed. Daniella, not quite convinced about the timing, understands my desire to see our life's trajectory un-interrupted and rattles off the listings enthusiastically.

Soon the tide turns again and storm clouds roll in. My head feels like a bowling ball, heavy and hard—it drags me down-ward. Mary brings Ativan, the drug of choice on the ward. Whether I'm nauseated, complain of headache or just plain scared, I get a dose of Ativan. How this anti-anxiety medication and cousin of Valium became a panacea for every ill of a bone marrow transplant patient, I offer no answer. Nor do I protest— it does the trick.

Later in the day, a pain develops in my left arm. It starts in the biceps area and radiates to the fingers. My mother is alarmed when I describe the symptom. She immediately thinks of a neighbor who dropped dead of a heart attack on the bas-ketball court. "Don't you remember, he had pain in his arm too. They thought it was nothing. I'm calling Dr. Young."

"Mom, come on, I'm thirty-one years old. Why would I have a heart attack? That's ridiculous. I must have slept on my arm funny."

Still, the idea sends a chill. Especially when I remember that one of the chemotherapeutic agents can be toxic to the heart. That was the reason Castro sent me for an echocardiogram. Only the Cytoxan hadn't been given yet and it's not supposed to cause heart attacks. Mary, responding to the panic-stricken faces staring at her from all directions, brings the famous elixir: 10 mg of Ativan, IV push. The pain lasts the rest of the day and disappears the next, as mysteriously as it appeared.

I sleep on and off during the afternoon, feeling tired and queasy, head aching, arm throbbing. But the evening witnesses another turnaround. My parents, cheeks icy red, arrive with shopping bags. It's below zero outside, the ninth snowstorm of the season has just replenished the roads with another six inches. Though my room is maintained within a narrow range of temperature, the white flakes falling outside my window combined with the brief surge of cold that radiates from my parents' flushed skin, invigorate me.

"I feel great. Had a nice nap."

"I'm glad," says my mother, "I brought some food. Your favorites."

After wiping the bedside table with a string of alcohol pads, Mom begins unpacking. Each item is wrapped meticulously in tin foil, placed in three consecutive plastic bags, each wound tightly with a twist-tie. Stricter decontamination methods would be impossible to find. If I develop an infection, she insists, it won't be from her. She lays out the smorgasbord. First, there's home-made matzoh ball soup. Then a tremendous hero stuffed with prosciutto, roasted peppers and Italian fontina. Fruit compote signals dessert. The eclectic spread reflects the best of my dappled heritage.

I devour the meal at once, ignoring the demands of a respiratory system that urge me to surface every now and then for air. Steven and Tom, who drop by during the feeding frenzy, can hardly get a word in edgewise.

Steven is familiar with my eating habits "Mrs. Biro, your son is a machine." He laughs. "We'll know he's really sick when the appetite goes, if that's possible. Even chemotherapy doesn't slow him down."

Steven recounts the story of our trip to Venice during Carnevale. "At two in the morning, we were about to board a train that would take us back to Rome. It was packed, people were hanging off the sides. David refused to get on. 'Steven,' he shouted at me, 'I'm not going unless there's a food car on board—I'm starved.' I told him I would kill him if he didn't follow. I had to drag him by the arm."

Everyone laughs. Everyone except Daniella. She is still uncomfortable with the number of visitors, who, though well meaning, take away from our private time.

"I can't deal with everybody on top of me like this," she says later. "The room is too small."

It doesn't matter, I tell her. Pretty soon, once the white count falls below 500, the normal range being between 3,500 and 8,000, I'll be in isolation and no one will be allowed to visit.

Daniella and I watch an action movie starring Steven Seagal after dinner. Seagal is a cook on a battleship that gets hijacked. Single-handedly, he rounds up and destroys the bad guys. I've always loved this genre of chase scenes, narrow escapes and biblical-style retribution. I'm sure Dr. Passik, the psychiatrist on service, would approve. It's a lot like guided imagery—except that a tanned, burly, ponytailed Seagal, instead of my immune system (of which, incidentally, I have none at the moment), is called upon to battle my mutant PNH cells.

CHAPTER EIGHTEEN

⌣

O N MONDAY, THE doors are officially closed. My white
count is 400 and falling. "The levels won't rise again for
several weeks," says Dr. Young. "I see you're also developing
some mucositis. That's not surprising, given the degree of
leukopenia."

He points this out to the residents with his penlight; there
are a few small erosions on both sides of the buccal mucosa.
They will get bigger, new ones will form.

I'm prepared. I know what chemotherapy and radiation do.
Targeting rapidly dividing cells, they destroy them by disrupting
DNA synthesis. Cancer cells, and in my case, bone marrow cells,
are among the most vulnerable because they proliferate constantly (unlike more static cell populations found in nerve, muscle and cartilage). Unfortunately, the treatment also harms
innocent bystanders; peaceful organs with quick turnover times
share in the devastation: skin, hair, nails and especially the lining
of the gastrointestinal (GI) tract; it has the highest turnover time
in the body, replacing itself every four to seven days. The conditioning regimen causes the skin to peel, hair to fall, nails to stop
growing and GI tract to ulcerate. This last side effect is the most

serious. The cells that line the GI tract separate the internal from the external worlds. When they die and slough, a critical barrier is breached, allowing infectious organisms to penetrate the body. In addition, the dead cells drag fluid with them and produce extensive diarrhea that can lead to dehydration and electrolyte imbalances. And finally there's the pain. Someone once described it as a giant canker sore running from mouth to anus. The process had begun.

Dr. Young and his retinue are the last people I see in the flesh. I hardly recognize Mary when she enters the room ten minutes later in full isolation regalia. She wears a yellow gown and rubber gloves. A mask covers most of her face.

"Dr. Young just gave the order. We put the red sign on the door. From now on, everybody has to wash up and put all this stuff on." Mary's head tilts to one side. I gaze into her still brown eyes, warm and receptive. I don't have to see the retraction of her cheeks under the mask to know how sorry she feels for me. "Don't be upset," she says. "It'll be okay."

After cleaning the catheter site, Mary hangs a bag of normal saline. She will do this every four hours for the next two days while Cytoxan is being administered. This chemotherapeutic agent can damage the bladder and kidney unless it's diluted with large quantities of fluid. That means several days of nonstop urination to match the furious inflow.

"Look for blood in your urine," advises Mary. "It's a sign of cystitis."

No problem, I tell her. I've become somewhat of an expert at urine-watching since the advent of PNH.

My parents and three sisters are peering into the room through the small window in the door. I wave. It takes them a while to carry out the instructions written above the sink; they don't want to miss a step. Masked and gloved, they finally enter, hesitant, almost stealthy, like a band of burglars. I'm afraid they might conceal things from me behind their paper and latex wrappings. They promise not to.

My mother and Lisa are obsessed with cleanliness. When I pick up the phone, they rush over to intercept, disinfecting the receiver with alcohol wipes before it makes contact with my vulnerable ear. They dust off the books on the window ledge and beg me to remove my slippers when I lie in bed; the floor is filthy, warns my mother. Although they've always been like this—toothbrush- and towel-sharing is strictly prohibited in my house—the obsession is now moving to more extreme levels. Michele and I take after our father, who is notorious for tracking dirt, sand and other earthly particles over our impeccably clean floors. He is also responsible for creating minor monsoons in the bathroom as he slaps water over himself in what might appear to the uninitiated as some bizarre Hungarian purification ritual. Debbie, the middle sister, stands somewhere in the middle.

During a pause in the sterilization process—like a government investigation, it is never over; the process remains ongoing—my father asks about Daniella, how she's holding up. Fine, I tell him. He persists, unsatisfied with my brief response. He would like to know why she seems upset when the family is around. Everybody wants the same thing, right? To make you as comfortable as possible, to get you through the transplant safely. We're all in it together. Everybody except Daniella. Why? He doesn't ask this directly. I see it in his roving eyes, his stuttering speech. I see it in my mother's attempts to redirect the conversation, to avoid conflict. I knew it was coming.

I try to explain. Daniella doesn't gravitate toward family the same way we do. That goes for her own family as much as ours.

"What about in times of crisis?" asks my father. "Doesn't that change things?"

No, to the contrary, it makes her even more detached. When too many people are around, telling her what to do, she gets annoyed and flustered. And on top of that, she's been working twelve-hour days, with no time to herself, no time to unwind. I'm sure Daniella feels guilty about not being here all day. She only gets to see me at night and in the early morning; we're asleep the rest of the time. She wants to be with me—alone—as much as possible. Can't you understand?

No. My parents can't understand. But they won't push. Neither will I. There is a chasm, of age and culture, between Daniella and my family. They're traditionalists with Old World values. Daniella is more modern in orientation. No way to bridge the gap, even, I suspect, in these extreme circumstances. I just hope the smoldering conflict doesn't erupt into full-scale war.

THE FIRST DOSE of Cytoxan passes through the large port of my catheter. I vomit shortly afterward. Mary gives me Zofran to alleviate the nausea. I don't feel like eating. I don't feel like doing much of anything. My mother paces back and forth, going through box after box of alcohol pads. She is cleaning my computer and wiping down, for the tenth time today, the row of paperback books on the windowsill. The room begins to reek of alcohol; if it didn't make me sick, I might laugh.

I arrived at Sloan-Kettering one week ago with the better part of my study: a suitcase of books, a stack of medical journals, my laptop computer. I had hoped to keep a diary, write a short story, perhaps even start a second novel. What a joke, my grand plans for this unexpected windfall of leisure time. Even when feeling good, I have no desire to read or write; I can't concentrate. My mind swiftly pushes me in other directions, away from Kundera and toward illness, away from Bellow and toward bone marrow transplantation, away from everything except the fear of complications and the uncertainty of my future.

Accepting this, I've tried to keep my mind a relative blank, to focus instead on cycling and push-ups, conversation (non-confrontational) and mindless Steven Seagal movies. So I tell my mother when she asks about the writing.

"I started a diary and stopped after two sentences. Haven't written anything since. Just take the damn computer home. Who would want to remember this anyway?"

"Maybe you'll change your mind one day," says my mother. "That's why I've been keeping a diary. Your father too. The doctors said that there may be a time when, even if you wanted to remember, you probably wouldn't be able to."

ON TUESDAY, THE second dose of Cytoxan is administered. I am in pain. New ulcers are forming on my tongue, along the sides of my mouth, around my gums. A cough develops; the thick, viscous matter accumulating at the back of my throat demands to be expelled. I bring up large globs of bloody phlegm, the remains of epithelial cells that once lined my upper aerodigestive tract, explains Dr. Young. It will get worse. He orders a morphine drip. The steady flow of narcotic into my circulation will make the pain tolerable. He doubts I'll be able to eat from here on in.

"I'm not hungry anyway," I confess.

"That's okay," replies Dr. Young. "Beginning Saturday, you'll be fed intravenously."

I don't talk much on Tuesday. The morphine leaves me hazy and confused. When a brief spell of clarity intervenes, I become nervous about what is happening to me, to my body. My parents don't know how to react. There are many pauses, deafening spaces of emptiness. Mom tries to divert. She mentions the steady stream of phone calls from friends at Oxford. They're waiting for me to get well so that we all can graduate together. Memories of Stilton cheese, pints of Guinness at the Eagle and Child, the Bodleian Library and the neverending rain make me smile. Most of the day, however, is spent in silence.

That night I talk to Daniella. The mask makes it difficult; she seems far away. "Honey, why do you seem distant with my family? I don't understand. They've been so kind. Every chance they get, they're here taking care of me. It makes me feel good. Aren't you glad?"

"Yes." Daniella doesn't want to talk.

I push. "Then why are you upset? This should be a group effort, with everyone involved. It's important to me."

"I can't be like that," says Daniella after a long pause. "I just can't. Your family is overbearing. They're stifling . . . your mother cleaning all the time, your sister making up schedules, your father telling me what to do, how to act . . . I need my space, David. This isn't easy for me, you know, it isn't easy." She is sobbing. Her mask bunches up as her face contorts underneath. "Everybody is different . . . people are different . . . they get through things differently." Daniella gasps between each phrase, unable to connect them. "If I'm going to make it . . . through this . . . I need my space . . . I need to feel like I have some control over things." Struggling to breathe, she manages to finish. "Your family is so dramatic, so neurotic . . . they worry about every damn thing . . . one minute you're going deaf, the next you're having a major heart attack . . . they're making me nervous. . . . Can't you understand?"

"Yes. But can't you try?"

"I'll be here for you, I promise. Every night, every weekend. But I have to do it on my terms. Otherwise I won't survive. Okay?"

Okay.

Daniella finally stops weeping. She pulls out her makeshift bed and climbs in, her feet dangling off the edge. She looks uncomfortable in her gown, mask and gloves. I don't know how she sleeps like that.

"I love you," I say, reaching across the space between us and grabbing her gloved hand. It's almost as though we're not really touching. Soon the same disconnect will extend to the emotional realm. The doctors warned that between the pain and the drugs to ease the pain, I will be incoherent much of the time. I had better hold on to these moments with Daniella.

CHAPTER NINETEEN

❦

WEDNESDAY, FEBRUARY 14, DIARY OF DOLORES BIRO

There are times when David is completely out of it. Dr. Castro warned us this was going to happen and would get even worse in the coming weeks. That's why it's more critical than ever to write everything down. I'm sure that some day, when he is better, David will want to know what happened to him, and to us, during this awful period in our lives.

It is difficult to spend so many hours in David's room. I feel helpless. This evening, I opened a package David received from a friend and tore my gloves. Later David asked for some juice. I touched the paper cup with my torn gloves, with my exposed skin. There could've been germs from the dirty floor. I'm very upset. I feel guilty.

THURSDAY, DAY 0, has arrived. Until now I've been on the negative side of the transplant calendar, which sounds as though nothing has happened. But that was only true for yesterday, the day after my last dose of chemotherapy and the completion of the so-called conditioning regimen. A radical

inversion of Creation, Wednesday (Day −1) was nonetheless labeled "a day of rest." And on the ninth day the doctors rested,
after wiping out a marrow and dismantling an immune system
that took thirty-one years to erect. Dr. Young informed me that
my white count was officially zero.

My pulse pounds against the hollows of my temples; I feel
its heavy beat. ZERO. What does it mean? How can there be *no*
white cells? How can I fight infection? How can I survive? I
have no answers to these questions. As a patient, the vanishing
number would be scary enough. But as a doctor, with too much
information, it is shattering.

And yet Dr. Young relayed the news so calmly. It had to be
zero, he reassured, that was the plan. Everything was going perfectly. As long as there were no nasty bugs that antibiotics
couldn't eliminate, I'd be fine.

Merciful morphine flowing through the IV tubing. Alongside it, I lay, dipping in and out of consciousness. For a day off,
Wednesday was no picnic. I was groggy and confused. Constantly nauseated, I vomited repeatedly. I had splitting head-
aches. Exhausted, I slept and dreamt weird dreams—people
upsized and downsized, clad in unnatural colors, saying and
doing bizarre things. I kept waking with a start.

I feel better today. Dr. Young, responding to my wife's concern, lowered the dose of narcotics. Daniella was up all night
trying to pacify me; I had been hallucinating. The fog is lifting;
there are more and more moments of clarity. My father and
Michele knock at the door at 9 A.M.

"Michele wanted to see you before she went down to
surgery," says my father. He is pushing her forward, practically
forcing her.

Is she scared?

I don't ask. In fact, I can hardly look at my sister. Better to follow the example of my doctors and think of her as the Donor, keeping it all very abstract and objective. Otherwise it becomes too humiliating—to face my baby sister, whom I once held in my arms, proofread book reports for, chastised for coming home late, my baby sister who is now about to save my life. Somehow, I resent her for this. I resent the hideous reassignment of roles. It makes me feel ashamed.

"I'm ready," says Michele tentatively. "My marrow is too."

My sister is scared all right—with the Illinois and Jamshidi needles waiting, who wouldn't be? But that hasn't stopped her from ardently preparing for her role as donor. Usually a vegetarian, for the past few weeks she's been overdosing on red meat. There are tons of iron and vitamins in red meat, she says, to beef up the stem cells. She is sure her marrow will work wonders in my body. I hope she's right.

"Good luck," I call out feebly as she's leaving.

DR. CASTRO VISITS in the afternoon. I've seen him only twice since admission and want to make sure he is following my progress. Every step of the way, he assures me. Dr. Young provides him with daily reports. He's looked in several times while I was sleeping. Today he brings news from the O.R.: "The harvesting was a success. We obtained plenty of cells from the Donor. She's in Recovery right now. She's fine."

"When do I get the transplant?"

"In a few hours. The marrow is being processed to filter out the T cells. We're right on track."

After thanking him, I urge him not to forget me.

"Impossible," he replies with a smile. A pause accompanies the gesture, imbuing it with a touch of irony; Castro uses the time to savor the humor internally and carefully choose his next words. "Don't worry, David. You're in good hands."

I believe him. But still, it's difficult to remain calm in the face of the gaping facts of my predicament. I've just received a lethal dose of chemotherapy and radiation. My white count is zero. If Michele's stem cells don't take, I'm dead. My marrow would never recover. I would be overwhelmed by infection.

I can't eliminate this knowledge. And yet, *that was the plan*, as Dr. Young had pointed out. The lethal dose of poison was necessary to insure that none of my marrow survived, that every last one of my mutant, PNH-ridden cells were destroyed. But now that the plan has moved from being an idea, a graph scribbled on Castro's notepad, a handwritten calendar taped to the front of my door, to a physical reality, one with incredible and now tangible risks, I stagger. How did I ever agree to this insanity?

There is no way to dissolve the tension in my hospital room. It pierces through isolation masks and saturates the stares of my mother, Lisa and Debbie. It halts conversation, disrupts sleep and deadens the comic effects of Peter Sellers. We are waiting breathlessly for the stuff that will make me whole again, that will fill my empty marrow, that will procreate and take me from zero to normal, that will remove the potential dangers bearing down upon my little world. We are waiting for Michele's bone marrow.

The destructive phase is over. Phase Two, a period of rebuilding, is about to begin. The coming weeks will be the most precarious. Conventional doses of chemotherapy and radiation for the treatment of cancer may also result in white counts of zero. While platelets and red cells can be replaced by transfusions from others, white cells cannot; because they are "mindful" and can differentiate between self and other, they would reject the body of another. Patients must therefore wait until their own cells recover from the toxic insult, which can take several days. In cases like mine, the recovery time is measured in weeks and sometimes even months since it depends on a far more complicated series of events. I must wait for Michele's marrow cells to locate, acclimate and then respond to my bone marrow, their new home.

The graft, composed of my sister's stem cells, will be infused into a vein through the catheter in my chest. From there it must find its way to the poison-depleted cavities of my bones. This journey is one of the most extraordinary events that takes place in the human body. How do Michele's cells know where to go? How are they able to exit the circulation and enter my marrow? Physicians have only recently begun to uncover some of the details involved in this homing process. It turns out that stem cells carry specific protein markers on their outer surfaces that can be called "addressins." As the cells circulate through the body, the addressins (Michele's) eventually recognize complementary markers (mine) on endothelial cells in the blood vessels of my bone marrow. The recognition leads to an embrace, causing the stem cells to attach to the vessel wall and thereby resist the flow of blood that pushes them forward. The cells will then use the same surface proteins to hoist themselves out of the vessel and pass into the marrow, much as a climber ascends a mountain, gripping onto the rock with his feet and hands. Diapedesis, the name given to this cellular means of locomotion, literally a "leaping across and through" body tissue, will cease only when the stem cells reach their final destination.

Next, Michele's cells must seize control of my marrow, a process known as engraftment. Although most of my marrow cells have been destroyed by the conditioning regimen, the few remaining ones will identify Michele's cells as foreign, despite their "perfect match." Weak as they are, they will put up a fight and attempt to oust the invaders. This can lead to rejection of the graft. To prevent this, I will receive large doses of corticosteroids and antithymocyte globulin (ATG) to suppress my immune system. The ensuing battle for control of my marrow prolongs the period of leukopenia.

Finally, once the graft takes, Michele's immature stem cells must adjust to an unfamiliar environment. They must learn how to communicate with other cells in my body, which will soon be sending SOS messages, in the form of chemical signals, alerting them of my dangerously low blood counts. Michele's cells must learn to respond to these urgent requests by procreating as quickly as possible so that my marrow can be replenished.

The overall process may take a month or longer before the white count reaches safe levels again. During this time I'm a sitting duck, vulnerable to attack from without and within. All visitors, including doctors and nurses, must wash thoroughly and put on gloves and masks before entering the room. Strict sterilization technique must accompany any direct contact with my catheter. These measures prevent infections with microorganisms from the external world—bacteria, viruses, fungi.

More worrisome, however, are the organisms that are already in my body, part of my natural flora. These bacteria and viruses have peacefully coexisted with me for a lifetime. Yet when the immune system is impaired, they can proliferate and wreak havoc. Infection with cytomegalovirus (CMV), herpes simplex virus (HSV), herpes zoster virus (HZV), Epstein-Barr virus (EBV) and a parasite named *Pneumocystis* contribute to many fatalities during the early period following transplantation.

I replay the sequence of events in the engraftment process over and over again. I can't help but list and relist the endless sources of infection. Likewise, I recall, with horrifying vividness, other potential complications that can develop. If my platelets aren't adequately replaced, I can bleed into my lungs and brain. Fatal thromboses of the liver can form in blood vessels damaged by the radiation. There is also interstitial pneumonia. And graft versus host disease.

Deep breaths into the nose, slow exhalations through the mouth. Frantic attempts to transpose myself to the sunny shores of Fire Island. I'm trying, Dr. Passik, I really am. I don't admit that his relaxation strategies aren't working. Morphine and Ativan are far more effective. So are our daily conversations. Passik applauds my continuing ability to exercise and laugh. "Not everybody does this well," he says. Whether or not all his patients are offered the same encouragement is irrelevant. I'm a competitive sonofabitch.

AT 7:30 P.M., Daniella arrives, winter-flushed and excited. "Did you get it?"

"Not yet."

"What are they waiting for?"

I raise my brow, shrug my shoulders, trying to conceal my nervousness. Castro was in hours ago. A white count of zero is flashing before my eyes. There's no time for putzing around. I want answers. So does Daniella. She pushes the alarm button. One of the night nurses responds to the call.

"Dr. Young just phoned," she informs Daniella. "He'll be up soon. He wanted to give David the transplant personally."

Less than a half an hour later, Dr. Young enters my room with a syringe in his right hand. He apologizes for the delay; preparing the marrow took a little longer than usual. "Are you ready?"

"That's it?" I ask incredulously, gazing at the 10 cc syringe, filled with a thick yellowish substance. Without the red flecks of blood, it could easily pass for egg drop soup from our favorite Chinese takeout.

"That's it," he confirms. "A little anticlimactic, huh?"

I'll say.

Dr. Young cleans the largest port of my catheter with an alcohol swab and injects heparin to flush the line. Then he sets up the transplant syringe. "Here goes."

"You don't inject it into his bone marrow?" asks Daniella.

Young shakes his head. "It'll get there on its own."

The injection takes a minute. When he's done, Dr. Young tosses the empty syringe into the red plastic "sharps" container on the wall. My transplant is complete.

"We heard the hematology Fellow usually gives the injection," I tell Dr. Young.

"As you can see, there's not much to it."

"I'm glad it was you. You've been so kind. We appreciate it."

Daniella and I are left dazzled by the simplicity of the event. A routine injection, my life hanging in the balance. I pray for my sister's cells, for their safe, swift journey through the blood vessels of my body; for their addressins, those remarkable postal codes that insure delivery to the right location; and for their nimble movements across the obstacle course of cells and stroma that lead to my marrow. I pray that once they arrive, they start reproducing as soon as possible and drive my counts up to normal levels again.

A small syringe filled with egg drop soup—the antidote for poisonous chemicals and gamma rays.

I AM STILL speechless when an unexpected visitor walks through the door and stands silently at the foot of my bed. I don't recognize him, gloved and masked.

"It's Dr. Luzzatto," prods Daniella. "Dr. Luzzatto, hi, it's

Daniella." Everyone is always introducing and reintroducing themselves in my isolation suite, never sure of who's who in this masquerade of protective clothing. "David just got the marrow."

"Yes, I know. I saw Dr. Young in the nursing station."

I am happy to see Luzzatto, happy to hear his soothing Italian accent. I tell him so.

Luzzatto smiles. He has been following my progress closely. He gets reports from both Young and Castro. Everything has been positive.

"I'm scared," I confess, "but glad I went through with it."

Dr. Luzzatto nods ambiguously; he's still not sure my decision was the right one. I will meet him on more neutral territory. "There's no way PNH could come back after all this, is there?"

"That would be unlikely." He is about to say something else but stops himself.

What is he thinking? Probably that I must first survive before a relapse of PNH becomes an issue.

I don't care. He is rooting for me. I see that and take his hand.

CHAPTER TWENTY

⋙

FRIDAY, FEBRUARY 16, DIARY OF LASZLO BIRO

Yesterday was Day 0 on transplant calendar. Had no chance to write. Got up 4 A.M. and left with Michele at 5:30. At Sloan by 6:30. David in bad shape with mouth sores. Mich insisted on seeing him before harvest. 8 A.M. she was taken to O.R. Watched David suffering from sores and stomach cramps. Michele throwing up all afternoon from the anesthesia. She took it so well. Only concern was her brother.

FRIDAY, FEBRUARY 16, DIARY OF DOLORES BIRO

David now has ulcers at the back of his throat and esophagus. He is hungry but cannot eat. Surprisingly though, he is still able to exercise. I don't know how. Anthony and Michael donated blood today. We left the hospital at 6 P.M. It was a nasty day, snowing more than eight inches. Les, Anthony and Michael shoveled when we got home. I made dinner for the family. We stayed together and talked until midnight.

I AM CYCLING WHEN the team arrives on Friday morning, February 16, the day after the transplant. Dr. Young asks how the mouth feels, whether I can still eat.

"No. The sores are bad." And so is my voice. The mucositis and buildup of phlegm is making it difficult to talk.

"It doesn't matter. Today we'll start feeding you intravenously."

During the examination, he spends considerable time poking around the right upper quadrant of my abdomen. A few spots are exquisitely tender. "Anything wrong?" I ask.

"Take a deep breath, David." As I inhale, Young palpates for the liver—I wince.

Dr. Young turns to the hematology Fellow. "Have a look, Dr. Rickert, tell me what you think." The Fellow looks, feels, reproduces the pain and then nods his head in agreement.

"Your liver is slightly enlarged and tender," Dr. Young explains. "Although this is most likely due to inflammation from the chemotherapy, we have to consider the possibility of thrombosis, of hepatic veno-occlusive disease, especially in a patient with PNH. We're going to start a heparin drip."

One day after my transplant and already a possible complication. I try to remain calm but am frantically dialing home as soon as the team is out the door. They're being cautious, my father assures me, that's all. Nevertheless, he promises to call Young after rounds.

The appearance of the hospital barber distracts me from visions of liver failure. My hair, shedding since Tuesday, covers my bed and makes me itch. Better to remove it all at once rather than be tormented by a slow molt.

The barber positions me on a chair and throws a drape over me. "Nothing fancy," I jest, more for my sister Debbie, who is sitting close by, than the razor-wielding stranger. "Just a clean shave." The electric razor buzzes monotonously while silent tufts of hair fall to the ground.

Afterward, I gaze in the mirror. The returning image is strange and unfamiliar. I pass my hand over the surface of my smooth, hairless skull. The hollows of my temples have become cavities. My complexion has taken on a bluish hue. The contours and proportions of my features are distorted. Is it me? Looking so sickly? Looking like some concentration camp survivor? Can it be? Or am I just part of the masquerade, the only one without a mask?

Images of the past, the healthy past, are resurrected to still my trembling hands. I am suddenly struck by the picture of Rema on the wall, beautiful Rema in her long, white wedding gown, smiling widely. Her hair, thick and curly, reaches down below her shoulders. She was devastated when chemotherapy caused it to fall out soon after that picture was taken. We all told her she looked great without hair; she did, she always did. Now a year later, the same words are repeated—this time by my sister Debbie to me. Irony is not just a trope we encounter in literature; it gallops through life, snickering.

I AM RELIEVED when the "Rinser" shows up with her cart of tricks. For patients on the transplant service, she is a goddess, worshiped more fervently than nurses and doctors combined; she provides relief where others consistently fail.

A knock, a poking head, a query from the Deity: "Busy?"

No, no, never busy for you, O Great One.

Regardless of my condition, I revive as the Rinser sets up

shop alongside my bed. She plugs her contraption into the wall: a simple glass bottle with a rubber seal connected by plastic tubing to a small motor. The Rinser fills the bottle with sterile water. She places a long, thin, hollow metal cylinder at the top of the contraption. Then she hands me a plastic container, shaped like a banana-split dish, and a stack of gauze pads.

"Now open up, nice and wide," she says, peering into my mouth with a penlight. "Some new ones today, I see. Starting to hurt, I imagine. Let's see if we can't help a bit."

She turns on the motor, positions the nozzle along the side of my mouth and releases the switch. A stream of water rushes forth, splashing over the dry, encrusted sores scattered throughout my oral mucosa—instant relief, momentary bliss, may it last forever! When my throat fills with cool, refreshing water, the Rinser pauses and allows me to expel it, along with the annoying phlegm, into the banana boat. She follows with another spraying. I can barely hold back tears of ecstasy; no amount of morphine can substitute for the soothing spritz.

I am shattered when the Rinser leaves, even when she promises to return for an encore performance in the afternoon. If she's late, my mother will track her down. If she doesn't spend enough time with me, my sisters will chastise her. They recognize, as my discomfort grows, the impressive healing properties of a good rinsing.

ON SATURDAY, I become febrile for the first time. This is not unexpected. There is no way to prevent infection during the period of zero white cell counts. Fortunately, doctors have a powerful array of antibiotics at their disposal to subdue most infectious organisms.

Dr. Young doesn't find a definite source for the fever when

he examines me; there is no abscess in the mouth, no rash on the skin; the pharynx is not injected, the lungs are clear. I offer no localizing symptoms that might help him pinpoint the area of inflammation. As a result, he will have to treat me empirically— that is, he will treat me without knowing the precise cause of the infection—with ceftazidime and gentamicin. These two antibiotics provide broad spectrum coverage against all but a handful of potential bacterial pathogens.

I tell Dr. Young that the sores in my mouth are getting worse—I can hardly swallow or talk. That the right side of my belly, where the liver is located, is still tender. And that my scrotum is starting to hurt. He lifts the bedsheet and removes my boxers to look.

"We'll have to raise the morphine," says Young. "Since the pain level is higher, the increased dosage shouldn't cause as many side effects. We can switch to a different narcotic if it does."

I'm becoming less aware of what is happening. Moments of clarity are dwindling. I don't fight the sedating effects of the medicine; the alternative is more pain, more anxiety. Instead, I doze on and off most of the day.

On Saturday night, I have a frightening dream. Somehow, I've managed to escape from the transplant ward and find myself casually strolling down Fifth Avenue. I decide to stop at the Public Library for an espresso at one of the tables out front. It's springtime. People, dressed in shorts and skirts, fill the marble staircase, smoking, snacking, chatting. I enjoy watching them. I enjoy the lovely weather, upset only for a moment at the discovery of my attire—a hospital gown and slippers. It doesn't seem to matter; no one notices.

I walk to a pay phone and call home. "What a glorious day!" I tell my mother.

"Where are you?" she asks. Alarm sets in with my response. "How did you get out of the hospital? Didn't anybody stop you? You're supposed to be in isolation. The white count is zero. Go back," she screams. "Hurry, hurry before it's too late."

Suddenly, I remember PNH, Castro, the transplant, the vanishing white count, the gloves and masks. Now I too am alarmed. I rush into the street and hail a cab. Within minutes a traffic jam materializes. I jump out and start running down crowded streets and intersections, banging into pedestrians that block my way. It's nighttime when I finally reach the hospital. Still the journey is not over. I am unable to locate the ward. A maze of corridors, leading to a series of underground passageways, delays my progress. There is no one around to help. The elevators are locked. Terrified, about to give up, I discover a staircase that leads to the sixth floor. I tiptoe quietly back to my room and slip under the covers so that no one should learn of my brazen indiscretion.

I am thankful to wake up in my hospital bed on Sunday. The dream served a purpose. I recognize this in spite of the narcotic high. It has completely revamped my predicament by applying the laws of relativity. There are always greater dangers. For the first time since my arrival, I feel safe at Sloan-Kettering. Astonishing how slickly the mind operates.

CHAPTER TWENTY-ONE

MONDAY, FEBRUARY 19, DIARY OF DOLORES BIRO

David called at 9 A.M. and said he had a bad night but was feeling better this morning. He was able to spit up a large mass of phlegm, allowing him to swallow and breathe more easily. He still has fever and the resident told him he might have to go on amphotericin. David was upset, he is scared of this medication. I bring food to the hospital, hoping he might eat, but he can't. I also bring special bandages for his nose. The nurse thought they might help David breathe by opening up the nasal passages. It gets worse at night. I pray they work.

MONDAY, FEBRUARY 19, DIARY OF LASZLO BIRO

Liver remains enlarged. Will not tell Dolores. Heparin still running. New worry today. Too much heparin may cause bleeding, especially with low platelet count. Can't stop thinking about possible complications. Driving me stir crazy.

ONDAY MORNING BEGINS on a positive note. After forcing myself to exercise, I start to cough and bring up sputum. Suspecting the mass at the back of my throat has loosened and could possibly be dislodged, I continue to cough even though it hurts. Large globs of thick, bloody matter pass into the toilet bowel. Feeling better, I drag my IV pole back to bed: air is moving more freely through my airways; talking has become a little easier. Daniella, initially alarmed by the grating noises emanating from the bathroom, is pleased to see me smiling.

Later on, however, there is a new source of discomfort. My scrotum is swollen and inflamed. The skin is beginning to slough, ulcers are developing. By evening, the entire scrotum is denuded and raw. I can hardly sit or lie down; any contact between my burning flesh and the bed causes excruciating pain. The nurse pages the transplant team.

Dr. Young and his staff take turns inspecting my groin. I am on display again, in the most degrading position to date. I watch the horrified expressions on the faces of the interns and junior residents. "Acute radiodermatitis," points out Young. "A common sequela after a radiation boost to the testes."

He gives me instructions on how to care for the wound. It must be kept clean so that bacteria are prevented from entering the body. The morphine level will be increased again to alleviate the pain.

I phone my father. "Radiodermatitis of the scrotum," I inform him in my raspy, scarcely intelligible voice. "It's bad. . . . Need some Telfa pads . . . some Silvadene. . . . They have nothing. . . ."

My mother arrives with both items in less than an hour. I put a thick coat of the soothing white cream over my scrotum, then cover it with a pad. The Telfa has no adhesive material and will be easy to remove. I try unsuccessfully to tape the dressing in place; the three dimensions of the wound make it impossible. I'll have to lie in bed, motionless and spread-eagle, until it heals. It could take weeks.

My mother spends more time at the hospital than anyone else. She arrives every morning by ten and leaves no earlier than seven. She rearranges my pillows and covers me with blankets. She brings water and ice chips, nose bandages and medication. She makes sure the room is cleaned, the sheets are changed, the Rinser never misses her cue and the nurses replenish my IV bags. She is tireless in her efforts. I am not surprised. My mother would do the same for all of her children.

I am surprised, however, by her composure, even now as she watches me bandage my radiation burn. My mother takes after Poppy Jim. She is emotional and expressive, the perfect counterbalance to my father's stoic calm; she cries and yells while he quietly contains and supports. Not so in this crisis. My father finds it difficult to look at me. He can't stay in my room for more than a few minutes at a time. His expression is often paler than mine. My mother, on the other hand, is full of energy. She races about, dusting, wiping, reorganizing. She smiles, comforts and encourages. I've never seen a tear, never a hint of fear. Surely they must surface sometime. Later perhaps, at home, alone, in the cover of darkness. My mother is being strong—for me, for my father, for the family; she is holding us together, sustaining us. I have never seen this side of her. I would have never expected her to assume the role of matriarch so easily, so gracefully. I'm glad my mother is with me. I want to tell her. But of course, I don't.

THE FEVER CONTINUES despite the antibiotics. If it doesn't break soon, I will need amphotericin. This antifungal medication is associated with severe allergic reactions. I remember administering it to patients as an intern, standing by with Demerol to stop the rigors, an intense, involuntary shaking caused by generalized muscle contractions. Fortunately, my blood level of gentamicin is not in the therapeutic range. Before proceeding with Amphoterrible, as we used to call it, Dr. Young will adjust the dose of gentamicin.

At this point, there are nine IV bags hanging from my treepole: antibiotics, narcotics, food, blood, platelets, fluid. I can't keep track of what is pouring into me. Yet I'm aware that the pole is getting heavier and the branches of tubing more tangled; an increasing number of items are required to keep me alive.

I no longer use the bathroom to urinate; it takes too much effort to lug my cumbersome companion. Instead, the nurse provides me with several bedside containers. I'm not ashamed to relieve myself in the open nor bothered by the lingering smell in the air. I am too tired to care.

On Tuesday, a new problem emerges. My entire body itches, from head to toe. Although the skin appears dry, there is no rash. "Many things can cause pruritus in your situation," explains Dr. Young. "The skin is sensitive after chemo and radiation. Medication, especially morphine, can make you itch. And finally, an allergy to one of the blood products is possible. I'd prescribe a cream but suspect you have your own preferences. We'll also order some Benedryl."

I'M A MESS. My mouth is one giant sore. I can't stop itching. My genitals are on fire. And I can barely talk—to vent my frustrations, to ask for help. Please, have mercy, just give me the Benedryl and let me sleep.

PART FIVE

DAYS OF SILENCE

Physical pain does not simply resist language but actively destroys it, bringing about an immediate reversion to a state anterior to language, to the sounds and cries a human being makes before language is learned.

ELAINE SCARRY, *The Body in Pain*

CHAPTER TWENTY-TWO

꩜

TUESDAY, FEBRUARY 20, DIARY OF DOLORES BIRO

I can't sleep. I can't stop thinking about David. He is in so much pain, from the mouth sores and ulcer in the groin. Now he's itching. David doesn't complain. He doesn't talk much at all. Talking just makes the pain worse. I also think he's afraid that no one can help him. It doesn't matter. From now on, Les and I will talk for David.

. . . David got ATG this afternoon, the horse serum that prevents rejection of the marrow. He wanted Les to be in the room when he received the medication in case there was a bad reaction. Mary hung the bag at 2 P.M. Les, Lisa, Debbie and I watched nervously as the fluid dripped into his IV. Mary had a syringe ready to give David if a complication developed. After fifteen minutes, Mary said we were home free and left the room. We were so relieved we made jokes. But an hour into the infusion, David began to shake, his lips began to chatter. The shaking got so intense that the bed started to move with him. It was horrible for him and horrible for us to see him like this. Les ran out to get Mary. She had to make up a new syringe of Demerol, the drug used to stop the rigors, because she had discarded the first one. Nothing happened after the injection. David continued

to shake. He started to foam at the mouth. It took ten minutes before the shaking subsided. The room became quiet. No one knew what to say. David looked so frightened, so weak. Thankfully, he just fell back on his bed and went to sleep.

Later, after we left, David received his second dose of ATG. There were no rigors this time, thank God. Instead, he had an attack of hives. Benedryl relieved the itch and made him sleep. Oh God, give David strength, please help Daniella and our family cope.

WEDNESDAY, FEBRUARY 21, DIARY OF LASZLO BIRO

David not well. Bad case of rigors yesterday. Itching and superficial peeling of skin continue today. David cannot even get on phone to talk. New and dreadful idea: can denudation of skin be first sign of graft versus host disease, or is this too early in transplant, as was case with liver thrombosis? Must get answer.

Recurring thought: In past, my bad back would only go so far but never too far. This is my Biro precipice theory, that our problems can grow and grow and grow but never get out of hand. Somehow we always know where to stop. And this must apply to David, I keep reassuring myself.

THURSDAY, FEBRUARY 22, DIARY OF LASZLO BIRO

Day +7, one week after transplant. Phoned David in morning. Extremely hoarse, can hardly talk. Scrotal ulceration painful. Went to give platelets, 2 P.M. Still on machine at 4 P.M., wondering when it will end. David needs platelets every day. Michele will donate tomorrow.

High dose steroids started yesterday. Like ATG, given to prevent marrow rejection. Added benefit, they help David's rash and lift his spirits, but unfortunately give bad nights of hallucinations.

Spoke to Castro and Young. Both very encouraging. One more week of suspense until marrow takes. Then waiting for infection or lack thereof.

THURSDAY, FEBRUARY 22, DIARY OF DOLORES BIRO

David slept most of the day. I'm happiest when he is asleep. It is his only relief. He needs the rest too. It will give him strength to fight the infection. . . .

FRIDAY, FEBRUARY 23, DIARY OF DOLORES BIRO

Michele and Debbie were at the hospital at 8 A.M. for the early shift. Les, Lisa and I got in at 2 P.M. From the beginning of David's hospitalization, Lisa insisted on making daily schedules so that someone would be with David at all times. I didn't realize at first how important this would be, not only for David but for Les and me, for our peace of mind. I wanted to be at the hospital early every morning, but this was impossible and I would have died if I knew David was alone.

David is very tired, irritable and uncomfortable. Today there is a new problem. He is unable to urinate. He feels the urge but nothing comes out. It is beginning to cause pain. The intern came and gave him Lasix, a diuretic. She said if it persists, they may have to insert a catheter. David became angry. He said he would refuse. He is worried that the catheter might lead to infection since his white count is still at zero. I'm shocked to see that he is still on his toes after all this.

Les is not feeling well. I think seeing David so sick is unbearable for him. He finds it difficult to stay in David's room for long.

SATURDAY, FEBRUARY 24, DIARY OF LASZLO BIRO

Calls and calls all day: Oxford, Tucson, Boston, Montreal. Friends of David, friends of ours. Make me feel better. Trying to shake lingering cold. Did not go in to see David this weekend. Watched old videotape of Rabin Memorial Service following assassination. Very depressing.

New transplant crisis: urinary tract retention. Cause unknown. Minor conflict between Castro and Young. Young wants to catheterize, Castro doesn't. David in agony. Hopeful it will resolve soon.

SUNDAY, FEBRUARY 25, DIARY OF DOLORES BIRO

Daniella is with David all weekend. I go in at 3 P.M. He is still in pain, from the mouth sores, scrotal ulceration and inability to urinate. Although it's hard for him to get around, he drags his pole to the bathroom and turns on the faucet, hoping the sound of running water may help. He returns to bed distraught. I can see the anguish in his face. Nothing comes out. It kills me to stand by so helpless. They plan to catheterize if this continues.

Fevers are another source of worry for David. They keep changing the dose of gentamicin because the blood level is never high enough. Dr. Young warned that if David's fevers continue, they would have to add amphotericin, regardless of the gentamicin levels. David is scared. He already experienced the rigors with ATG and doesn't want to go through it again with amphotericin.

Hallucinations from the high dose of steroids are also a problem. They give Haldol for this, which only adds to David's disorientation and confusion. I don't know how he survives, between the pain and all these medications. I can't stand to see him like this. I try to control my feelings and remain positive in front of him.

I am back home at six and begin cooking. Les has been home with a cold. We eat dinner at eight. I try to let him vent his feelings, which is always difficult for him. I think this nightmare has been a little easier for me because the girls have been so supportive and protective. They are always around helping at home or taking care of David in the hospital. I can see they have the same effect on Les. When they are home, he is much more relaxed. And when he can't go to the hospital, he knows that they will be with David.

My way of coping is nonstop doing. I am a machine that never stops. When I'm completely exhausted, I feel numb and cannot think. I am grateful for this state of being. No time to think, I will just keep going from one day to the next.

MONDAY, FEBRUARY 26, DIARY OF LASZLO BIRO

Another day, another crisis. Fever to 102.7 despite one week of powerful antibiotics. Will they give amphotericin? Young worried about fungal infection. Fourth dose of ATG went in without complication. By 2 P.M., fever resolved, hopefully for good. 8 P.M., urination still a problem, catheter still a threat.

TUESDAY, FEBRUARY 27, DIARY OF DOLORES BIRO

Susan Merker, the mother of David's friend Neal, visits David every Tuesday. She has been a volunteer at Sloan-Kettering since her husband passed away from leukemia. She is always positive and considerate. Today she showed me where the hospital gowns and pajamas are kept so I don't have to keep washing David's clothes late at night when I get home. Susan said she would do anything to help. She is donating platelets today and will have her children do the same. "David is pure gold," she said to me, "one of the best people I know. He's going to make it, I'm sure of it." I always knew David was well liked by his friends and their parents but now I see their loyalty and love.

WEDNESDAY, FEBRUARY 28, DIARY OF LASZLO BIRO

Office at 9 A.M. Nice to walk into library, look at David's desk, see David's patients. When will life come back to us?

10 A.M., David phoned: white cells have risen from the dead thirteen days after transplant. Count is now at 200. Is this already new marrow? Hard to tell. Fever gone. David finally urinates after morphine switched to Dilaudid.

THURSDAY, FEBRUARY 29, DIARY OF LASZLO BIRO

If David doesn't phone in morning, I'm nervous and imagine all sorts of dreadful problems. Relieved at noon when white count returns at 300. Young says this is trend, bone marrow grafting. Only threat now is CMV infection. Notice confidence for first time in David's voice.

Lunch with my associate, Dr. Ragi. He asks about David, tears in his eyes.

WEDNESDAY, MARCH 1, DIARY OF LASZLO BIRO

White count dropped to 200. Like Dow Jones, gyrating up and down, taking David's spirits along with it. Dr. Young not upset. Counts will fluctuate for a while, he says. Nice man. Wish he was staying on service. But Sloan-Kettering merry-go-round moves on. Lady doctor named Jakubowski will be in charge for March.

SATURDAY, MARCH 2, DIARY OF LASZLO BIRO

Walked into hospital room at 3 P.M., David broke down crying. Steroid withdrawal and cabin fever. Stood there with Michele, helpless.

How must he feel? Mich was ready to cry. She became very close to her brother since she literally saved his life. I felt awful.

Saw Daniella. Still a visible distance between her and family that I can't understand. Otherwise holding up well through these horrid weeks.

Most important, count rose again to 600. Must keep David's spirits up and up and up.

PART SIX

MARROW RESCUE

Our only health is the disease
If we obey the dying nurse
Whose constant care is not to please
But to remind of our, and Adam's curse,
And that, to be restored, our sickness must grow worse.

T. S. ELIOT, Four Quartets

CHAPTER TWENTY-THREE

⌖

F OR THE FIRST TIME in days, I pick up my phone before the answering machine turns on. Steven is calling from Denver, roaring over the Rockies, about my counts, my ever-climbing, ever-yearning counts. "Davie boy, this is big. Big. You're out of the woods. In a few days, you should be back in the normal range."

"Let's not get carried away," I reply. "But thanks, I'm feeling better."

"Your voice sounds better too. The mouth must be healing, right?"

Yes, it is. In fact, the Rinser only comes by once a day now. A new group of transplant patients with more extensive sores must be attended to. Time is moving in a circle. After hitting a peak a week ago, my sores are starting to improve; they're smaller, shallower, less confluent. I've returned to the early stages of mucositis.

Steven shouts his approval and promises to visit as soon as he gets back.

I force myself to focus on the numbers. Steven is right, this is big. We've reached day +18 on the calendar, a month since my arrival at Sloan-Kettering. The last two weeks have been a blur: flashes of pain from different parts of my body, the obfuscating penumbra of narcotics, a steady stream of paralyzing fear. Every time I felt ready to emerge from stupor, the precariousness of my situation filled me with dread: No white cells, no immune system, how will I survive? So I welcomed the blur and every opportunity to shut out, shut down.

Then came Genesis. New cells, new marrow. My entire world is revolving on its axis, even the numbers. The days of zero are no more. My counts are beginning to sound respectable again. Movement down is followed by movement up. The circle must complete itself. I take comfort in the necessity of geometry. I will recover.

Dr. Jakubowski, the attending doctor on service for the month of March, corroborates my theory. Michele's cells are grafting, declares Jakubowski. The counts will continue to rise. There has been no fever in the last three days and a CMV culture was negative. "We're happy with your progress," she says. "Hang in there."

"I will. But can we start tapering the Dilaudid—I have to feel normal again. I have to wake up."

"As long as you can tolerate it. We can always turn it back up again."

No way. The laws of geometry are propelling me forward. I'm not as hoarse as I was yesterday. There is less phlegm obstructing my airways, less pain when my tongue touches a sore. And even though my mouth remains dry as a dusty old rag and I still can't swallow, I am determined to accelerate my recovery.

Signs of healing are not limited to the mucosa. My liver is no longer tender. The heparin was discontinued once the threat of thrombosis had dissipated. I can urinate at will, without having to run the water or stand over the toilet in agony. And the itching has become bearable. My father brought in a mixture of

Sarna lotion and hydrocortisone. I splash on the menthol-smelling salve, like aftershave, whenever another area of skin demands to be scratched.

Meanwhile, a fresh layer of epidermis has grown over my ulcerated scrotum. While the skin is still inflamed, I can finally get comfortable in bed without wincing. I no longer scream in the shower when the water hits the area straight-on, instead of rolling indirectly down the sides of my body. A thick coat of Desitin suffices to relieve the residual discomfort. I like the smell of the pasty cream, baby-clean and fresh. Much better than the odor of latex gloves, alcohol pads and recycled detergents that waft through my room after the morning cleaning.

The rising white count is followed by a falling body temperature, more evidence of movement in the right direction. Michele's stem cells have given birth to a young and feisty cadre of lymphocytes and neutrophils. They are winning the battle against the unknown infection that has produced fever during the last two weeks. A week ago, I cringed at the prospect of reliving the rigors of ATG with amphotericin. Now, after a few days of afebrility, there's talk of an end to all antibiotics.

I don't mention my ruse, which may have helped matters in this regard. Since the fevers usually registered in the morning, I would place a cup of ice chips on the armrest of my cycling chair. Just before seven, I would swish a few under my tongue. That would predictably lower the temperature when the nurse, a moment later, inserted her thermometer in the same spot. Anything to stave off Amphoterrible, though I'm beginning to doubt the appropriateness of my judgment, now that I'm on the mend.

MICHELE AND DEBBIE come by in the afternoon with a movie. I'm excited about the diversion, but before long my

mind begins to wander, away from *Forrest Gump* and Tom
Hanks's twangy voice, to the window and the world beyond my
tiny cell, to my picture gallery of faraway friends. The transplant
experience has impaired my concentration, leaving me jittery
and labile; my mood swings back and forth between positive
and negative poles.

The picture of Rema on her wedding day continues to
haunt me. So many emotions cling to it: pity for all her suffering, longing for her friendship, fear that our fates may turn out
the same. Now there's a new one, a new image, shed from memory's negative, flickering about the walls of my chamber. I see
Rema's family and friends, the people she left behind. Her parents sitting at the funeral, her brothers and sisters. I see their
tears, their stumblings, their stammerings. And Billy, Rema's
husband, singing the song he had written with his wife before
she died, "Chasing the Sun." The survivors. Have they recov-
ered from their loss, their incomprehensible, inexplicable loss?
Will they? Can they?

A sequence of images, racing across my restless mind, leaps
from Rema's world into mine. And what about my family, my
wife? What happens if I die, in spite of the ever-climbing, ever-
yearning counts, the positive prognoses of my doctors? I'm tee-
tering on the edge of a precipice, clearly at the most tenuous
point in my life since the mythical days of young David and
Goliath. Things can go either way. What happens to my family?

Debbie and Michele are following the movie less closely
than they would have me believe; they repeatedly glance over in
my direction to make sure I'm all right. They have been so
good. My entire family has been so good. They would have sac-
rificed their own lives to save mine, every one of them. I know
from Rema how hard it would be for them, how intolerable,

how unbearable. But at least they have each other, a close-knit family, with a deep well of collective strength to draw from.

Daniella concerns me more. I'm afraid that she wouldn't be able to absorb the shock, that she would refuse support from others. Always so sure she could do everything on her own, Daniella rarely asks for help. It would humiliate her to find that she needed others to survive. I had always suspected this was misguided. Now I'm convinced. No one can endure life's absurdities alone. No one can be that strong.

I am worried about Daniella. She has been operating on overdrive since my first day at Sloan-Kettering. Her office, ignoring my illness and slow to replace an associate that recently quit, demands more from her now than ever before. She is in a daze, floating between fashion houses and cancer wards. She never complains, never asks for help. Just keeps on going, indefatigable. I'm not sure how long it can last. Or how she'd react if something went wrong.

When Daniella arrives that evening, she comes over to the bed and hugs me. I grab her tightly, not wanting to release her. "I need to talk to you."

Suddenly, I am sobbing hysterically. This upsets Daniella and she starts crying too. It's the withdrawal of steroids, I explain. I can't help it. "But listen," I say, squeezing her arm. "Let's try to get closer to our families, mine and yours. It's so important, a family coming together in a crisis. We have to spend more time with them. I want you to promise."

"Honey, you're very emotional today. Did Dr. Passik come by?"

"Yes, I'm emotional, but this is important. I want you to promise. Promise we'll do things with our families, more so than we've done in the past. Please."

Daniella promises, although I doubt she understands my sense of urgency. She probably thinks the medications have wound me into a delirium. Daniella is confident that life will soon return to normal; no one, no matter how persuasive, could convince her otherwise. I hope she's right.

CHAPTER TWENTY-FOUR

～✦～

From early on, David would call for things he needed, food he wanted. These requests were important for me. At least I could help in some small way, at least I could make his life a little easier. You can stay in a hospital room for hours and feel so helpless.

Yesterday he asked for saline spray to help with the dryness in his mouth and nose. Today he wanted San Pellegrino water. He hasn't asked for or eaten anything in three weeks. He must be getting better.

D R. PASSIK HAS abandoned meditation exercises, finally acknowledging their ineffectiveness in my case. Instead, I receive Haldol, initially for steroid psychosis and now for the emotional volatility associated with steroid withdrawal. Passik believes this is temporary and will sort itself out over the next week or so. Today he decides to add Klonepin, a relaxant in the Valium family that also acts as a sleeping agent.

"I'm amazed at how quickly you've bounced back. Everybody should do this well." Passik never leaves without celebrating a patient's fortitude. All part of the job.

Praise and sedatives notwithstanding, my mood continues to oscillate. The morning typically opens on an optimistic note. My head is clear, there is less pain than the day before. I can exercise and shower without having to assume awkward positions to protect my tender genitalia. I'm excited about the rising counts, the prospect of recovery. As the nurse draws blood from the Broviac, my breathing rate quickens, a nervous gurgling sounds from within my belly. I watch the test tube fill with the deep red liquid. It looks normal to my eyes. How will it look under the microscope? How many of those young, vibrant white cells will they count today?

Impatient, I wait for results. They are due back around midday. I stare out the small window of my door for Mary or Dana. No one comes. I send Lisa to reconnoiter.

On Tuesday, Day +19, almost three weeks after the transplant, Mary enters the room with an index card.

"Well?" I ransack her eyes for expression, fumbling for a pen in the drawer. I keep a daily log of the numbers.

"They're lower today," says Mary regretfully. "But that's normal," she is quick to explain. "They always fluctuate a bit in the beginning."

The white count dropped from 1,800 to 1,500. The platelets fell to 9,000, a dangerously low level. And most disturbing of all, the Blood Bank called: My reserves were exhausted. They needed donors immediately. For now they would send up two units from an anonymous source.

The walls collapse around me. Visions of recovery dissipate and distort. I am crushed. There's a problem with the marrow; I can see it on my log. A downward trend, a slippage, a progressive erasing of all those healthy new cells. My marrow is failing. I'll never leave the hospital.

No one can extricate me from these descents into hell. Mary tries. "This is normal," she insists. "You have to be patient." My mother no longer bothers. She has learned that talking only makes me more upset. Instead, she endures my silence and waits for the mood to pass.

Today my mother intercedes in a novel way. She takes out the hand massager, a gift from Lisa, and pulls her chair closer to the bed. She begins moving it over the soles of my feet. I want to resist, but it feels good, the smooth wooden wheel slowly turning over the tense surface of my skin. Memories of Arturo, the aromatherapy masseur, kneading my twisted body the day before admission, peek through the icy cloud cover of consciousness. I soon become attached to the miracle object, a soothing replacement for the rinsing apparatus.

THE NEXT MORNING, Dana barges into the room beaming. White count is back up to 2,000, the platelets have skyrocketed to 30,000 after the transfusion from the unknown donor. "Who knows, kiddo," she giggles, "maybe you'll be able to go home in a week or two."

The thrust of a rocket launcher couldn't boost my spirits any faster, any higher. All I can think of is escape, an official one this time, as opposed to the earlier dream-induced variety. My mother and Lisa, having befriended the families of other patients on the ward, encourage me with news from abroad. The Stanwick girl is scheduled to be discharged tomorrow.

"Really?" I ask, astonished. In the beginning, I didn't want to hear about other patients, their progress or their difficulties. It made me nervous. Besides, the nurses and doctors discouraged it. "Everybody is different," advised Castro. "What happens in one case has nothing to do with another."

All this has changed now that the success of my transplant seems more certain. I eagerly await every new report. Nancy Stanwick, a year younger than me, resides on the opposite end of the floor. She and her husband live in Hoboken, a few blocks from Lisa. Occasionally, Joe Stanwick gives my sister a ride home. They talk. The next day Lisa talks to me.

"So, how is she doing?" I ask, never having seen or spoken to the phantom in 602 but increasingly jealous of her strong lead in the race home. Nancy received her transplant twelve days before mine.

She started eating a couple of days ago, replies my sister. Dr. Jakubowski believes the infection is gone. Joe is picking her up tomorrow.

The doctors never figured out what caused Nancy's fever. Or the diarrhea and abdominal cramps she developed a week after transplant. Beyond routine isolation precautions, additional measures were taken so the mysterious infection wouldn't spread to other patients. I bombarded my sister with questions: What measures were taken? What bacteria or fungi did they suspect? What antibiotics was she getting? Lisa wasn't sure. She'd investigate.

My mother brings news from 638, the older lady two doors down. A religious Jew from Borough Park, Mrs. Hershfeld always has a crowd of pious Hasids gathered outside her room. The Grand Rebbe himself has made several appearances, conducting Friday evening services over a flickering Sabbath candle in the hallway.

His prayers have fallen on deaf ears. Mrs. Hershfeld, my mother learns from her husband, is in bad shape. Her transplant didn't take. The counts have remained perilously low. If they don't recover soon, the doctors may try another infusion of donor marrow. Otherwise she will die from infection. My mother responds to the grieving husband in the way she knows best. Can she bring him anything? A book, a newspaper, some food perhaps? No thanks, he would manage.

"She's an old lady," my mother rationalizes, for me as much as for herself. "You can't compare yourself to her. Your body is young and strong. It can withstand a lot more." Lisa concurs.

Dana likes to listen to our gossip sessions. Occasionally, she donates an item to the mix. "Did you hear about the boy next door?" she asks with an impish smile.

Alberto, also thirty-one, is a leukemia patient. He used to follow me down at Radiation, ages ago it now seems. My mother has become friendly with his wife. She brings gifts for Alberto's two small children.

"He's really sick, isn't he?" I ask. There is always commotion surrounding my next door neighbor's room. A few days ago, I heard a loud thud, followed by screams. Alberto, in a daze, had fallen out of bed. Consultants were called in. X-ray machines entered and exited the room all night long. I felt terrible for him.

"He's better now," reports Dana. "You'll never guess what his wife brought him last night?"

We all look at Dana, perplexed.

"A Big Mac. He asked for a Big Mac and his wife went to McDonald's and got him one." Dana is laughing so hard she can barely speak. "No white cells and he's ordering fast food. Thank God he's all right."

"You mean he ate it?" I ask incredulously, wondering how he could possibly have an appetite.

"No, we stopped him after the first bite. He couldn't swallow it."

I'm not happy about this information. Poor Alberto, still recovering from a nasty bed spill, has just lapped me in the transplant race. Big Mac? Just envisioning the twin patties dripping
with special sauce makes me queasy.

Dana's story prompts a radical rethinking of my predicament. If I ever plan to catch up to Alberto and Nancy Stanwick, who may be crossing the Holland Tunnel at this very
moment, I must force the issue. Since recovery hasn't come to
me, I must come to it.

"My appetite is back," I announce to my mother and sister
the next day. "I'd like to start eating again." I look over at the
bulging TPN (Total Parenteral Nutrition) bag, the heaviest object hanging from my IV pole and sole source of nourishment
these last few weeks. Won't be needing that anymore, I tell the
nutritionist. She advises me to proceed slowly. First liquids.
Then high-protein drinks like Ensure. And if all goes well, I'll
graduate to semisolids and solids in a week.

Gazing at the map of Italy on the wall, I focus on the top of
the boot. An elegant green bottle flashes through my mind. San
Pellegrino. I want San Pellegrino, I must have San Pellegrino.
My recovery program will commence with sparkling water
from the babbling brooks that wind across the Italian Alps. A
balm for my dry, aching mouth. My mother promises to bring
some in.

I discuss strategy with Dana and Mary. They explain that
discharge from the hospital won't be considered until I'm no
longer dependent on transfusions and intravenous medication.
They point to the lush overgrowth on my IV tree. Bags of
steroids, antibiotics, acyclovir, Diflucan, Haldol and saline rest
on top of each other in a tangled mess. A unit of red cells or
platelets is added to the heap every day. It takes considerable ef-

fort to push my fecund friend across my narrow quarters. I recognize the problem.

"Once you can swallow," says Mary, "we can give you most
of the medication by mouth. Be patient. We'll work on debrid-
ing your IV pole every day."

My tree, my faithful companion. Close as we have been
these past few weeks, you are now an obstacle that stands in my
way. You are now my enemy and I am determined to sever our
connections.

CHAPTER TWENTY–FIVE

⌇

Sita, the woman from South Africa, was readmitted to the ward last week. I don't want David to know. She had just spent three months in the hospital. Now, a month later, she's back with CMV pneumonia and rejection of her transplant. Her only hope is a sample of her own marrow that was frozen earlier. The doctor will try to remove the cancer cells before giving it back to her. Sita's husband is friendly but it's not hard to see how much he's hurting inside. They have five children. He always asks about David. I once mentioned an article in a medical journal that I heard about from one of the nurses. A patient had two bone marrow transplants that failed and is still living twenty years later. He asked me to go in and tell Sita about the case. It would give her hope, he said. I didn't want to go. I felt terrible for Sita, her husband, her children. But I was afraid I wouldn't be able to speak if I saw how sick and desperate she was. I never went.

Whenever I meet Sita's husband in the corridor, he begs me to visit his wife. He told her about the patient, but she doesn't believe him. It would be better to hear it from me. I finally gathered the courage and went to see her today. I found Sita praying. She prays all day, she told me, and hopes that God will answer her prayers. I felt so uncomfortable in front of this poor woman. I only wanted to leave. I feel very guilty about this. She kept thanking me for coming.

F ROM MY BED, I watch the snow falling at an angle across the bruised sky of dawn. It is Thursday morning, March 7, and another snowstorm in a record-breaking winter is about to blanket the city. Daniella, asleep on the rollout, gloved and masked, limbs drooping over the floor, is unaware of the silent invasion. A layer of white powder already covers the balconies and roofs of nearby buildings. I can almost smell the crisp chill in the wintry morning air. The landscape is peaceful, full of beauty.

I exercise before the curtain of falling snow, able to do more leg lifts and squats than yesterday. I cycle for forty-five minutes and would have continued if the nurse hadn't interrupted to draw blood. It won't be long before we can go back home, I tell Daniella as she's leaving for work. I feel great.

Dr. Jakubowski and the team arrive at nine. "Your mouth is healing," she says after examining me. "How does it feel?"

"Extremely dry. Gargling with saltwater helps."

"How about the pain?"

"Not bad," I reply. "Let's keep lowering the narcotic dose. It'll make it easier for me to concentrate. I'm starting to eat today. I'd like to go home as soon as possible."

"Don't rush things, David. You're doing very well but this is not over yet. We're stopping the antibiotics. You haven't had a fever in almost a week. That's the first step."

"So when do you think I can leave?"

"I can't answer that question and please don't keep asking me. Remember, there are a few pentamidine treatments left and we still have to taper your steroids. Be patient. We all want you to go home, but you have to be ready."

"I'll be ready. You'll see."

As the team leaves, Debbie enters with a big smile and a bottle of San Pellegrino. I pour a cup, watching the gas bubbles bounce, listening to them sizzle. Cautiously, I drink. The liquid feels good against my tongue and the sides of my mouth. But moving farther down, it begins to burn. I can't swallow.

I am upset by the failure. Sensing this, Debbie offers an explanation: "It's the carbonation and cold. Mommy's bringing some hot soup later. That should go down easier."

As a grade school teacher, Debbie is used to consoling frustrated pupils. She's always been a patient person. Lisa and I take some credit for this. We used to torment our younger sister for the thick, ugly glasses she wore as a child; our cruelty must have taught her empathy. Besides which, Debbie got the last laugh, when in adulthood, her looks eclipsed the rest of us entirely. I'll try again later, I tell Debbie.

Outside my door, the pulmonary technician is setting up my third pentamidine treatment. Debbie wants to stay, but the medicine, warns the tech, will be aerosolized; she could breathe it into her lungs. She'll go for a walk instead.

I sit down on the chair. The tech throws a plastic tent over me and puts together the plastic nebulizer. He fills it with pentamidine. This antibiotic prevents infection with *Pneumocystis carinii,* an organism that parasitizes the lungs of most healthy people. When the immune system is compromised, however, *Pneumocystis* can proliferate and cause a life-threatening pneumonia. Aerosolized pentamidine is used in this setting to keep the number of organisms at bay.

The nebulizer fits into a tiny opening in the tent. For twenty minutes, I take in the metallic air. Besides the bad taste, the spray leaves my mouth drier than it already was. I suspend treatment periodically to gag. There are only two more sessions left.

DEBBIE RETURNS WITH a Carnation instant breakfast drink. She pours the powder into a cup and fills it with skim milk. "Try this," she says encouragingly. "It might be easier to drink than San Pellegrino."

I drink the milk even though it turns to solid as it moves down my pharynx, a large solid mass that must be forced through with great effort. I swallow painfully.

Rita Klein, the nutritionist, is happy to see me drinking. If my appetite picks up, she says, she may be able to lower the TPN level.

"I'd like to stop it completely," I say, shaking my head. "That's the only way they'll let me leave. Tell me what I have to do."

"You're getting a lot of calories and vitamins with TPN. Don't forget, you've lost over thirty pounds. It'll take a while to regain that. You need to maintain a certain level of intake. I don't think you can do it without the TPN."

"Just tell me what I have to do."

Rita smiles. She's not annoyed by my stubborn determination. "You'll need at least a thousand calories of food per day before we can stop it. The Carnation drink has a hundred and fifty. That's a start. Keep a list of everything you eat and I'll tally it up at the end of the day. Good luck."

My mother telephones in the afternoon. She's been delayed by the snowstorm. There are ten inches of snow blocking the staircase to our house in Bay Ridge, Brooklyn. But the soup is almost ready. She'll be in by 4 P.M.

My mother arrives at three. She heats the soup in the mi-

crowave at the nursing station. The warmer liquid passes with
less effort. I try some of the chicken. No way. Still, there is
progress. Everyone is relieved.

I do better on Friday: two Carnation drinks, half a glass of
soy milk, a cup of soup, some mashed potatoes and a dollop of
custard. Rita whips out her pocket calculator and plugs in the
numbers. "Congratulations. You went from two hundred to
eight hundred calories in a day. We'll probably be able to stop
the TPN next week."

The truth is, I'm starving. My appetite has returned with a
vengeance. The regenerating marrow evidently needs a plenti-
ful supply of nourishment to continue propagating. Unfortunately, the physical apparatus, not yet healed, is unable to
comply. Although the proximal portion of my GI tract appears
normal, there are still sores farther down the pharynx and
esophagus. "It'll get easier to swallow every day," promises Rita
before she leaves.

Suddenly, I have the urge for kapostas kotcka, a Hungarian
dish my cousin Catherine makes: bow-tie noodles with shred-
ded cabbage and a dash of spice. When Daniella arrives later
that evening, I can only think of Chinese. It's Friday night, I remind her. Time for dumplings, chicken with cashews, pork lo
mein and a movie. It's our tradition.

"Stick to the chicken soup, honey. We won't be ordering in
from Empire Szechuan for a while," says Daniella.

It doesn't matter. The return of desire is as big as the rising
counts. I'm back. I know it. Daniella knows it. My family
knows it.

CHAPTER TWENTY-SIX

꧅

Office empty after snowstorm. David calls. White count at 2,200, neutrophils, 1,900. He is eating again and talking about returning to work. Castro hinted David might be able to leave hospital at end of next week. May not be soon enough. David already getting antsy.

I CYCLE FOR AN hour this morning and breakfast heartily afterward with two instant Carnation drinks (total, 300 calories). At lunch, I feast on another bowl of Mom's chicken soup (150 calories, 300 when we include the crushed bits of chicken and noodles). Food is moving down my digestive tract with less resistance; the quantity is picking up.

At noon, Mary delivers the lab results, which are then logged on a white sheet of paper taped to the wall. The white count likes to dance—up to 2,200, down to 1,800; up to 1,900, then over 2,000 again. My mood swings back and forth with each half-step. Today we're at a high, 2,200. But the daily fluctuations are not as worrisome. With an enlarging series of numbers before me, it is clear that the overall trend is upward. I've passed the critical period of engraftment.

I feel good, I feel strong. But the most significant changes have taken place in my mind. Released from the zombie-like trance induced by narcotics, I'm once again aware of what is happening to me and around me. It's not simply a matter of re-learning how to eat, exercising more vigorously or responding to the daily counts with more emotion. I now appreciate each and every returning facet of life, however simple, and consider its implications. I can think again, I can plan and strategize. My brain has awoken from a deep sleep.

Surely this awakening corroborates my sense of recovery and nourishes hope. But there's a negative side too. The resumption of mental activity inevitably generates anxiety and fear—about what I've been through, about what lies ahead. It also reminds me that I've been trapped inside a room for the last five weeks. The days of panic are not far behind.

The transplant schedule beneficently provides the mind with a respite during its most precarious and physically debilitating periods. It permits, even nurtures this temporary suspension of consciousness, this *epoché* as the philosopher Maurice Merleau-Ponty might call it. Radiation and chemotherapy cannot selectively wipe out a bone marrow and immune system without having systemic consequences on the organism as a whole. In the same damaging sweep, the conditioning regimen depletes the body's strength and energy reserves until a simple task, like raising the eyelids, becomes impossible. And if by chance an opening is accomplished, the narcotic drip flows in to dim the lights and cast a haze over the vanishing landscape. There is little opportunity to move beyond oneself, to communicate with others. Mucositis enforces the imprisonment by destroying speech. I've been living in a semi-vegetative state, oblivious to everything, exiled from the world.

It is over now. One by one, the plastic bags filled with medication and nourishment are being pruned from my IV pole; they are no longer needed to sustain me. My tree is shrinking, withering away. Soon it will be removed and replanted in another patient's room.

The paroxysms of pain are also diminishing, their memories receding into the crevices of consciousness. My body is reviving, its voice and appetite returning. The will to live once again powers through my circulation, along with my new blood cells. I am awakening. Only, as with all awakenings, I'm a little startled by what I see, where I find myself, when I lift my head from the pillow. Now that I can move again, now that I *want* to move again, I realize there is nowhere to go. My room is a tiny box, tightly sealed.

A lifetime ago, when considering bone marrow transplantation, I was concerned about claustrophobia. Could a person who has always resisted buttoning shirt collars for fear of accidental suffocation possibly survive this degree of confinement? Until now, it hasn't been a problem. But suddenly, as I emerge from the slumber of leukopenia, fevers and narcotics, I feel like blasting through the walls. I need more space, more air to breathe, another set of walls to stare at. Recognizing the early symptoms of a panic attack, Dana rushes for the coveted transplant elixir, Ativan, and summons Dr. Passik.

"Ah huh," mumbles the spectacled psychiatrist. "Sounds like a case of cabin fever. Absolutely normal, I assure you. Good thing you won't be around much longer."

"I have to get out. It doesn't have to be for long, just a small walk."

"They won't allow it," replies Passik.

"Dr. Castro promised. I have to. It's the only thing that will help. I'm starting to get depressed. That can't be good."

"No, you're right. I'll write something to that effect in my note. But try to concentrate on all the positive stuff that's happening."

Passik tries to change the subject, unsuccessfully. I'm not in the mood to chat, rehash the rising counts or revel in my strength. It doesn't make the room any bigger. And so, when words fail, my psychiatrist inevitably turns to drugs. "We'll increase the dose of Klonepin then. That should help."

Daniella suggests reopening the room to a limited number of visitors. We had asked our friends not to come once isolation precautions were imposed. Now that I'm better and there's less risk of infection, company might be just the thing to cheer me up.

Kenny is our first choice. Vivacious, idiosyncratic, at times hilarious, he would surely make me laugh. Not today. We hardly talk. I don't respond to his questions. He soon becomes uncomfortable. I don't care. I'm mad at Kenny, mad that he can come and go as he pleases, that he can slip on his coat and boots at will and trudge happily through the snow. The tension, growing inside me, begins to spill out into the room. I may explode at any minute. Kenny doesn't stay.

Neither do my in-laws. They stop by later and quickly sense my frustration.

"He's getting a little crazy in the room," explains Daniella. "My baby needs to get out, right?" She sits next to me on the bed and hugs me. "And he will, soon. The doctors say he may be able to leave next week or the week after."

"Friday," I correct her, my one word contribution to the conversation. I'm rude and don't give a damn. Manners and decorum had been jettisoned long ago. You might say I've returned to the pre-social days of my childhood, concerned solely with my own needs and desires. There is no shame when, a moment later, I stand up, grab the container next to the bed and begin urinating. Fuck everyone.

SUNDAY IS NO better, even after Mary's news flash that the white count "soared" to 2,500. Daniella and I sit quietly by the window. The balconies and rooftops are still covered with snow from Thursday's blizzard. I dream of moving outside, frolicking in the white powder, building a snowman. These urges originate somewhere deep within. Not being able to satisfy them fills me with infantile rage. And when the rage settles, I become depressed.

Dr. O'Reilly has seen this before. Head of the transplant service at Sloan-Kettering, O'Reilly has performed more transplants than anyone in the country. That's what Mary said when she informed me that he was making rounds today.

"Dr. Biro," says O'Reilly in a deep, booming voice. "I'm glad to meet you. I've heard a lot about you from Dr. Castro. We're very happy with your progress. I can see, though, you're feeling down at the moment."

O'Reilly is a big man, tall and broad-shouldered, with a big voice to match. He is standing in the doorway, filling its entire opening, another door that shuts me in. I am sitting at the opposite end of the room, slouched against the windowsill. Although he addresses me as a colleague, I feel very unprofessional. Across from this impressive figure, I seem small, smaller than I had ever imagined. My arms are thin and frail, my scalp hairless, my voice weak. I am a dwarf in the presence of a giant.

"Now is the time," bellows O'Reilly, like a platoon sergeant, "when you must hunker down and wait. In some ways this is harder than the physical part of the transplant. But it's temporary. Remember that."

"If I could just get out of the room for a bit." My request is hesitant, barely audible.

"Not possible. We can't risk infection. You've come too far. It's only a matter of time. Hang in there."

I cry when O'Reilly leaves, not because he denied my request. It was the image of myself he left me with. I have changed during my stay at Sloan. I've become small.

DANIELLA TRIES TO revive me. She flips through the Sunday *Times* and takes out the real estate section. "Come on, honey, let's go through the listings. Where should we start?"

No answer.

"Uptown or downtown?"

I submit reluctantly. Daniella could somersault across the room and she wouldn't pry a smile from my sullen face. The day grinds on in silence.

Sometime after the sky turns dark, I become frantic. I have to escape, with or without official authorization. In my telephone book, I find Castro's number and dial. He's not in the office, says someone from the answering service. "It's Sunday night. Is this an emergency?"

"Yes it is, ma'am. This is Dr. Biro. I must reach Dr. Castro immediately. Call him, page him, do whatever you have to, just get him on the line." My voice sounds whiny, agitated. I wonder if the operator takes me seriously. Daniella is shaking her head, flailing her hands, trying to stop me.

"Dr. Castro, it's David. I'm calling from the hospital."

"Yes, I should hope so."

"I'm sorry to bother you, but you have to help me."

"Relax, David. What's wrong?"

"I have to get out of the room, I have to. You promised. Dr.

O'Reilly said no. I asked Dr. Jakubowski. She said no too. You have to do something. Please." I am shouting into the receiver deliriously.

"I'll talk to Dr. Jakubowski tomorrow morning, I promise. We'll work something out."

"It would help me, I know it would."

"I agree."

"I'm sorry for bothering you."

"That's what I'm here for. I'm your doctor. Call me whenever you want. Now get some rest. We'll talk tomorrow."

He's going to let me out, I tell Daniella after hanging up the phone. A boon from the gods of Castro-Malaspina. I feel better already. Poor Castro, his vision has been confirmed: His patient is a raving lunatic.

CHAPTER TWENTY-SEVEN

꩜

O N TUESDAY, MARCH 12, when the Kettering clocks
strike 10 P.M., I am allowed out of my room, released
after thirty-one days in captivity. A short stroll around the ward
when visiting hours had ended and the halls were empty—that
was the compromise Castro worked out with Jakubowski. Daniella is not present to witness the glorious occasion. She had to
fly to Milan for the spring show; she'll be back on Saturday. Lisa
and Michael, staying past their usual shift, will escort me.

Barely able to contain my excitement, I slip on a mask and
pair of gloves and rush out the door with my IV pole. The
dramatis personae have changed roles; now I'm the one in cos-
tume as my sister and brother-in-law toss theirs into the garbage
bin. It's good to see their faces and hands again. I wish Mary and
Dana were around. I wonder if I'd recognize them in the flesh.

Lisa points out famous landmarks along the way. There's the
kitchen where Mom microwaves the food. Here's Nancy Stanwick's old room. Two doors down is Mrs. Hershfeld, who
miraculously appears to be doing better. I pause for a minute in
front of the nursing station and gaze at the doctors writing
notes, at the row of charts along the wall. Which one is mine?

What does it say? Perhaps I should enter the restricted sanctum and reintroduce myself as Dr. Biro, demand to have a look at my chart—Dr. David Biro that is, up-and-coming dermatologist from Bay Ridge, Brooklyn, temporarily disheveled by a series of violent winter storms, clad in bathrobe and rubber gloves, with not a single strand of hair on my head, emaciated and frail. It wouldn't be Passik they'd call to pacify me but a team of orderlies from the psych ward, straitjacket in hand. The thought makes me smile—I can laugh at myself again.

I'm winded after a lap around the ward. Still, I'd rather attempt a second than return to my cell. The world is just around the corner, ready to spread its vast fields before my feet, ready to open up its seas, the world of possibility and adventure. My prison days, so frustrating, so demeaning, are almost over. I am free, free at last.

When we reach my room, I inspect the schedule on the door. Many days have passed, many things have happened. But the squares from March 12 onward are empty. The last pentamidine treatment was given on Monday. There are no more activities left. Nothing but the end.

Lisa insists on staying over. I haven't slept alone at the hospital since the first night. Daniella, occupying the tattered rollout and branding it her own, has watched over me through the darkness without fail or complaint. She deserves the break, though her harried Italian schedule doesn't quite merit the designation.

"I'll be fine," I tell Lisa, "now that I know I can leave the room."

In addition to my new excursion rights, plans for departure are in progress. Yesterday, the head nurse, Anne Young, came by to prepare me. Going home will be a happy time for you, she said, but also a difficult one. The recovery process is slow. I will be very weak at the beginning. Someone should stay with me at all times, at least for the first few weeks.

Most importantly, infections must be prevented. "As you know," said the nurse, "your immune system will take time to mature. That makes you susceptible to bacteria and other microorganisms. You must be extremely careful." All meals should be prepared at home. Meat should be well cooked. No aged cheeses, cold cuts, grapes or raspberries. No contact with cats or dogs. Stay away from small children. Refrain from dusting and cleaning. Don't water household plants or handle the soil. When allowed outdoors, a mask and gloves must be worn and crowded areas and construction sites should be avoided. My mother took extensive notes during the meeting even though nurse Young assured us that everything was written down in the pamphlet—another Sloan-Kettering special publication, *Returning Home After Bone Marrow Transplantation*.

Yesterday's list of warnings and restrictions was daunting. As Anne Young went through them, one after another, in her quiet but forceful manner, I began to see her as a preacher delivering a sermon, one of those fire-and-brimstone sermons that are intended to instill fear in the hearts of parishioners: Danger is present everywhere; it lurks in every cranny, every crevice, waiting to seize an unsuspecting victim; even the smallest misstep can be fatal.

And the nurse-preacher was not wrong. The world is indeed full of deadly threats to a man with no immune system. The potential for disaster is great. I saw it in my mother's eyes, twitching in terror.

But I wasn't so impressed. Only one thought, one image stood out in my mind: Home—I was going home. Beyond that, nothing mattered, not even those nasty, ubiquitous bugs parading about my universe. Just as long as I was able to cross the sacred threshold once again.

When my sister leaves, I grab the pamphlet and begin reading. There are several things about my homecoming that Anne Young failed to mention. Because the regenerating marrow often can't produce enough red cells and platelets at the beginning, I may need transfusions. The low counts will make me fatigued and predisposed to bleeding. I should continue to use a soft toothbrush and an electric razor. I must avoid strenuous activities. Sexual intercourse is strictly prohibited until the platelet count exceeds 50,000.

The reference to sex is jolting. Suddenly, I realize that an entire sphere of my life had been obliterated along with my marrow, one that had always been rather important to me. True, the conflagration that consumed my genitalia would have prevented the most rakish Lothario from pursuing satisfaction. But that time has passed; the skin has healed; everything appears normal. Everything except for the lack of feeling, the absence of desire. Another section in the pamphlet indicates that hormone levels are often affected by radiation treatments and that this can diminish libido. I touch myself under the covers, stroke my flaccid penis. There's no response. None.

Have I been deprived of sex? Neutered like some animal? The doctors warned me about sterility but not this. Regardless of the platelet count, no matter how feeble the sex drive, as I close my eyes to sleep, I vow to make love to my wife the minute she returns from Italy.

ON WEDNESDAY, DR. Jakubowski arrives to perform a bone marrow biopsy. I have become her most annoying patient.

Every morning during rounds, I plead and argue for a definite departure date. What are we waiting for? The counts have been stable, there hasn't been any fever (even without the ice-under-the-tongue trick), I'm off TPN and eating again, and the steroid taper is almost finished. What's holding me up then?

Jakubowski finally gave in yesterday. If the marrow biopsy showed full engraftment, she promised, I could leave on Friday. So today, for the first time, I am overjoyed to see a hematologist wielding her favorite weapons, the Illinois and Jamshidi needles. I am ready for the pelvic stick. I rather look forward to it.

CHAPTER TWENTY-EIGHT

❦

THURSDAY, MARCH 14, DIARY OF DOLORES BIRO

I am scared. I understand that David wants to go home. But is he ready? He tells me that he will get better at home, that he will recover more quickly there, as if by magic. He is wrong. He doesn't see himself. He is so thin and weak, much more so than he realizes. He thinks he will be able to take care of himself, alone. He is wrong.

I understand David wants his privacy but not at the expense of his health. In the hospital, he has his family around twenty-four hours of the day. There are nurses and doctors if something goes wrong. At home, he has no one until Daniella comes home from work, no one to feed him, no one to divert his attention when he's not feeling well. If he doesn't want me, then we will hire a nurse.

I am also scared about cleanliness. David's apartment must be thoroughly washed—blinds, cabinets, refrigerator, floors, air conditioner. I'll do a large food shop so there's plenty to eat. So many things to do, so little time. He may leave tomorrow.

J AKUBOWSKI GIVES THE green light Friday morning. The marrow looks healthy under the microscope. She goes over the list of medications I will take at home. On Monday, Castro will see me in the outpatient clinic.

The surgeon comes by at noon to pull the catheter in my chest. The pulling is more like a wrenching since the tubing seems to have sprouted roots in my skin. He will order Percocet for the pain. No need, I'm going home. I crank the stereo when he leaves. With the Broviac gone, my last tie to the hospital is severed. I dance to Bob Marley, ecstatic.

Entering the room without masks, my three sisters find me swaying to the beat of reggae, screaming: "Everything's gonna be all right." The isolation sign has been removed, the door to my room left open. Lisa helps me pack my clothes. Debbie disconnects the phone and answering machine. Michele takes down the maps and pictures from the wall.

A phone call from my mother interrupts the moving process. She needs more time. She has been at my apartment with her cleaning lady since six in the morning. They still haven't sterilized the bathroom. Give her another hour.

We leave after lunch. I wear a mask and gloves and will do so whenever I venture into public places during the first hundred days posttransplant. We run into Castro at the elevator, smiling. If I need him before Monday, I can call. Anytime, he winks.

Outside, the winter air is bracing. I'd like to stand on the corner for a while, perhaps take a stroll along the East River. Instead, I am whisked into the car by my protective sisters. Traffic swarms around us, horns are honking, taxis screeching. Armies of people crowd the sidewalks. We pass small mountains of snow with blackened peaks as we drive farther and farther away from the tower of Memorial Sloan-Kettering Hospital, away from its weathered-white stone face with a thousand brown-windowed eyes.

PART SEVEN

RECOVERY

But precisely because my body can shut itself off from the world, it is also what opens me out upon the world and places me in a situation there. The momentum of existence towards others, towards the future, towards the world can be restored as a river unfreezes.
MAURICE MERLEAU-PONTY, *The Phenomenology of Perception*

CHAPTER TWENTY-NINE

⌇

A RRIVING AT MY apartment building, I am greeted by
Willie, the doorman, and Tony, the super. They are not
surprised to see me bald and wearing a mask; my mother had
prepared them. She also made sure they'd be waiting for me
downstairs.

"It's good to see you back," says Tony, grabbing my duffel
bag. "Let me know if you need anything. I'm here for you
around the clock, buddy."

Five years ago, the same man barred the moving company
I'd hired from entering the building. "No way," he announced
calmly, standing in front of the door with folded arms like a
bouncer at a nightclub. "We have strict moving rules around
here. If you're not in by five, you'll have to wait until tomorrow." Tony wasn't swayed by any of my arguments that day: The
movers were late, my apartment was empty, there was no bed to
sleep on, and I'm a doctor who needs his rest to take care of sick
patients. After a good deal of screaming and stomping (on my
part), he yielded on one item only; we were allowed to take our
mattress. The rest of our stuff went into storage and had to be
brought back the following day. This merciful act was the beginning of a beautiful friendship.

"It's good to be home," I tell Tony.

I march into my apartment like Caesar crossing the Rubicon and inspect the premises with renewed appreciation for a sorely missed home, a home that a few months ago my wife and I were eager to abandon. It looks the same, only much cleaner and with a heavy scent of disinfectant in the air. My mother, standing on a small ladder, is hosing down the blinds. She looks over and waves.

Now what? I ask myself collapsing on the couch. My victory celebration is short-lived. Although I'm happy to be home, there's something wrong, something missing. It's not the same. I'm not the same. I rip the mask off my face and toss it on the coffee table. The apartment feels empty, I feel even emptier. Daniella is not here; she won't be back from Italy until tomorrow. What happens next?

Nothing. In fact, I can hardly move. My body, exhausted—after walking from hospital to car, from car to apartment, no more than fifty feet in all—needs the couch to support its weight. The doctors warned me this might happen. The combination of radiation, continuous intravenous medication, six weeks in bed and a thirty-pound weight loss would decondition Michael Jordan, much less David Biro; it would take months to recuperate. But I was determined to stay in shape. No matter how sick I felt waking up on that damn hospital bed, I forced my body into position for squats, pushed firmly back and forth against the wall and pedaled away on my cycle. So how can I be this weak? How is it possible? I try to lift myself off the couch but can't; no strength, not a particle of energy. I close my eyes. The room spins.

Recognizing the downturn in my mood, my sisters and mother try valiantly to cheer me up. You're home David, they say. No more IV bags and doctors; no more nurses sticking thermometers under your tongue. You'll feel better again soon, you'll see. To accelerate my recovery, Michele volunteers to swing by the butcher shop for some red meat—T-bone, filet mignon, porterhouse, whatever my pleasure.

My father brings Grandma Helen, Poppy Jim's wife, to dinner. She hasn't seen me since Thanksgiving. Vacationing in Florida with my aunt, she has been kept in the dark about my illness and the transplant. My mother told her yesterday. Granny can't help crying when she sees me. She doesn't stop until the salad plates are cleared from the table.

My mother places an impressive piece of steak in front of me with a smile. "You can't get meat like this in the hospital, now can you?"

Slicing into it, I notice the inside is a dusky gray. No one seems bothered. The doctors warned us, explains Lisa, no raw meat; everything must be well done.

"Don't you think you're going overboard, Ma? You can't eat steak like this."

"It's delicious," she replies, after taking a bite, "and good for you. Eat. You have to gain weight."

My parents want someone to stay with me overnight, in case I feel sick or need help going to the bathroom. "Remember," says my mother, "you can't ring for the nurse anymore."

I'm not a child, Mom, I reply. I need my privacy. I've been surrounded by people for months. Daniella will be home tomorrow. I'll be fine. Besides, I'm tired and will be asleep a few minutes after you leave. Reluctantly, my parents leave.

I am alone now, in my own home, about to lie down on my own bed, once again. I've been dreaming about this moment for weeks. But I'm not as happy as I thought I'd be. Not happy at all, really. This whole thing is far from over.

———

DANIELLA IS DUE to arrive in New York at 12 noon on Saturday and should be home a half hour later. There's no word at 1 P.M. Excitement gradually turns to concern, concern to worry and by 1:30, panic sets in. Although it requires all my strength to move from couch to bedroom (less than ten feet), I make the trip repeatedly. Television doesn't divert; I'd rather look out the window for Daniella.

Swarms of cars zoom down Thirtieth Street, stop at the light, pass through. Cabs pull over, discharge their passengers, swing violently across the street for the next fare. No sign of Daniella. My heart hammers against my chest, it is beginning to impede the expansion of my lungs. Could something have happened? To her plane? To her car? Where is she? I need her. I'm too weak, too vulnerable. I won't be able to manage alone. I'm scared for her, scared for myself.

For two hours, I pace the room, clenching and unclenching my jaw until my head begins to throb. Then the phone rings. It's Daniella, her voice booming over the receiver and into my midst. She's been detained at Customs. She'll be home soon. I can relax.

Strange how upset the delay has made me. I am usually not the worrying type. Evidently, that has changed. I guess I no longer trust in the goodwill and predictability of Fate. Accidents have happened. They can happen again.

I AM REUNITED with my wife at five. Her run-in with Customs officials has left her harried, though she's glad to see me home. After unpacking, she makes dinner, risotto with asparagus, a dish she somehow mastered in between meetings in Milan. By eight o'clock we're in bed, both of us spent. Nevertheless, I will insist, remembering the vow I made during my final days at the hospital. There's hardly any desire on my part, even less on Daniella's; proximity and touching would be enough right now. But I'm determined to see it through. I need reassurance—that my apparatus still works, that I'll be able to use it effectively. Forget the fact that my platelets were a feeble 20,000 on Friday.

Daniella, despite the absence of passion in my request, understands. She reaches over and slips her hand beneath my T-shirt. It takes considerable effort to arouse me, incompletely as it turns out, but enough to produce, rather prematurely, a brief surge of orgasm. We remain interlocked in the darkness until Daniella's grip relaxes and sleep separates us. I roll over on my back wondering whether the experience was any more fulfilling for Daniella than it was for me.

CHAPTER THIRTY

⌇

SUNDAYS ARE LAZY days, to lounge on the couch, nosh on
bagels, peruse the *New York Times*. Today that spirit reaches
hyperbole. Lethargy permeates my body, chilling the atoms into
a motionless silence. I cannot finish a single article; I feel too
weak to walk to the bathroom, to pick up my glass of orange
juice. I cannot do—only sit, passively, staring into space.

"Honey, what's wrong?" asks Daniella. "Aren't you excited
about being home?"

"Yeah, I'm excited. I just didn't think I'd be so weak. One
trip to the kitchen and I'm destroyed."

"You were lying in bed for six weeks, what did you expect?
They told you it would take time. You have to be patient."

They told me. But I imagined they were talking about patients in general, not me. Not someone who did laps around the
sixth floor during his last week at Sloan. It makes no sense.

"I just want to feel normal again." That's what I expected.
Only it was clearly a fantasy. One barrier had been removed
when I left Sloan; another was erected in its place. The road to
recovery was so much longer than anticipated.

"You *will* feel normal—soon," promises Daniella and promptly steers the conversation in another direction. "So, my love, what shall we have for dinner tonight? I'll stop at Todaro Brothers and make something special. I'll rent a movie. We'll have fun." Daniella puts her arms around me and squeezes.

I feel small in my wife's embrace, small and passive. I am depressed by my physical condition. I feel trapped in my apartment. Little has changed as a result of my momentous return home. I've swapped a small cell for a slightly larger one, three rooms instead of one. But I'm still in prison. One hundred days is my sentence. Nothing to do for one hundred days except scrutinize the walls and wait. I'll go crazy.

"How about taking a walk outside?" suggests Daniella. "We'll bundle you up."

Yes, maybe that will help.

Joe, the weekend doorman, opens the lobby door for us and greets Daniella. I mumble hello under my mask. Joe nods. He doesn't recognize me at first. Then a look of horror spreads over his face. He takes a step back and stammers: "Dr. Biro, is that you? My God, Dr. Biro, I didn't know . . . I didn't know anything was wrong."

"That's okay, Joe. I got back from the hospital yesterday. I'm fine now."

We leave Joe speechless as we step outside into the chilly March air. We walk around the block, arm in arm. I'd like to do this every day, I tell Daniella, gradually increasing the distance to build up stamina. It feels good to be on the other side of the window.

Daniella drops me off at the apartment before going shopping. She is happier, more relaxed since we've moved back home. Life has become much simpler. No more doctors and

nurses, fevers and transfusions, threats of infection and complications. And my sisters and parents, with their anxieties and
schedules, have long since departed. Just Daniella and me.

Daniella returns with a shopping bag full of groceries. We
feast on a four-course gourmet Italian dinner, then retreat to the
couch with a bowl of popcorn for tonight's special feature, *Once
Around*. Richard Dreyfuss plays a quirky older man who falls in
love with a younger Holly Hunter. Sinatra's "Fly Me to the
Moon" is their wedding song, the same as ours. After working
out his differences with Hunter and her doting family, Dreyfuss
becomes sick. He dies in a wheelchair on a frozen lake, hugging
his newborn baby. His wife skates around him, unaware.

My carefully guarded tears escape involuntarily. I begin to
sob. Although I've always been a sucker for melodrama, I rarely
lose control like this. I can't even blame it on the steroids this
time. The emotion simply erupts from some hidden well, deep
within my body. There's no stopping it.

"It's only a movie, David. Don't be upset."

I can't help myself. The image reminds me of just how tenuous my hold on life was, how tenuous my hold on life *is*. And
it reminds me of Rema—of the devastation that follows in
death's wake. I feel for this woman. She lost the man she loved,
forever. How sad, how incredibly sad, I think, holding on to my
wife and crying.

THE FOLLOWING DAY, Monday, March 14, Daniella and I return to the outpatient wing of Sloan-Kettering to visit Dr. Castro. The clinic is packed. Many patients are masked and bald like
me. Everyone, with the exception of the receptionist, looks
sick.

After check-in, I stop at the lab for blood tests. Castro ordered a chemistry panel to assess the function of my liver and kidneys, a type and cross in case a transfusion is necessary, and a CMV culture. Most importantly, a CBC, or complete blood count, is drawn to evaluate those all-important counts.

Eventually, I am ushered into a small examining room where a nurse takes my vital signs. "Fever?" I ask anxiously, as the nurse reads the thermometer. No, thank God. I can relax. Fever during the next hundred days will catapult me right back into the hospital—a constant source of dread. The nurse measures and weighs me: 73 inches, 151 pounds. I was 190 pounds six weeks ago.

Dr. Castro enters with a smile. "How is my favorite patient feeling today?"

Lousy. Weak. Scared. My hands are shaking. "Not so good," I confess.

"That's normal, David. You've been through a lot. Recovery will take time."

I am silent, my face empty, expressionless.

Castro senses my frustration. "Maybe you should have a talk with Dr. Passik."

I shake my head. No more psychiatrists.

"I don't want you to feel depressed. You have to remain positive. If this continues, I'll insist."

"I'll be okay once I get a little stronger."

"We'll see. Now for some good news—the counts were excellent: white count, 2,200; hemoglobin, 9.6; and platelets, 31,000. You won't need any transfusions today."

I write down the numbers in a notebook. Castro's affinity for statistics has rubbed off. I've become obsessed with data and documentation, viewing and reviewing my numerical progress repeatedly throughout my long days on the couch. It shifts focus away from the absence of progress on the physical and psychological fronts.

"Let's have a look at you now," says Castro, moving closer to the examining table. "Open your mouth. It's very dry, isn't it?"

Extremely. Radiation damages the salivary glands that lubricate the mouth. Nerves exacerbate the problem; here in the hospital, surrounded by doctors, sick patients, and the ever-looming threat of being admitted on a moment's notice, I am so exquisitely dry, I feel like gagging.

"It will get better over the next six months. Just keep drinking."

"But then I'm up all night urinating."

Castro nods sympathetically. "How about your eyes?" he inquires.

"Pretty dry too." The lacrimal glands also suffer at the hands of gamma rays. But they're not as resilient as the salivary glands; they may never recover.

Castro peers into my mouth with a penlight. "All clear," he remarks. There is no evidence of thrush, or infection with a yeast named candida; no whitish papules on the mucosa, an early sign of graft versus host disease. He then feels for adenopathy in the neck and along the collarbone. Swollen lymph nodes—of which thankfully there are none at the moment—might indicate lymphoma caused by the EBV virus. He listens to the lungs for signs of pneumonia due to either the *Pneumocystis* parasite or the CMV virus. He examines the heart for damage from chemotherapy, the belly for enlargement of the liver and spleen, the legs for water retention caused by kidney dysfunction. I follow every hand movement apprehensively until the final verdict is in. "Excellent," says Castro, patting me on the back. "We'll see you again in a week. I want you to be more optimistic, David. Everything is going perfectly."

Before I leave, we review my list of medications: acyclovir twice a day to contain the herpes simplex virus (the cause of cold sores) and the herpes zoster virus (shingles); Mycostatin swish-and-swallow twice a day to prevent candidal thrush; aerosolized pentamidine treatments once a week to subdue *Pneumocystis;* Klonepin at bedtime for anxiety and sleep; folate vitamins to nourish a growing marrow.

Unlike many transplant patients, I do not require immuno-suppressive therapy. Ordinarily cyclosporine is taken to suppress both host T cells (responsible for graft rejection) and donor T cells (which cause graft versus host disease). But since I had a T cell–depleted transplant, this is not necessary. Michele's marrow had been purged of its T cells before it was given to me. And the conditioning regimen I received was more aggressive than those used in routine transplants; the tremendous dose of chemotherapy and radiation has shattered my immune system; it will not revive for some time.

This profound immunosuppression is one of the reasons that T cell-depletion remains controversial—yet another in-stance of division in the medical community that haunts my ex-perience as a patient. In fact, many hematologists, including those at Seattle's Fred Hutchinson Cancer Research Center, the largest transplant center in the world, no longer perform them. They believe a small degree of GVHD is essential to rid the host of any diseased marrow that remains after conditioning. They also find the delay in immune reconstitution unacceptable since it renders a patient more susceptible to infection and cer-tain viral-induced cancers. That is why Dr. Castro must remain especially alert for any suspicious signs and symptoms.

I am aware of all this, deeply aware. I too will remain on the alert.

DANIELLA AND I hail a cab downtown. She drops me off at home and then speeds off to work. I am back on the couch by 11 A.M., a vast windfall of time ahead of me, to gather my thoughts, to contemplate the cosmos.

CHAPTER THIRTY-ONE

꩜

I AM NOT PREPARED for this homecoming. Horrifying as my fainting spell before the radiation engine was, or the conflagration of my scrotum, or the rigors from ATG, I was able to find a place for each of these events in my fight against PNH. But returning to a desolate apartment after the battle had ended, so physically debilitated, and with miles to go before my old life could resume—this I could not account for, I could not rationalize.

There's an emptiness inside of me, full of empty feelings, gray and hopeless. I try desperately to fill the void with things from the past, things that used to give me pleasure. Scanning my bookshelves, I take down *Our Mutual Friend*. Dickens, a favorite, could always be counted on to entertain. Not today. I can't get through the first paragraph. The emptiness inside is alive. Feeding on itself and my anxieties, it erases words before I can read them.

I am not prepared because I don't recognize myself. I used to love spending time at home, reading and writing. My schedule was arranged accordingly: mornings at the computer or on the couch with a novel, afternoons and evenings at the office. It was difficult to tear myself away, always at a critical juncture in a story, mine or someone else's.

I don't remove my laptop computer from its case. I drop Dickens a minute after taking him in my hands. Even the easy lure of TV cannot distract me.

My mother, who had promised to stay away, comes in the afternoon with shopping bags. "Don't worry, dear, just dropping off some food," she says in response to my angry looks.

"I'm fine, Mom. Everything is fine. Don't treat me like a baby."

After she fills the kitchen cabinets with cans of tuna fish and soup, we take a walk. I push it—five blocks down First Avenue, five back up Second, a fierce wind slapping my masked face. Not bad. One proud moment in an otherwise bleak day.

Later that night, between frequent trips to the bathroom, a pain develops in my abdomen. It gradually worsens until I can't lie still in bed. I search for the thermometer and take my temperature. No fever. I palpate my belly, then tap on it; nothing appears abnormal. Finally, I rummage through the closet and find my old stethoscope, a relic since my area of medical expertise had narrowed to the realm of skin.

"It's two in the morning. What's going on?" asks Daniella, as the familiar grumbles of peristalsis are being transmitted to my ears.

"My stomach hurts."

"Maybe you should call Castro," she suggests.

"It's probably just gas. I'll be all right. Go back to sleep."

I lie down on the living room floor, massaging my belly, waiting for the pains to pass, wondering whether anything serious was happening, dreading any unscheduled return to the hospital.

There is no improvement the next day. Cramping continues throughout the morning. Rhonda, a friend from residency, calls before noon. She wants to visit. I'm happy to see her, to see anybody. We talk about business, we talk about personal stuff, even manage to find room for a joke. None of which alters the fact that I'm still besieged by pains marching across the underside of my belly. Rhonda wants to help. She convinces me to page Castro. "I'm sure it's nothing but at least he'll set your mind at ease."

And as usual, Castro is reassuring. He is not concerned by my symptoms. Many patients, he says, complain of cramps when they start eating regular diets again. He recommends antacids. If the pain doesn't subside, I should call back.

As she's leaving, Rhonda offers to pass by the pharmacy. Don't worry, I tell her, Daniella will pick up a bottle of Tums after work. Ten minutes later, Rhonda returns with a bag full of every imaginable variety and flavor of antacid.

BASTA. ENOUGH MOPING. It's time to revive before Daniella comes home; she mustn't see me so depressed. Though attempts to recover my literary passion have failed, I should still be able to exercise. We'll start with push-ups, the real kind, not the silly ones against the wall the physical therapist had me doing in the hospital. Ten, rest; ten, rest; then another ten. Afterward, I pedal away on my stationary bike, working up quite a sweat. I vow to do more tomorrow. Now for my small reward—a nice, hot shower.

The steam rises along my sides as I stand beneath the faucet. It feels good, loosening the phlegm at the back of my throat. Suddenly, I am coughing, my body trying to expel every last drop of cellular debris. The steam continues to rise, covering me in a white haze, enclosing me, penetrating my pores. Still coughing, I feel light-headed, woozy, my eyes are starting to flutter. As the light dims, I begin to fall, fall, falling faster, falling into the darkness . . .

I WAKE WITH my lips pressed against a cool, hard surface, wondering where I am. Water is running into my nose and mouth. I try to pick myself up, but gravity and the weight of my body pushes me down. I rest on the ground, the soothing sound of water lapping against my skin. I could sleep here forever. Only the water is rising and filling my mouth. If I don't get out soon, I will drown.

Slowly I lift myself, fear propelling me upward. I grab onto the edge of the tub, the soap dish, then the shower door. My foot hurts, the left one; I can't stand on it. The faucet resists my feeble turn. The towel has disappeared. Dripping, tottering, I hobble to the phone and press the familiar sequence of numbers.

"I passed out," I tell Daniella.

"Are you okay?" She sounds alarmed.

"Yeah. Except for my foot. I may have sprained it."

"Don't move, I'll be right there."

When Daniella arrives, I'm lying on the couch with an ice pack over my rapidly swelling foot. "What happened?" she asks.

I'm not sure. I felt hot, very hot. And then I was sprawled out in the tub, face down. But I'm fine now. Just glad I didn't break anything.

"You should call Dr. Castro."

"I'm fine, honey. Really."

"What about the foot? And the bruise on your forehead? Did you hit your head? Let me see that." Daniella moves closer to inspect my forehead. "I want you to call Dr. Castro right away. Please."

I refuse. I refuse to do anything that might result in an emergency visit to Sloan-Kettering. Even the injury to my head, which I wasn't aware of until Daniella pointed it out, doesn't prompt reconsideration.

Daniella insists. We compromise by calling Naftali Bechar, my friend from internship, and explain the details of my accident to him. "But I feel fine now. You don't think I need to go in, do you?"

"I don't think, I know," says my friend. "And so do you. Get your ass over here."

"No, Naftali, I can't. I'm sure it's just a sprain."

"Fuck the ankle," replies Naftali. "It's your head I'm worried about. Remember the counts, the platelets—who knows what they are at this point. You could easily have a subdural hematoma."

"That's ridiculous. I have no symptoms."

"You've got to come in. I'm calling Castro."

"Okay, fine—I'll call him myself."

Not surprisingly, Castro shares Naftali's concerns. He wants to take some tests. I may need a transfusion. He'll notify the E.R. Naftali will be paged once I arrive.

It's Tuesday night, only four days since my discharge from Sloan-Kettering, and I'm on my way back, back to the odious gray prison tower with a thousand eyes. I couldn't have dreamt a more horrifying dream. Tom, who lives nearby, picks us up. I stumble into his Jeep, Daniella pushing me in from behind. It's pouring outside, we are soaked. The wind is howling. Tom can barely see the road as the rain ricochets off his windshield.

Naftali is waiting in the E.R. He shakes his head with a disbelieving smile. "Let the nurse draw some blood first," he then says. "I'll page Ortho and we'll get an X ray of your foot. How does it feel?"

"Not bad. The icing helped."

After several tubes of blood are taken, Naftali performs a neurological exam. Abnormalities could mean bleeding into the brain. There are none.

"You're still not out of the woods. A bleed could take twenty-four hours to develop. You'll have to stay overnight for observation."

"No way, Naftali. I'm a doctor, goddamnit. I can do my own observing. I'm going home tonight. That's all there is to it."

"We'll see."

The orthopedic Fellow introduces himself. He listens to my story, then examines my foot. "It's swollen but not very tender. Let's see what the X ray shows."

Daniella and Tom try to make light of the situation. We joke about my clumsiness, recall numerous instances of similar mishaps in the past. But our laughter, saturated with unease, doesn't last. Across from me is an older man admitted with fever. Part of his workup includes a spinal tap. Several unsuccessful attempts have been made. The patient is crying. His wife pleads with the nurse to leave her husband alone. A younger man to my right is vomiting into a basin. He is emaciated and sickly-looking. His wife strokes his hair while he heaves.

My wife draws the curtains around my stall.

NAFTALI EVENTUALLY RETURNS with the counts. They are low. Anemia, the drop in red cells, may have precipitated the fainting episode. They will give me a unit of red cells and one of platelets. Naftali is considering a CAT scan to rule out a subdural hematoma. Next the young orthopod enters with a series of negatives in hand.

"Only a sprain, right?" I ask.

No reply.

"Are you sure you're not in any pain?" inquires the doctor, pressing down against my foot. "Does this hurt?"

"No, not at all. Nothing's broken, right?"

"Wrong. You have three broken bones, three metatarsals. It's called a Lisfranc fracture. It usually happens after major trauma, not a minor slip in the bathroom." He appears perplexed. "It's also supposed to be very painful." More perplexity.

"You're joking?"

"See for yourself." The doctor points out the fractures on the film. "Lucky for you the bones aren't displaced. If they were, we'd have to bring you to the O.R. and put in a few pins."

The orthopod will make a temporary cast. If there is no change in the X rays after two days, when the swelling subsides, a permanent cast will be placed.

"How long will I need it?"

"Six to eight weeks."

I close my eyes and sigh. The news is devastating. I had hoped to continue exercising, build up strength, resurrect my life. Now this. Delay. Infinite delay.

"It could've been worse," argues Naftali. "Listen, David, it's already midnight. The blood will take another hour or two. You should stay the night."

"No. I'm leaving as soon as the transfusion is over."

Naftali doesn't push. Instead, he advises Daniella to wake me every hour. If she notices anything peculiar, she should bring me back immediately.

The last drop of blood flows into my arm at 2 A.M. Daniella puts my mask back on and helps me to my feet. Tom hands me the set of crutches. We drive back in the pouring rain, drained and dejected.

I'm exhausted when I finally lie down in bed. I was weak before the fracture. Now I have to drag my entire body along on crutches. And then there's the nocturnal urination problem. How will I get to the bathroom? Daniella brings me a plastic container. We revert back to life at the hospital, urinating bedside again.

I am moving in the wrong direction.

CHAPTER THIRTY-TWO

⚘

THE ORTHOPEDIC FELLOW was puzzled by the absence of pain following my fracture. He considered the possibility of nerve damage and was tempted to call in a neurologist. That proved unnecessary. On Wednesday morning, I awake in excruciating pain. Daniella pages the Fellow. He is relieved that my wayward foot has found its way back into a classic textbook case of a Lisfranc fracture. "It was only a matter of time. You'll need some narcotics. I'd start with Percocet."

Although the mention of narcotics stirs up unpleasant memories, the pain is dizzying. Tylenol doesn't help. Daniella telephones my father. He'll be over with medicine in less than an hour.

I spend the day on the couch, gazing at my extended leg, wrapped in a temporary cast, stretching from mid-foot to mid-thigh. My father sits on the rocker to my right, my mother on a chair to my left. The leg throbs. Perspiration drips down my forehead, from the Percocet, from the pain; it moves in cycles, reaching piercing highs, then leveling off, receding. My mother brings cold water and compresses. She wipes the moisture from my brow. My father talks about the office, some of my patients

he's recently seen, anything to steer me away from the throbbing.

They are upset, they have mixed feelings. On the one hand,
they are angry with me and Daniella. They had insisted that
someone should stay with me, at least for the first week or two.
You could barely walk to the bathroom on your own, they
warned. How will you cook and clean? What will you do all
day, alone? Who will you talk to?

I need my space, I answered. I need to feel like an adult
again. Daniella agreed. As much for me as for herself. Another
full-scale invasion by my family would have landed her in the
hospital.

My parents are also upset because they feel guilty. If Daniella and I were wrong, if we acted stupidly, they, as parents,
should have overruled us. They knew best, yet watched passively as the worst unfolded. They were responsible for my self-
imposed isolation. They were responsible for my fall in the
shower, my fractured foot. For Christ's sake, they could've killed
me.

I watch my father shaking his head, rolling his eyes, the
rocker moving back and forth with nervous jerks. "What could
you have possibly done, even if you were here?" I ask. "I
would've still taken that shower. I would've still fallen and broken my foot."

"It could have been worse. You could've injured your head.
You might never have made it out of that tub. There was no
one here to help you." He is mad. He feels guilty.

My mother will no longer listen to me. From now on, she
will come every day, make sure that I'm eating properly, that the
house is as germ-free as possible, that every imaginable detail is
attended to. No amount of protesting will change her mind.

Sweat rains down my forehead into my eyes. Through a wa-

tery film, I glance at my parents, at my bandaged foot, at the uri-
nal and crutches on the floor beside the couch, at the walls and
ceiling of the living room, surrounding me, enclosing me, helpless, a helpless hostage, once again.

AN APPOINTMENT AT the Orthopedic Clinic for another series of X rays and the placement of a permanent cast is scheduled for Friday. I won't go. I will not return to Sloan-Kettering.
Dr. Aldo will take care of me, I tell my father. An orthopod and
close friend of the family, Dr. Aldo has a private practice in Bay
Ridge. He is gentle, he is compassionate, a warm-hearted Sicil-
ian from Sciacca. I also have a better shot at convincing him to
reduce my cast sentence. As long as Dr. Castro agrees, says my
father. Castro agrees.

On Friday morning, my father is waiting for me in the
lobby. Hobbling to the car on crutches—gangly, bald, masked
and now casted—I feel like a freak. At least the pain has subsided. It lasted twenty-four hours. By Thursday, Percocet was no
longer needed. As we drive through the Brooklyn-Battery Tunnel, I cling to a wish, planted in the fertile fields of my imagination the day after my fall and nurtured there ever since: the
orthopedic Fellow at the hospital, young and inexperienced,
had made a mistake; the fracture was bad but not bad enough to
warrant a cast; a new series of X rays would confirm my suspi-
cion; I may even be able to start jogging again. A wonderful,
wishful wish.

The patients in the waiting room gawk at the masked freak
stumbling into their midst. Fortunately, I am quickly escorted
into an examining room. Dr. Aldo wraps his arms around me.
"It's good to see you. Your parents were so worried. I felt terrible for them. But it's almost over, thank God. And don't you
worry about the foot. It'll heal in no time."

Dr. Aldo takes several X rays after removing the cast. Findings are the same, interpretation the same: three broken metatarsals, a Lisfranc fracture. Permanent cast is necessary. Permanent cast is placed.

"They said six to eight weeks. Do you think we could cut that in half?"

"We'll see," smiles Dr. Aldo. "You'll need the crutches for another week or so. Then you should be able to walk without them." He hands me an open sneaker with Velcro snaps, the only footwear option for the bulky white extension on my left leg.

My father and I drive back to Manhattan in silence. I'm mad at myself. Replaying the shower scene over in my mind, I change the sequence of events, hoping to alter the outcome. If I hadn't made the water so hot . . . If I had just grabbed onto the soap dish or the shower door . . . Such a small mistake, such enormous repercussions. I desperately wanted to start exercising again. The remaking of my body would lead to a remaking of my spirit. Instead, I am left with a cumbersome, cement casing over my leg, an open sneaker with a Velcro snap. There will be stasis instead of rebuilding. I am an invalid—to be nursed by my mother, by Daniella, while I watch and wait for an increasingly elusive recovery.

THE FOLLOWING DAYS are among the worst in my transplant experience. They are filled with restless nights. Klonepin neither relaxes nor helps me sleep. Insomnia, an old friend, returns to celebrate my misfortune. She brings along a new friend—depression. We stay awake together in the darkness. I see bad things, terrible things; they fill my thoughts in the quiet of the night. No hope, not a shred of hope to chase away the demons.

I review the list of transplant complications. The fractured foot has left me feeling more vulnerable, more susceptible to the advancing army of hostile organisms around me, inside of me: CMV, EBV, HSV, HZV, PCP. Nasty little fuckers with their innocuous-sounding trio of letters, poised to strike a man when he's down. Lymphoma, graft versus host disease, radiation pneumonitis, and the list goes on.

The pains in my belly, which had taken a sabbatical during the height of my foot fiasco, have returned. They seem to worsen in the darkness. And in their ashy lulls, an image gradually arises—a nodule, the size of a tomato, red and slimy, growing in the lymph nodes of my stomach, pushing against a nerve, causing me to wince. Lymphoma? Could it be? Rising up in the night like a thief to pounce on an unsuspecting victim? And if so, what treatment would it require? More chemotherapy? More radiation? More days and nights at Sloan-Kettering? Please, dear God, let me be.

As I'm about to shriek, a new symptom sets in to accompany my belly pangs—shortness of breath. I begin to wheeze. Is it asthma? Or something more serious, like CMV pneumonia? I can visualize the fuzzy infiltrates on the chest films, blocking out my lungs, consuming them. Another catheter will be placed inside a large vein. They will feed me intravenous gancyclovir for weeks, months, indefinitely, until I recover. Or die.

Sitting up, gasping for air, I reach for the inhaler in my bedside drawer. Deep, slow breaths, in through the mouth, out through the nose. Or was it the other way around? I can't remember. Confused, I alternate inhalations and exhalations between the two orifices, hoping that one of the sequences will calm me before Daniella wakes up.

She was exhausted this evening. Arriving home after an eleven-hour day at work, Daniella prepared dinner, listening, as she chopped, to my barrage of exasperating instructions from the couch: Sterilize the vegetables, don't let the raw chicken touch the silverware, cook everything thoroughly. Afterward she cleaned, my job in the old days. Yesterday, she even managed to get me through a round of sex, awkward as it was with the cast. It used to make me happy in the past. She had hoped it would do the same now.

Daniella lies on the pillow with her face to one side, my side. Her eyes are closed, her mouth open. She, too, is vulnerable, even as she sleeps. I am contagious. The gloomy scenarios envisioned in the darkness easily enlarge to accommodate my wife. Daniella sitting at the bedside of her sick husband, feeding him, consoling him, watching him die. There she is alone. By his grave. Crying. A lonely widow. Mourning.

Wide awake, I anxiously wait for the morning light.

ON MONDAY, MARCH 25, I am back at Dr. Castro's clinic, surrounded by a horde of sick patients. I no longer feel different. I am just as sick, just as despondent. Castro is quietly perceptive. He looks unblinking into my eyes and appropriates my innermost feelings. I find myself turning away from his gaze.

"A minor setback, David," he decides. "That's all. Don't get upset. I can call Dr. Passik. Talking with someone might make you feel better."

I shake my head.

"He wanted to get outside more," explains my mother, on behalf of her silent son. "He wanted to walk so that he could build up strength."

"He will in time," promises Castro, patting me on the back. "Your counts were excellent today. The platelets are up to 50,000. I doubt you'll need another transfusion. Your new marrow appears to be sustaining itself. I listened to your lungs; they sound clear. David, you're doing fine."

"What about his stomach pain?" asks my mother.

"I'll prescribe some medicine. It should get better. If not, we may have to scope him."

"Why?" I ask, breaking my silence. "To look for what?" I'm afraid of new tests, new tests that may uncover new problems. Has Castro seen the red nodule, the large tomato sitting quietly in the lymph nodes of my belly?

"Nothing, David, relax. I'm sure it won't be necessary. Let's wait and see. In the meantime, I want you to be more positive. It's important for your recovery."

I know that, but the terrifying visions keep coming. They're beyond my control.

I WALK OUT of Castro's clinic, brooding. I mope around my apartment, brooding. My mother is never far away, busy with some chore, trying to be discreet, but checking in on me, nevertheless, every five minutes to make sure I'm all right. When our eyes meet, she quickly retreats, embarrassed, while I scowl like a crotchety old man, like a vicious animal. All of my fear turns into rage, rage directed at my mother, my poor, selfless mother. All of my frustration about to be unleashed on her tireless shoulders. How is it possible, this irrational behavior? Where does it spring from? A son's resentment toward his mother, toward his persistent feelings of dependence? Some psychic misinterpretation of devotion for guilt? I have no answers. And yet still, in the midst of its blatant inappropriateness, and my self-disgust, I am unable to stop it.

"How about some chamomile tea, dear?" asks my mother hesitantly. "It's good for your stomach."

I want to scream but manage a quiet "No thanks" instead and return to my barren world of TV, magazines and wall-gazing. Minutes pass, hours, and days. Time filled with nothingness moves incredibly slowly. My inner world is as empty as the outer one. I am frozen in a kind of shock state—mouth open, pupils dilated, eyes fixed on something terrible before me, paralyzed by an unwillingness to either run or fight, waiting for a merciful annihilation.

CHAPTER THIRTY-THREE

⌒⌒

THERE COMES A POINT when terror, unrealized, loses its capacity to shock. Time moves on, nights turn into days, the balance tilts from darkness to light, and I am still around to witness the morning sun slipping in through the blinds. It's a matter of survival. One learns to disregard consciousness, acknowledging its self-destructive impulses, overruling them, demanding to be revived, to move on, rather than involute and wither.

Contact with other patients at Castro's clinic, sometimes inspiring, sometimes disheartening, plays a role in my turnaround. Every Monday at 9 A.M., my parents join me for the weekly pilgrimage to Sloan-Kettering. After check-in and blood drawing, we wait to see the doctor, anywhere from thirty minutes to two hours. During this time, we converse uneasily and glance over at familiar faces in the waiting room. We wonder about their stories, from afar mostly. No need to get too close; it might depress me even further. But curiosity gradually overcomes my fear.

A week after the fall, my mother spots Nicole Montaldo across the room. Go on over, she whispers in my ear, say hello. Nicole, several years younger than me, had a bone marrow transplant for leukemia six months ago. My father had recognized her and her parents, patients of his from Bay Ridge, in the clinic two weeks before my transplant; she gave me some tips on what to bring to the hospital. She was thin and bald that day, tentative and still shaken by her ordeal. Today she is another person—lively, smiling, back at work. I am envious. "It takes time," she tells me. "But soon you'll be able to take the mask off; that helps a lot." The change in her appearance is dramatic. I envision the same changes for myself.

A week later, a young man, my age, sits down next to me. With his full head of hair, ruddy complexion and confident stride, he appears too healthy for Castro's clinic. I ask him whether he's a patient or here with someone else. "Castro's my doc," he answers. "I had a transplant two years ago. I'm back every six months for a bone marrow biopsy." Rick had a chronic form of leukemia that didn't respond to chemotherapy. Bone marrow transplantation was his only option. However, he had no brothers or sisters, he had no match. He was placed on a national registry. Three months later, miraculously, a donor was found. "A woman from San Francisco. That's all I know," he says.

"What do you mean?" I ask.

Donors remain anonymous, explains Rick. Those are the rules. Still, he hopes to find out where his marrow came from one day. He wants to thank the person who saved his life.

Rick tells me he used to run the New York Marathon. "Are you running now?" I ask. Yes, he is.

"When? When did you start?" I ask. "I can't imagine doing anything very strenuous. I feel so weak. I didn't think it would be like this."

Neither did he. Returning from the hospital, he tried to get back into shape. No way. It took three months before he had enough energy to run around the block. "It doesn't happen all at once. Each week, you gain a little more. I didn't feel a hundred percent until a year out. You've got to be patient. It'll work out. Just look at me."

I am looking and looking makes me feel better. Others have experienced the same feelings, the same weaknesses, and have overcome them. Nicole is back at work, Rick is running again. I will be too. The minute this damn cast can be ditched.

These success stories accelerate my recovery. So too, I'm embarrassed to admit, do the less sanguine tales that unfold in the waiting room. One day I run into Loretta, a beautiful black woman in her late thirties, whom I hadn't seen since November. She is a fellow zebra, the only other patient I know with PNH. Loretta had been doing well without any medication until recently, she confides, when she became disoriented and had a seizure. An MRI showed some bleeding in her brain, a result of severely low platelet counts. She is now on steroids and receives weekly platelet transfusions.

Loretta speaks slowly. Her cheeks are swollen and shapeless; they used to be thinner, the contours more defined, almost polished. She walks unsteadily. No makeup today, no form-fitting dress, her old elegance gone. And yet she is genuinely excited to see me. "I was worried about you," she says. "I'm so glad you're all right."

I don't know how to respond. The sympathetic glimmer in her eyes is disabling. I feel terrible, sick to my stomach. How can she worry about others, about me, in her state? And why am I not more like that? Why am I always so competitive? Will I ever be as compassionate as Loretta?

"What will you do?" I mumble. "Bone marrow transplant?"

"No," she says. "Don't you remember? I don't have a

match. They are thinking about a partially matched, unrelated donor, but I'm afraid. Too risky."

I had forgotten. I had also forgotten about PNH, the bad things it could do, the difficulty in predicting what might happen. And the unfair odds of the genetic lottery, the slot machine of HLA matching—the only definite means of escape from the nightmare.

These thoughts cause a sudden shifting of the wind. They push me away from Loretta's uncertainty and toward my small but definite advances. My situation now appears less bleak; the laws of relativity, moving gracefully between the physical and psychological realms, support the transition. Despite the bum leg, the overwhelming weakness, I am, after all, cured of the dreaded disease that brought me to Sloan in the first place. I *will* eventually recover.

The following week, I am reunited with my next-door neighbor at the hospital, Alberto, the man with a soft spot for the Golden Arches of McDonald's, whose wife smuggled in a Big Mac across the rigid barriers of isolation, only days after her husband sailed out of bed and landed on the floor with a thud. It is less than a month after we were discharged from the hospital. Alberto is sick. His skin is red and scaly, his lips dry and cracked. There is a yellowish tinge to his eyes. "Graft versus host disease," he explains. "They are giving me cyclosporine. That's why I shake so much." He holds up his quivering hands. "The medicine affects the nerves."

As a dermatologist who recently passed his boards, I am familiar with graft versus host disease since it commonly affects the skin—familiar, that is, with its textbook descriptions and Kodachrome images. But here beside me is a living example. I peer into Alberto's body and imagine a fierce army of circulating T cells, cells from his brother's marrow. They don't recognize Alberto's skin, his liver, his glands. Instead, they brand these organs "enemies" and declare war. The result is an itchy rash, extreme dryness, diarrhea and jaundice.

Alberto has other problems. He was recently diagnosed with a CMV infection and spent two weeks in the hospital. Another catheter was placed in his arm. He will need intravenous medication for three months. Listening to Alberto's tremulous voice makes me shiver. How can I feel sorry for myself in the presence of Loretta? Of Alberto? Besides the fractured bones, which will ultimately heal, I've had no complications. None. Nothing, at least that I am aware of, is threatening my life. I feel ashamed.

It is unsettling to acquire strength from the weak. I remember feeling the same in the hospital when Vincenzo used to accompany me down to Radiation. Observing the old lady heaving before me, a sickly Alberto dozing off after me, I felt invincible, the sweet refrain of relativity ringing in my ears. What an ugly, selfish way to think. I couldn't help myself then. I still can't.

IN MY MOST desperate hours, I discover hope. And with hope comes the desire to expand again, to send out feelers, to make contact with objects and people beyond myself, to speak to them. That desire was nonexistent when I first arrived back home. I had shriveled, contracted, sealed myself off. But the momentum of existence toward others, toward the world, is returning. I welcome its soothing embrace.

I carry with me another vision of Rema. A month before she died, we went to a nightclub to watch her husband Billy, a musician, perform. Rema was smiling, full of pride for the man she had fallen in love with. Later that evening, however, I realized that beneath her gracious exterior, Rema was in pain. Her legs were swollen; she could hardly walk; she clutched her belly. Rema never cried, never complained, never wallowed in self-pity as I have been doing these last few weeks. She picked herself up and moved on. I will try to do the same.

CHAPTER THIRTY-FOUR

⌇⌇

TEN DAYS AFTER my fall, I can walk without crutches. Gradually, more and more time is spent away from the couch and wall-gazing. The plastic urinals are dumped in the trash bin; I'd rather hobble to the bathroom than live in the perpetual midst of yellow vapors, a constant reminder of my infirmity. I force myself to exercise, undaunted by the clumsy apparatus weighing down my left side—thirty minutes on the stationary bicycle followed by push-ups and sit-ups. It was all preapproved by my favorite orthopod, Dr. Aldo. "You'll know what you can do. Just don't push it."

I resume my outdoor jaunts, ever eager to feel the slap of air against my face. During the week my mother chaperones; Daniella fills in on weekends. Drooping along with a bandanna covering my scalp stubble, a mask sealing my mouth, large round sunglasses that dip below the cheeks and a bulky cast opening onto a Velcro sneaker—I am quite a sight. Nonetheless, I am out and about, increasing the distance traveled every day.

My forays into literature are gathering momentum. The first paragraph of *Our Mutual Friend* leads to the second; one chapter yields to another. Not to say that I'm completely engrossed; images of confinement and transplant complications continue to intrude. But there is progress—I'm emotionally involved in a world other than my own. Unfortunately, the writing taboo remains in effect. I still can't remove my laptop computer from its case. Writing is too solitary an enterprise for someone desperately trying to escape solitude. I'm not strong enough at the moment.

On Mondays, my parents accompany me to Sloan-Kettering. We now have many friends at the clinic—patients who have been through transplants and patients who are considering the option. We encourage potential candidates, pointing out the landmarks of my recovery as they occur, praising the medical and nursing staff on the transplant team. After socializing in the waiting room, we visit with Castro. Everything seems to be going smoothly. There are no signs of complications. The counts are stable. Final results of the bone marrow biopsy done the day before I left the hospital show a healthy new marrow with the right proportions of each cell line; moreover, chromosomal analysis indicates that all of the cells possess two X chromosomes—that is, they are 100 percent female. My marrow has been replaced by my sister's. None of my feeble, underperforming, mutant stem cells have survived. "I didn't expect anything less," says Castro, beaming. "Now we wait for your immune system to recover."

"How long?" I ask.

"Between six and twelve months. We'll start testing you at the hundred-day mark. When the numbers fall in the normal range, we can begin vaccinations."

The systematic dismantling of the immune system may be the most terrifying part of bone marrow transplantation, even more so than the shifting of marrow from one person to another. In fact, the conditioning regimen of chemotherapy and radiation, explains Castro, has wiped out my immunity to polio, measles, rubella, tetanus, mumps and thousands of other organisms—an unfortunate but unavoidable consequence of destroying all the white cells in my body, including those T cells that would have rejected Michele's marrow had they survived. I am an infant again and will eventually have to repeat the entire childhood vaccination series.

And yet the leveling of my immune system is a lot easier to comprehend than the miracle of its reconstitution. How is it possible for all the broken pieces of the puzzle to be reassembled, pieces that took years of exposure to a wide array of antigens to develop, shape and fine-tune? And how can Castro be so sure that it will happen in just a few months?

Of course, there is some comfort in the fact that a basic level of immunity is already operating in my body. As soon as my white count was resurrected from dead zero and entered the normal range, an army of neutrophils and macrophages had begun to circulate throughout my bloodstream and tissues. These cells, though untrained and somewhat primitive, are innately responsive to many deadly organisms and provide a limited degree of defense against them.

What is missing, however, is the more sophisticated and learned arm of my immune system that is directed by mature T cells. Unlike neutrophils and macrophages, T cells have many qualities that we associate with mindfulness. These intelligent cells can distinguish self from other. They can respond to organisms and tumors with exceptional specificity. They can coordinate the activities of other white cells to combat a foe more effectively. And most remarkable of all, they possess memory; T cells will remember an infectious agent when they encounter it a second time and be more prepared to deal with it. This adaptive response accounts for the lifelong immunity that develops

after a primary infection with certain organisms and after a series of vaccinations.

I have no T cells with such qualities at the moment.
Michele's stem cells have given rise to a group of immature
pre–T cells. In order for them to function effectively, however,
they must be educated. Ordinarily, this takes place in the thymus, an organ located in the neck. There, T cells learn their
trade. The best students receive diplomas and graduate. The
worst—those, for example, that are unable to differentiate self
from other and can potentially cause an autoimmune disease—
are expelled in a process known as negative selection and ultimately destroyed. During this period of intensive immunologic
training, much of which occurs *in utero* and during infancy, a
baby is protected from hostile threats in his environment by the
mother's immune system, its steady flow of antibodies passing
first through her circulation and then through her breast milk.

I am afforded no such protection during my vulnerable period. Furthermore, in medical school I was taught that the thymus begins to atrophy after puberty, when its role as T cell
university has concluded. I may well have very little thymus left
at the moment. So how will my T cells mature? When and
where will they be educated? There's no point in asking these
questions; hematologists, including Castro, though full of possible theories, aren't quite sure. Better not think about it then.
Somehow, somewhere, the process will take place. My immune
system will recover. Castro is confident about this. I'll just have
to trust him and concentrate on more concrete matters.

"WHEN WILL I be able to return to work?" I ask my doctor.
There is no way I can remain cooped up in my apartment for
another six months, waiting and wondering. As soon as my hair
grows back and I no longer look like a patient, sometime in the

next few weeks according to the Sloan-Kettering transplant manual, I am determined to resume practicing dermatology. Castro promised. I'll hold him to it.

"As long as you're careful, I don't see why not." Dr. Castro doesn't like to disappoint, even after the slew of objections raised by my mother. She is afraid that I may be rushing into things prematurely.

"You're son is going to be as healthy as you are, Mrs. Biro," reassures Castro, "and will be able to do everything you can do."

These words are heavenly music to my ears. They provoke more radical requests. "Can I take the mask off?" I ask in mid-March. "How about ordering in some food?" comes the next petition. "I'm dying for Chinese." And tired of soup and pasta, in its myriad manifestations, compliments of my two live-in chefs, Mom and Daniella. It's not a question of uninspired preparation. I simply want a little variety.

Each visit with Castro, I negotiate a different culinary item. Pizza, chicken wings, curry, pad thai and whatever other delicacies are being offered at the local takeout places. "Is that all you ever think about, David—food?" cries my exasperated doctor.

"It's a biggie," I admit with a smile. I don't bother mentioning my ultimate fantasy, the succulent taste of sushi, beginning with an order of uni, followed by two of ika. It's obvious that raw fish is light-years away right now.

Castro finally concedes to pizza in early April. Next comes paella from our favorite Spanish restaurant. And by the end of the month, seventy-five days after my transplant, I am rewarded with fried dumplings and chicken with cashew nuts from Empire Szechuan.

FORTIFIED BY AN expanding, multicultural diet, I am ready for visitors again. They appear in droves, my circle of friends, as

they did the first week at the hospital. Tom reports his most recent successes in the O.R., Steven discusses his firm's latest
transcontinental leveraged buyout. Ellen and Kenny substitute
for my mother on the daily stroll around Kips Bay. The
Rothenbergs stop by in the evening before dinner. Rema's husband Billy appears with his guitar one afternoon and plays songs
from his new album. And like clockwork, at the beginning of
every month, Dr. Luzzatto checks in. He is delighted with my
progress. I am delighted that he still thinks of me.

Surveying the landscape as it fills again with friends and
well-wishers, I notice a few changes. There has been some re-
structuring in the wake of PNH; certain relationships have
flourished, others have foundered. My closest friends stood by
me throughout the ordeal as I knew they would; it has brought
us even closer. More surprising, however, were responses from
people I considered good friends. Some were compassionate to
a degree I would have never expected; they visited and called
every chance they had. Others I no longer speak to. They were
absent when I needed them; they will remain absent evermore.
Daniella urges me to reconsider: People feel awkward in these
situations; they're afraid of imposing. I don't care.

My three sisters also visit my prison cell with news from the
land of the healthy. Lisa and Michael are actively trying to con-
ceive. With any luck, I'll be an uncle around the time of my
one-year anniversary. We might even be able to coordinate my
vaccination schedule with the baby's. Perfect! Debbie continues
to be worshiped by fourth-graders at P.S. 48; she receives letters
and gifts every week from appreciative parents. And Michele
raves about the wonders of occupational therapy; among her
never-ending list of new ideas is a plan to design a clothing line
for patients with arthritis and other disabilities.

My sisters have returned to their respective worlds. After months of intense contact, fraternity, the sharing of blood and marrow, we are back to our pretransplant routine, spending less and less time with each other. How strange and natural this coming together and moving apart now that the danger has passed. It happens seamlessly, both phases, and without many words, much like the human body works—an instinctive, inarticulate ensemble.

I never asked anything of my sisters. They gave spontaneously, somehow always knowing what I wanted, what I needed. Our lives have moved on—almost as if nothing had happened, nothing had changed. A small damaged part of the *corpus familias* was swiftly repaired and is now running smoothly again.

And yet everything has changed. The bonds that join me to them have shifted since PNH, they have been redefined. My sisters have literally become a part of me, Debbie and Lisa just as much as Michele. The gift of marrow came from them as a unit, an indivisible group. I see, I speak, I move with the blood cells of all my sisters.

As Michele thanks me for the anatomy book I recently lent her, Rick's words suddenly flash before my mind. He desperately wanted to thank the anonymous donor from San Francisco. "She saved my life."

She saved his life. Like Michele saved mine. Like all my sisters saved mine. When a stranger saves your life, she deserves vast praise, whole fields of appreciation. But my sisters are family and that's what families are supposed to do. I hardly thanked them—that is, in the words we use with our friends and colleagues, in the words we use to get things done in the world. And yet they must know how grateful I am. Somehow, in that sign language of family, they must know, and with and without each other, we move on.

"Thanks for the book," says Michele. "It helped me study for the last exam."

Don't mention it, I reply.

MY FATHER BRINGS me home to Bay Ridge every Wednesday, his day off. "You can't stay in that apartment forever," argues my mother. "You need a change of scenery." She's right. It's wonderful to recline on a different couch, peruse different walls, admire the contours of a different TV set. When the weather permits, lounge chairs are positioned under the shaded dogwood tree in our backyard. There, my father and I, bundled up in winter coats, sit and discuss the practice. We plan my return in exquisite detail. I'll start in early May reviewing charts and insurance contracts, learning how to use the new computer. Then we'll start booking patients, a few hours a week at first, gradually extending my schedule as tolerated. I should have my hair back by then, at least an acceptable amount of it, and enough strength to battle stubborn verrucae and skin cancers. These visions of my reentry into life are exhilarating.

One Wednesday, headed south along the FDR Drive, my father stumbles into uncomfortable territory; he does so on purpose. "I wanted to talk to you alone, before we got home, about . . . Daniella." The subject makes me cringe; I feel groundless in its midst. I understand how my family feels. They are upset that Daniella has remained aloof, hardly calls, never invites them over.

"Maybe she's angry," he suggests, "that she wasn't here when you decided to go ahead with the transplant, that she wasn't involved in the decision?"

"No, that's ridiculous. She knew what was happening." I

neglect to mention that we never exactly discussed it. Still, I'm sure she agreed.

"Are you sure?"

Yes I'm sure.

Am I? Perhaps I assume too much, that the love between two people obviates the need for overt communication. That language flows inaudibly beneath the surface of things, as it does with all matters of family. Maybe I'm wrong, maybe this is just a selfish and distorted view. Doubtless I'd make an excellent case study for some deft psychoanalyst. Outwardly, I'm talkative, gregarious, always ready to embrace friends and strangers, a trait inherited from Poppy Jim by way of my mother. But when it comes to anything that strikes an emotional chord, I turn inward and silent like a mollusk. In this way, I am my father's son. But the stoic's tough exterior betrays a hidden insecurity; extending oneself and one's feelings into the realm of others comes with a price: vulnerability. Perhaps I was afraid to tell my wife everything and perhaps she was just as afraid to confide in me.

As we enter the Gowanus Expressway into Brooklyn, it occurs to me that I may have missed something in my explanation of Daniella's behavior. Yes, my wife is strong. But that strength depends upon an ability to exert a level of control over her environment. She lost that ability back in the winter of '96. Suddenly, she could no longer take care of, even help, her husband. Information and medical details were kept from her. She hardly entered the decision-making process after my summit meeting with Castro and Luzzatto. And at the hospital, my family made up schedules and timetables without consulting her. In no time, she became powerless over my life, over her life, over our lives. My father is right. She must have resented that.

But those days are over. I'm better. We're home. Daniella is back at the helm, taking charge, confident again. I can see it in her determined gaze, her easy laugh. "Don't worry, Dad," I tell my father. "Things are going to change. Life will return to normal and we'll forget all this." My father is skeptical. I don't know what else to say.

We pass a construction site on the highway, and my father reminds me to raise the window. I have been warned to avoid such areas; the drilling aerosolizes microorganisms in the ground, enabling them to enter the lungs; immunocompromised patients like myself are often unable to defend themselves. I push down the button. The window doesn't move. My father reaches over and tries. The window is stuck. Already disturbed by our previous conversation, my father is now frantic. Get on your mask, he screams, button up your overcoat. He tries to slip off his coat to furnish me with another layer of protection, but the car swerves into the next lane as he drops the wheel. He curses under his breath, afraid I may catch pneumonia before we reach home, afraid my mother will never forgive him for it.

Arriving in Bay Ridge, we pull into the auto repair shop. My father, ordinarily calm and even-tempered, is yelling at the mechanic who had assured him only yesterday that the windows had been fixed. My son is sick, he shouts, can't you see. It's winter and the goddamn windows don't work. The mechanic apologizes profusely. He offers us a ride home while someone attends to the car.

We don't mention the incident to my mother.

My father slowly recovers under the dogwood tree in the backyard, discussing our favorite topic, office affairs.

BY THE FOURTH week in a cast, my leg won't stop itching. I call Dr. Aldo and plead for its removal. One more week, he in-

sists. At the end of April, an electric saw is blasting through cement, freeing my captive limb. Despite the brittle, brown sediment above my skin that secretes an unpleasant odor, I am
overjoyed to be reunited with my leg again. "When can I start
running?"

"Give it some time, the bones aren't healed yet. We'll take
another X ray next month." Dr. Aldo believes the healing
process may be delayed because of the heavy dose of radiation
and steroids I received in the hospital. He prescribes a calcium
supplement.

Without my cast, I am ready to pick up where I left off before the fall. Just thirty days to go. Thirty days to reach one
hundred—the end and the beginning.

CHAPTER THIRTY-FIVE

～

A LTHOUGH THERE IS movement in the right direction as
April winds into May, I am far from happy. These last two
months have been the most difficult part of the transplant. I've
never become accustomed to the many restrictions imposed on
me because of my impaired immune system. Wearing a mask,
taking a handful of different medications, eating certain foods.
No shopping, movies, parties—too many people and things
around, harboring too many germs. I worry about the germs
constantly.

There is plenty of time to worry. Despite many phone calls
and visitors, I am alone most of the day. Even when my mother
is around—"No more than a half hour, then I'm leaving," her
famous last words—I still feel alone. Waiting and wondering, in-
terminably, and still not strong enough to enjoy the solitude.

Yet time pushes on, however grudgingly. Every day I walk,
sometimes uptown along Fifth Avenue to Central Park, sometimes downtown to Union Square and Greenwich Village. The
bandanna has been discarded. I no longer feel embarrassed by
the stubble on my scalp; cropped hair seems to be the fad in the
spring of '96. I admire the sights and architecture of New York
City along the way, from classics like the Flatiron Building and

the Pierpont Morgan Library to small details on a façade, like the curling of a gargoyle's tongue. There is plenty of time to admire. And to appreciate the elegant renovation of Bryant Park, the quaintness of the Little Church Around the Corner.

As I walk, I talk to myself. I plan my return to work. First, the necessary catching up on journals and applying to HMOs. Next, reorganizing the office to improve efficiency. And then gradually, the real thing—seeing patients again. Naturally, all this hinges on the acquisition of a better means of transportation, trading in my restless legs for a set of wheels. I compare the various models parked along the street. Hours are spent imagining myself sitting in the driver's seat of different sedans and sport utility vehicles.

On weekends, Daniella joins me in my musings. She proposes a relaxing vacation in the Caribbean in the fall. After exhausting the list of potential islands, she moves on to real estate. We design our dream apartment and then discuss what section of the city to put it in. When Ellen is around, we discuss my novel and the changes I might make before sending it out to publishers.

I'm aware, of course, that these are games played entirely on the mental sphere. But they're all I have at the moment. I am repopulating my world with people and things, filling a gaping emptiness with possibilities, carving out a future. Although more imaginary than real, the process nurtures my recovering psyche.

ON MAY 27, THREE months after my transplant, I appear before the mighty Castro. "You've reached the hundred-day mark," he says, patting me on the back. "Congratulations, you've made it." My counts have been stable during this critical period. He is sure they will remain so. There has been no sign

of infection or graft versus host disease. Better yet, a sample of
blood sent off two weeks ago shows that my immune function
is almost in the normal range.

"I'm very pleased," says Castro, smiling confidently. "Aren't
you glad you went through with the transplant?"

"Yes. But I'll be even happier when I don't have to come
back here anymore."

"One step at a time, David."

Dr. Castro informs me that a blood culture for CMV done
last month was positive. Some of his colleagues had urged him
to admit me to the hospital for treatment. Relying on the absence of any symptoms or signs of an active infection, my doctor decided to wait. Sure enough, just last week, a repeat test
was negative. "I didn't want to worry you unnecessarily," he
explains. I'm surprised Castro kept the information from me,
though in retrospect I realize it was an excellent idea—it would
have had devastating consequences on my fragile state of mind.

ONE HUNDRED DAYS have passed. I can remove the mask,
return to work. Some medications will be discontinued now,
others in the near future. Soon my immune system will fully recover and vaccinations can start. No more restrictions after that.
Daniella is allowed to book our Caribbean vacation.

As I walk back into the waiting room, maskless for the first
time in three months, a group of patients begins to clap. I recognize Loretta, my friend and fellow zebra with PNH. And
Rick, the long-distance runner. They are smiling at me, cheer-
ing for me. I made it. I'm a survivor.

At least one in every four patients dies from a bone marrow
transplant. For no reason, I happened into the better group of
three.

LETTING GO

❧

After great pain, a formal feeling comes—
The Nerves sit ceremonious, like Tombs—
The stiff Heart questions was it He, that bore,
And Yesterday, or Centuries before?

. . . .

This is the Hour of Lead—
Remembered, if outlived,
As Freezing persons, recollect the Snow—
First—Chill—then Stupor—then the letting go—

EMILY DICKINSON

S TORIES HAVE NO endings, in life or in fiction. A period is nothing more than an artificial pause created by the human imagination in its quest for closure and meaning. The pattern of the organic universe, individual and collective, is more circular than linear; it repeats itself over and over again; there are no discrete stoppings and startings, creatings and destroyings; only the continuous flow of time and its repetitions.

But even though I believe, intellectually, in the endlessness of things, I am unable to forgo the possibility of closure. I still hope, in spite. When the mighty Hugo Castro-Malaspina offered me the chance to end the story of my disease, to wipe out PNH once and for all, I grabbed at it as a falling man might grasp at a hand. Yes, I want to efface the last four months of my life. Perform this miracle of modern medicine, give me a new bone marrow. Then I will be healthy again and the threat of PNH will no longer hang over my head. Together we will stuff its evil spirit into a box and bury it forever in the bowels of the earth.

I believed in the story.

Naiveté? From a doctor who, by then, had had a few years of experience in the profession? From a doctor who had learned that cures were just like endings, pipe dreams except in a handful of cases? Who had witnessed the consuming embrace of medicine, steadily tightening rather than loosening its hold over patients?

It is now January 1998, almost two years since my transplant, and my story is far from over. I am still waiting for my immune system to recover. An early positive test was ruled a fluke when subsequent ones showed subnormal readings. "I'm not worried," Castro assured me, "it's just taking a little longer than usual." Typically the immune system reconstitutes itself within a year. However, there are a few patients, he recently informed me, who are still immunocompromised four years after their transplants. Is there a chance they won't, I won't, ever recover? Castro doesn't think so.

More troubling is another unexpected problem that surfaced after the critical one hundred days had passed. On a routine visit to the clinic in June, four months following the transplant, Castro gave me the unsettling results of my last bone marrow biopsy. Ten percent of my marrow had become male; somehow, some way, a stubborn cohort of my own cells managed to survive the conditioning regimen. "I wasn't going to tell you," said my doctor, "but I thought you might be suspicious when I ordered another biopsy. Don't worry. I doubt it's significant."

A shocking revelation, it sucked the wind right out of me. I fell backward into a chair, dizzy, as Castro delivered the next blow. "The counts have also been dropping," he went on hesitantly. "We're not sure why." Castro mentioned several possibilities, including a reaction to medication, a subclinical infection or least likely (but most worrisome), delayed marrow rejection. My white cells were predominantly affected, making me more susceptible to infection. He would prescribe Leucovorin, an antidote for the toxicity of Bactrim, one of the medications I had been taking, and daily injections of Neupogen, a growth factor that stimulates white cell production. A repeat bone marrow biopsy was scheduled.

The scare ended a month later when the counts returned to normal levels, as mysteriously as they had plummeted. No rhyme or reason for the sudden downturn was discovered. A virus, perhaps, suggested Castro. Neupogen was discontinued.

Subsequent bone marrows, however, continued to show a persistence of host cells. Fortunately, the percentages hadn't changed. My marrow is now referred to as chimeric; it is a hybrid, part female, part male. Castro believes the balance will be a stable one, that my cells won't grow and overtake Michele's. He also points out that my remaining cells have been tested for chromosomal abnormalities and PNH. The results have been repeatedly negative. "You have nothing to worry about," says Castro.

I'm not so sure. I ask him how many such transplants have ended like this. "Not many," he replies. "How many?" I persist. "Well, you're the first, at least in the case of T cell–depleted transplants." That is not encouraging. I've gone from mutant to chimera, which doesn't sound like I've left the animal kingdom. In fact, I remain a zebra, through and through, with endless uncertainties whirling around my striped coat.

My story is far from over.

Questions remain. What will happen to those rogue cells of mine? Will they, as Castro believes, coexist peacefully with my sister's brood? Or will they live, like the Israelis and the Arabs, in a constant state of war? Will my disease return, now that some of the conspirators have survived?

No answers to these questions. There are not enough patients with the same story. We must wait and see. Meanwhile, I'll go along with Castro's version, the happy one: My immune system will recover; my residual cells will cause no problems. I'll believe it too, only a little less naively than I might have in the past. I realize there will likely be no finale or curtain call. For even if Castro's prediction comes true, other issues still remain. I have been exposed to damaging levels of radiation and chemotherapy, which can result in complications down the road— cataracts, thyroid disease, secondary cancers. I will be followed for the development of these and other conditions, indefinitely. Cure? Depends on what you mean, who you ask. In my book, no. I will always remain a patient at Memorial Sloan-Kettering; my story continues there, echoing against its stark white walls.

I don't mean to sound ungrateful. I am not. I believe that I made the right decision back in the winter of '96. I am a lot better off today than I was then. Despite a few restrictions still in place—no sushi, ocean swims or long airplane flights—I lead a normal life, very similar to the one I led prior to my illness. The thrombosis in my right eye has resolved without leaving any permanent damage. I am back to my original weight, my hair has regrown and the horizontal lines across my nails, a side effect of chemotherapy, have vanished. I exercise every morning. I see patients in the office, attend dermatology conferences and teach residents. Daniella and I go to the movies. We subscribe to the theater. We dine out with friends.

And I'm finally writing again. It took a full year before I was strong enough to sit down in front of the computer. After spending so many days alone, I feared the quiet and solitude of writing. I preferred noise and crowds instead, talking and laughing with others; the ongoing dialogue reassured me that I was alive and still part of the world. Being able to write is proof that my recovery is almost complete.

I am very grateful—to my wife; to my family and friends; to the nurses and doctors who tried their best, even though their godlike armor no longer appears flawless. They don't have, they can't have, all the answers. Their promises will never be absolute.

I'm also grateful for a relatively easy transplant course. Just ask Castro. He'll tell you a few of the more tragic stories he's encountered in his tenure at Sloan. I am familiar with some of them—my next-door neighbor at the hospital, Alberto, for example. I saw him last week at the clinic. Finally, after a hellish two years battling graft versus host disease and CMV infection, he looks healthy again, no longer shaking, his skin smooth and moist. Although he still suffers from a chronic (and mysterious) respiratory ailment, he has returned to work and leads a happily productive life. Another patient recounts his long list of troubles while we wait one morning in the clinic for the doctor. Since his transplant four years ago, he's been hospitalized eight times, had two open lung biopsies, countless scans of every sort and a near fatal bout of the chicken pox. These two patients are among Castro's healthiest, the "cured." "Hey, I'm a survivor," boasts Alberto. "I still tuck my kids into bed every night."

Many transplant patients have not been so lucky. Some have

watched their anemias and leukemias return with a vengeance. Like the patient with the anonymous donor that used to run the New York Marathon. Rick recently told me that his bad cells were back; he wasn't sure what, if anything, could be done. Others have died along the way. A few months ago, a Scandinavian woman brought her son in to see me at the office. The boy worked as a lifeguard during the summers. His mother was concerned that his light complexion might predispose him to skin cancer. Please check his moles, she asked. I don't want anything to happen to him.

It turns out that Mrs. Halvorsen's youngest daughter passed away last year. I'm sorry, I say. What happened? She had leukemia and was hospitalized at Sloan-Kettering for a bone marrow transplant. Under whose care? I stutter. Dr. Castro and Dr. Jakubowski. A week after discharge she was readmitted with a cough, a slight one, says Mrs. Halvorsen in a faltering tone. It was CMV pneumonia; she died within the week. Mrs. Halvorsen is crying. I shudder inwardly. Why this poor girl and not me? Why her parents and not mine?

I have been very fortunate. If you saw me today and compared me to what I was two years ago, you'd hardly notice a difference. Has the experience changed you in any way? is a frequently asked question. I'm not sure how to respond. Perhaps in the way I practice medicine. I've become a more tolerant doctor, perhaps even more empathetic, interested in patients and their stories as much as in their diseases. But then again, I've also become more intolerant. When a patient with a chronic disease decides to vent his or her frustration, I'm less apt to coddle. When they angrily ask, How can there be no cure for psoriasis?, I'm tempted to snap: Psoriasis? Consider yourself lucky that it's only a skin problem and nothing more life-threatening.

The real changes are more subtle. They have taken place

below the surface, in my psyche. I've become more insecure. In the days before Nemesis, I was invincible; no goal was beyond my reach, nothing was capable of harming me. I'm more tentative today. I worry about things—catching a cold, the cleanliness of restaurants, carcinogens in my dry cleaning. Every so often, I experience attacks of panic. Suddenly, while driving to work, singing along with Bob Dylan, I recall my run-in with PNH and Sloan-Kettering and am gripped by fear. What will happen to my immune system, my surviving marrow cells? Will I develop a secondary cancer? Will I live another ten years? What about twenty?

My tentativeness has a physical dimension. Daniella sees it in my walk. I used to have a more confident stride, she says. This, I suspect, can be traced back to that brief but momentous encounter with Dr. O'Reilly, head of the transplant service at Sloan-Kettering. A tall, powerful man looming over a small, powerless boy, advising him to hunker down. The image has found a permanent place in my consciousness.

I am hopeful that time will heal my insecurities. There are signs. I have started to dream as energetically as I once did. During a run, I imagined living part of the year in Rome, a small but comfortable garret in the old section, with a view of the Campo dei Fiori. I have some good ideas for a new novel. And last week, Tom phoned and invited me to rejoin him in the safari of medicine; he wants us to publish my case, my extraordinary case of PNH presenting with retinal vein thrombosis. My world is enlarging every day with new and exciting possibilities.

Meanwhile, the story of my bone marrow transplant continues without end. In this way, it is no different from any other story, in life or in fiction.

ACKNOWLEDGMENTS

I wish to thank Dr. Luzzatto, Dr. Castro and all the other dedicated doctors and nurses on the bone marrow transplant service at Memorial Sloan-Kettering; Rema Hort Mann, my late friend and first critic, whose courage in a situation far worse than mine was a source of strength throughout my ordeal; the many wonderful teachers I have had over the years—Gil Feldman, Robert Palmer, Elaine Scarry, Stephanie Kiceluk, David Rothman, Dr. Thomas Garrett, Dr. Alan Shalita, Dr. Edward Heilman and Terry Eagleton—whose enthusiasm for literature and medicine continues to inspire me; Will Dana, Marshall Sella, Stephen Dubner and Eric Copauge for their help with my "Lives" article; my agent, Julie Merberg, who was there from the beginning; my editor at Pantheon, Dawn Davis, for guiding me and my manuscript, with patience and constant encouragement, through its last several incarnations; and my friend Ellen Tien, who more than anyone has helped me fulfill my greatest dream.

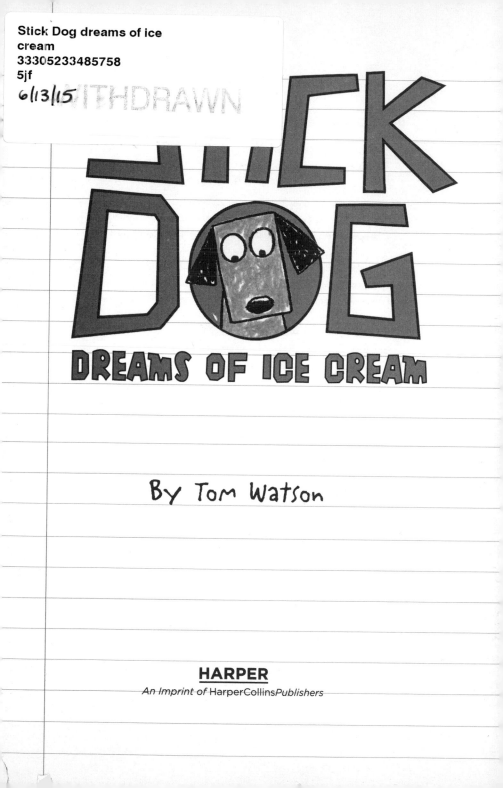

DREAMS OF ICE CREAM

By Tom Watson

HARPER

An Imprint of HarperCollinsPublishers

Dedicated to Carol, Donna, Susie, Richard,
Jim, and Tom

Stick Dog Dreams of Ice Cream

Copyright © 2015 by Tom Watson

Illustrations by Ethan Long based on original sketches by Tom Watson

All rights reserved. Printed in the United States of America.

No part of this book may be used or reproduced in any manner whatsoever without

written permission except in the case of brief quotations embodied in critical articles

and reviews. For information address HarperCollins Children's Books, a division of

HarperCollins Publishers, 195 Broadway, New York, NY 10007.

www.harpercollinschildrens.com

Library of Congress Cataloging-in-Publication Data

Watson, Tom.

  Stick Dog dreams of ice cream / by Tom Watson ; illustrations by Ethan Long. — First
edition.

    pages cm. — (Stick dog)

  "Illustrations by Ethan Long based on original sketches by Tom Watson."

  Summary: Stick Dog and his feral friends are looking for relief on a very hot day—and this
time they have their eyes on a ice cream truck.

  ISBN 978-0-06-227807-4 (hardcover) — ISBN 978-0-06-238092-0 (int.)

  1. Feral dogs—Juvenile fiction. 2. Dogs—Juvenile fiction. 3. Ice cream, ices, etc.—Juvenile
fiction. 4. Friendship—Juvenile fiction. 5. Humorous stories. [1. Dogs—Fiction. 2. Ice cream,
ices, etc.—Fiction. 3. Friendship—Fiction. 4. Humorous stories.] I. Long, Ethan, illustrator.
II. Title.

PZ7.W3298Su 2015   2014030713

[Fic]—dc23   CIP

                                                                                              AC

Typography by Tom Starace

15 16 17 18 19   CG/RRDH   10 9 8 7 6 5 4 3 2 1

❖

First Edition

TABLE OF CONTENTS

Chapter 1

ESCAPE FROM THE HEAT

It was really, really hot.

Stick Dog, Stripes, and Poo-Poo looked forward to some brief relief from the heat.

And Mutt was just back from the creek to provide it.

He was sopping wet. He didn't say anything at all but simply sidled up close to the others. They all knew the routine. This was, after all, Mutt's fourth trip to the creek in the past hour. Stick Dog, Stripes, and Poo-Poo stood at the ready.

And then Mutt began to shake. He started slowly at first, spraying the others with big droplets of water from his shaggy fur. But then his shaking sped up, until he trembled and vibrated so hard the dry dirt around his paws puffed up in little brown clouds. With this vigorous shaking, Mutt was able to spray his

companions not with big droplets of creek
water but with a fine, cooling mist.

The other three sighed as they felt the wet,
cool relief.

"That feels wonderful," whispered Stripes
when Mutt finally stopped shaking.

"I never get tired of that smell," Poo-Poo said.

Stick Dog enjoyed the temporary respite. He
needed a little break from the dry, hot day as
much as anyone. "Thank you again, Mutt. That
really does feel great," he said. "Come on, you
guys. Let's help him retrieve some of this stuff.
That's the least we can do."

Immediately, Poo-Poo and Stripes helped
Stick Dog gather all the things that had come

flying out of Mutt's fur with the water. They picked up a crushed Ping-Pong ball, a blue marker, two bottle caps, and an old gray sock. They returned them all to Mutt, who tucked everything back into his fur except the old gray sock. He took that to the shade of a beech tree and began to chew on it.

Poo-Poo and Stripes shared some shade under an old oak tree. And Stick Dog settled beneath a leafy maple. Unlike Mutt's shaking, the shade provided little help. They all heated up again quickly.

"Stick Dog," Poo-Poo said. "We have *got* to do something about this heat."

"There's not much we can do," Stick Dog answered. He seemed to be conserving his energy as he spoke. He didn't even turn to address Poo-Poo. "My pipe is even warmer than out here. The air doesn't circulate in there. We're not going to find better shade anywhere. I guess we could go down to the creek and get another drink of water. That always helps a little."

"I'm sick of drinking creek water," Stripes said. She sounded frustrated. "It's too sandy and gritty. And on a day like this, it's not even cold."

"Let's go look for some new water," suggested Mutt. "Maybe we can find a better place to get it."

Stick Dog considered this. "A new water source, hmm? Cleaner, colder. I think it's a good idea."

"You do?" said Mutt. "Really?!"

Stick Dog nodded. "Let's just wait for Karen to get here and then we'll go look."

"Did you hear that, you guys?" Mutt asked Poo-Poo and Stripes. There was genuine excitement in his voice. "Stick Dog thinks

we should go find a new place to get water.
It was my idea! Did you hear me suggest
that?"

Poo-Poo nodded his head, and Stripes
closed her eyes.

"Another great idea by yours truly," Mutt
whispered to himself as he shifted around

a little in the shade. "Old Mutt comes through again."

Stick Dog took pleasure in seeing Mutt act this way. And he took even greater pleasure when a random summer breeze whooshed through the woods for a few seconds. He closed his eyes and waited for Karen.

He didn't have to wait long.

Chapter 2

GOING NOWHERE

Karen soon came through the woods and entered the small clearing at Stick Dog's pipe. She joined him beneath the maple tree.

"Can you believe how hot it is?" Karen said as she plopped down.

"Don't remind us," sighed Stripes.

"Where have you been?" Poo-Poo called from beneath the oak tree.

"Nowhere," Karen answered. She panted and added, "It's so hot!"

"I said, 'Don't remind us,'" Stripes complained. She seemed really agitated. "And you can't be 'nowhere.' That's impossible."

Poo-Poo nodded in agreement.

Mutt ignored the entire conversation. He had now chewed through the heel of the old gray sock and was working on the toe area.

"Look," Stripes said to Karen. "You don't have to tell us where you've been. It's your business. But you have to agree that you can't go 'nowhere.'"

"Yeah," Poo-Poo said. "You have to admit that."

Karen's chin rested on the ground. She didn't respond, but she did shift her eyes to look at Stick Dog next to her. It was almost as if her eyes were saying, "I really want to prove these two wrong, but I don't know how. Can you help me?"

Stick Dog got the message. And he thought it was just too hot for this back-and-forth conversation. On a nicer, cooler day, it would be fine—maybe even amusing. But not today. Not in this heat.

"Listen, Stripes
and Poo-Poo.
Do me a quick
favor, will you?"
Stick Dog
asked. He stood
and stretched
his legs. He knew they would leave soon.
"On the count of three, will you two go
and climb into my pipe? It's not a race or
anything. I just want you to get into my pipe
for a second. Okay?"

It was an odd request, but neither Poo-Poo
nor Stripes saw any harm in doing so. They
nodded to indicate they would do it.

"One, two . . . ," Stick Dog said, and then
paused. He waited. Poo-Poo and Stripes
were ready to move from the oak tree's

shade to Stick Dog's pipe, but they held still, waiting for the signal. Then Stick Dog said, "Forget it. I don't want you guys to go to my pipe after all."

"You don't?" asked Stripes.

Stick Dog shook his head.

"Why not?" Poo-Poo asked.

"Just changed my mind is all," said Stick Dog. He winked at Karen and turned to Stripes and Poo-Poo. "Can I ask you both a question?"

They nodded.

"Where did you guys go?"

Stripes looked at Poo-Poo. Poo-Poo looked at Stripes. They both looked at Stick Dog, shrugged their shoulders, and answered together, "Nowhere."

NOWHERE.

"Yes!!" Karen exclaimed, and began hopping up and down. "I knew Stick Dog could prove it! I knew he could! You two just went 'nowhere'!"

"Wait a minute, wait a minute," Stripes began to complain.

"That's not right. That's like word magic or something," Poo-Poo said, and shook his head. "That's what it is: word magic."

Stripes turned to Mutt, hoping that he could help them. She called over, "Mutt, what do you think about all this?"

Mutt lifted his head. The other dogs were too far away to see it, but gray and white threads hung from the corner of his mouth. He seemed to take the question very seriously. He tilted his head a bit to the left as if pondering something that concerned him quite deeply.

"Well, what do you think?" Stripes called again.

"I think," Mutt said, "that was the best darn sock I've ever eaten."

Stick Dog smiled and said to them all, "Come on. Let's go find some nice, cold water."

Karen followed Stick Dog with light, happy, and energetic steps.

Poo-Poo and Stripes followed as well— glad to end the conversation.

And Mutt came along too. He was eager to find something to help wash down the final threads of that old gray sock.

Chapter 3

POO-POO IS QUITE SPECIAL

Halfway through the forest, Poo-Poo skidded to a halt. He snapped his head left and right, up and down. He sniffed continuously as he jerked his head all around. The other dogs had all slowed and stopped to watch this display.

"What is it, Poo-Poo?" asked Mutt. "Do you smell something?"

"Oh, I smell something, all right," Poo-Poo

declared. He inched closer to a large oak
tree. "I just can't put my paw on it. But it
smells familiar."

"Is it hamburgers?" asked Karen with real
hope in her voice.

"Or frankfurters?" asked Stripes.

"Maybe pizza?" Mutt asked.

Poo-Poo answered all three questions by shaking his head. "Up in the tree," he whispered as he stepped quietly toward the big oak's trunk. "Squirrel."

This is what Stick Dog was afraid of. He knew that Poo-Poo could stalk a squirrel for hours. And it was too hot—way too hot—to be delayed by this.

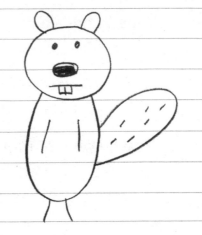

Poo-Poo circled the tree a few times, stopped, and peered up through the leaves and branches. He took a couple of short, quick sniffs. "There's a fuzzy-tailed, acorn-munching chatter-mouth up there, all right," Poo-Poo whispered. "If I could see him, I'd get him."

"Can't you see him, Poo-Poo?" Karen asked.

He shook his head but kept peering up into the top branches.

"Then how do you know there's a squirrel up there?" asked Stripes.

"Are you kidding me?!" Poo-Poo exclaimed, taking real offense. "I can smell a barbecue potato chip three miles away. I can smell a smoking grill in the next county. I can distinguish whether a tortilla chip in a garbage can on the other side of Picasso Park is nacho cheese flavor or cool ranch flavor. You think I can't sniff out a nasty, nutty-breathed tail-shaker?!"

"Okay, okay," said Stripes.

Mutt didn't pay much attention at all. He was twisting his tongue around inside his mouth trying to get the sock strings dislodged from between his teeth.

Sorry. I just need to interrupt the story here for a minute—because this thing that's happening to Mutt drives me crazy too.

You probably remember from the previous stories that I need to make little comments here and there sometimes. I can't help myself. And, umm, you're not going to hassle me about it, right?

Thanks.

Anyway, I can't stand that feeling of having something stuck in my teeth.

Worst food for getting stuck in your teeth? Celery.

I love celery. It's crunchy and tastes pretty good for, you know, a vegetable. Dip it in a little peanut butter, and you almost forget that you're eating something healthy and green.

But it's the worst for getting stuck between your teeth. It's kind of stringy to begin with, and those strands have a special way of getting stubbornly stuck. And here's the worst part: they're a little bit slimy because the spit in your mouth combines with the moisture in the celery, and that makes the stringy parts impossible to grab. Believe me, I've tried. I've shoved my whole hand in my mouth trying

to get a celery
strand out. I grip
it real good and
then—SLIP!—I
can't get it.

It's super
annoying.

So I can totally relate to what Mutt's trying
to do here with the strings from that old
gray sock. While he did his best to get those
strings out, Poo-Poo continued to circle the
tree trunk as he stalked the squirrel. Karen
and Stripes had found some shade several
steps away, where they settled in to observe
the whole affair.

"That sneaky, sniveling villain," Poo-Poo muttered to himself when he stopped once to glare up into the tree for a moment. "If I could just get my paws on him, then I—"

"Poo-Poo?"

It was Stick Dog.

Poo-Poo jerked around for a moment, surprised out of his squirrel-stalking trance. He snapped his head toward Stick Dog and then yanked it back around to stare up into the tree again. "Yes, Stick Dog?"

"I don't mean to interrupt you here," Stick Dog began. "And if I'm ruining your concentration or something, just tell me and I'll stop bothering you."

"It's no problem. I can do more than one thing at a time. I can circle the tree while we talk," Poo-Poo said confidently. He proceeded to pace again. In just a couple of steps, he stubbed his front right paw on a tree root, stumbled, and rammed his shoulder into the tree trunk, knocking off a big chunk of brown-and-black bark. "Go ahead, I'm listening."

"Well, I was just thinking about what you said a couple of minutes ago," Stick Dog commented. "About how you can smell things from really far away? Like the flavor of a tortilla chip across the park or a grill from a long way away?"

"Mm-hmm, that's right," Poo-Poo said. He nodded his head at Stick Dog, and this seemed to throw him off balance again. He hit his head against the tree. Poo-Poo rubbed it, smiled, and before continuing to circle, whispered to himself, "Just like old times."

Stick Dog allowed Poo-Poo to regain his footing before he asked, "But can you smell *water?*"

Poo-Poo stopped. The timing of the

question came just when he was on the opposite side of the trunk from Stick Dog. He didn't move his body but did stretch his neck out and around the tree to look directly at Stick Dog. "I can smell anything, anywhere, anytime," he said with absolute confidence. And then, with increased emphasis, he added, "I'm Poo-Poo."

Stick Dog pressed his lips together and nodded his head in full understanding. He then came closer to the tree. By this time, the heat had made Stripes and Karen feel drowsy. They were both lying in the shade with their eyes closed. Mutt did the same, but every now and then you could see his tongue press his cheek out as he probed around to get the sock strings out from his teeth. None of them were close enough to hear Poo-Poo and Stick Dog.

"I don't want to embarrass the others," Stick Dog whispered, and nodded toward Stripes, Karen, and Mutt. "But I think you might be the only one here who can smell water. And I'm not sure the four of us can find any cold water without your refined and ultra-sensitive sniffing capabilities."

Poo-Poo nodded and whispered back, "I see. Yes. I am quite special."

Stick Dog nodded and continued in the same hushed tone. "Without your help, we might be in danger. It's awfully hot. And we're all awfully thirsty."

Poo-Poo nodded again in understanding. "You guys might not stand a chance without me."

"That's right. It's all up to you," Stick Dog whispered. "You can stay here and try to get the squirrel. Or you can come with your friends, who are in desperate need, and help us find something to drink."

Immediately, Poo-Poo cleared his throat.

When he did, Stick Dog backed away, and the other dogs all opened their eyes.

"I have an announcement," Poo-Poo declared loudly. "Despite the fact that my arch-nemesis resides somewhere in the branches above me, I have decided to leave this place. I'm quite certain that it would only be a few minutes before I figured out a way to corral this tail-twitching nuisance. But those are minutes I choose to forfeit so I can use my expert sniffing abilities to deliver my friends from thirst and anguish."

Poo-Poo lifted his head and took a great and authoritative snort. He turned in several directions, sniffing and pondering. Finally, he pointed with his nose and said, "There is water this way! Follow me, my dry-mouthed comrades!" Poo-Poo then ran off into the forest.

By this time, Mutt, Karen, and Stripes had sauntered up to Stick Dog. They all had puzzled looks on their faces.

"Stick Dog?" Karen asked.

"Yes?"

"Didn't Poo-Poo just run off in the exact same direction we were going before he stopped to look for the squirrel?"

Stick Dog thought for a moment before answering. "Yes. Yes, he did."

And off they ran.

Chapter 4

RUNNING AROUND IN UNDERWEAR

It only took a couple of minutes for Stick Dog, Stripes, Karen, and Mutt to catch up with Poo-Poo, who was running with his nose slightly elevated through the woods. And it was only a few minutes after that when they all reached the other side of the forest. They stopped to survey their surroundings from behind a couple of big logs.

They could see the backs of four houses. Between them and the houses were four good-sized yards. Each yard had something different in it. From left to right, the first yard had a swing set, the second had a patio with some furniture, and the third had a badminton net.

But it was the fourth yard that caught the attention of all the dogs—except for Poo-Poo.

You see, in the fourth yard, three small humans were running in, out, and around a water sprinkler.

"Stick Dog," said Mutt, "I think that funny machine is spraying wat—"

Quickly, Poo-Poo interrupted. "Shh!" he said loudly. His eyes were closed, and his head swayed back and forth in a rhythmic, almost hypnotic pattern. "I'm sniffing for water."

"But if you just look over—" Mutt started to explain.

"Quiet. Please. I'm trying to work,"
demanded Poo-Poo. He crossed his hind
legs and went into a meditative position. He
then whispered, "I am becoming one with
the smells."

"But all you have to do is open your—"
Stripes began, but she was interrupted by
Poo-Poo as well.

"Really, I must insist," he said. There was no
meanness in his voice, but you could tell he
took his water-finding role very seriously.

Mutt, Karen, and Stripes all looked at Stick
Dog. They opened their eyes wide and
pointed toward the water sprinkler.

Stick Dog said nothing. He simply nodded
his head in recognition and raised his right
front paw calmly. Together they waited
patiently for Poo-Poo to finish.

In a moment, he did. Poo-Poo lowered his
head, opened his eyes, and then turned

directly toward the yard where the little humans played in the sprinkler.

"There!" he said triumphantly, and pointed. "I have smelled out our new water source. It's over there!"

Stripes, Mutt, and Karen just looked at Poo-Poo with blank expressions on their faces. They truly didn't know what to say.

"I know, I know," Poo-Poo said, and smirked a little in an attempt at modesty. "It's hard to understand, I know. I just have a talent for smelling out solutions like this. I can't help it.

It's just a gift, I guess. Sometimes I can't even believe the things I do myself."

Stripes, Karen, and Mutt still did not know what to say.

So Stick Dog spoke up. "Sometimes, Poo-Poo, I can't believe the things you do either," he said. And then he added, "Great job."

Karen turned away from Poo-Poo and toward Stick Dog and asked, "How are we going to get to the water? Those little humans are all over it."

"What are they doing with it anyway?" asked Stripes.

"I'm not sure," answered Stick Dog. "Let's get a closer look. Stay by the forest line."

Mutt, Poo-Poo, Karen, and Stripes followed Stick Dog along the edge of the woods. They snuck behind sticker bushes, cattail reeds, and tall, thick weeds. Soon they were staring out from behind a neatly stacked pile of logs.

They stared for a few minutes without saying anything as the three small humans

darted in and out of the spraying water.
Safely concealed behind the woodpile, the
dogs gathered around Stick Dog after this
brief period of observation.

"Okay, what are we looking at here?" he
asked.

Karen spoke first. "It's raining up from the
ground," she said confidently and without
hesitation. She motioned with her paws to
demonstrate how the water rose up from

the ground. "I believe somehow a small storm cloud has crashed into the earth in that yard. During the crash, it flipped over and is now raining up instead of down."

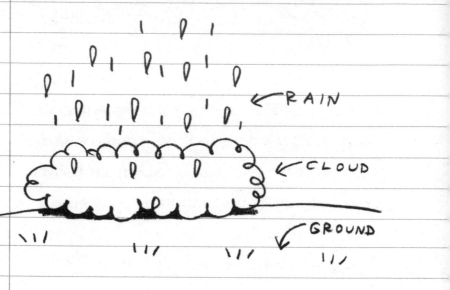

"All right," said Stick Dog slowly.

"Yes, that makes sense," Mutt said. He was kind of mumbling because he was still poking his tongue between his teeth to dislodge the strings from that old gray sock. "Upside-down rain cloud. That's it for sure."

"I don't think that's true," said Stripes, who had another idea altogether. "I think the water is actually attacking them. Just look at it! It's shooting all over the place trying to get them. And those little humans seem awfully frightened by it. They keep running up to it and then running away from it over and over again. Yep, it's definitely a water-attacking machine of some sort."

Stick Dog looked through some of the cracks and cavities in the woodpile. The little humans were, in fact, doing exactly what Stripes described. But he didn't think they looked very scared at all.

This is when Poo-Poo spoke up.

"These are not normal little humans," Poo-
Poo said. "They're afraid of water, and they
run around in their underwear. They're
bizarre—even for humans."

Stick Dog looked through the woodpile again. He saw one of the small humans walk to the side of the house and turn a knob. When he did, the water stopped spraying. After they each grabbed a towel from the grass and dried off, the humans went inside the house.

"See? I told you they were a strange bunch," said Poo-Poo. "Why would you want to dry off on a day like this? The wetter, the better, I say."

"Hey, where'd the water go?" asked Mutt.

Karen shrugged her shoulders. "Stopped raining, I guess."

Stick Dog backed away from the woodpile

and addressed the others. "I don't think it's actually a rain cloud, and I don't think it attacks. It could be some kind of machine, though," he said. "Let's wait just a minute to make sure they're not coming back out. Then we can run in and get something to drink. I'm sure there are still some nice-sized puddles there."

The others nodded along with this idea—and got ready to run.

Chapter 5

A WATER MACHINE ATTACKS

They sprinted out of the woods and into the yard. They lapped at several small puddles in the grass.

There were not as many puddles as they hoped. They were small in size too. And they were absorbed quickly by the ground—and evaporated by the heat of the day.

"I think you were right, Stripes," Karen said as she paced around looking for a puddle. She noticed the mechanical nature of the sprinkler. "I think it is a water-attacking machine."

Stripes was too busy drinking from a small puddle that was quickly disappearing to say anything, but she did nod and smile. She was glad to be correct.

Stick Dog smiled too. He said, "I'm just glad it's not attacking now."

When the few puddles were gone, Stripes

and Mutt licked at the sprinkler itself as it
continued to drip and bubble refreshing, cold
water. Karen and Poo-Poo saw this and tried
to nudge themselves in for a drink too.

Stick Dog stood back. He noticed that his
friends were bumping and shoving more than
they were actually drinking. There was really
only room for two dogs at a time.

"Karen, Poo-Poo," he called.

They lifted their heads. This gave Mutt and Stripes ample room to continue drinking these few new drops in comfort.

"What is it, Stick Dog?" Karen asked.

"Follow that long, green tube that's connected to this water machine," Stick Dog said, and pointed. "It goes all the way to the side of the house. It looks like it's dripping over there too."

This is exactly what Poo-Poo and Karen did. And even though they could see the end of the hose attached to the faucet at the side of the house, Karen and Poo-Poo did not run in a straight line to it. Instead,

they lowered their heads and followed the
hose along its path in the grass. It twisted
and turned and looped all over the yard.
When the two of them ultimately reached
the side of the house, they were happy to
discover water dripping where the hose
connected to the spigot. This outside
faucet dripped a single drop of water
every second or two.

KAREN & POO-POO'S PATH

Karen and Poo-Poo took turns lying on
their backs. They opened their mouths and

let the cool, clear water drip in. It tasted terrific, but it was an awfully slow process. Poo-Poo needed to keep his mouth open for nearly a minute just to get a full swallow. And for Karen, who had a much smaller mouth, it still took nearly thirty seconds.

After a couple of turns each, Karen got an idea. She came closer to the spigot handle.

"Poo-Poo," she said. "Can you look at this for a minute?"

After getting a mouthful of water and swallowing it, Poo-Poo stood up and came next to Karen. "What is it?"

"I think this thing might control the water drips."

They both stood there at the faucet for several seconds, tipping their heads left and right in thought.

"If it's dripping a little, maybe we can make it drip a lot," suggested Poo-Poo. "Maybe if you move it, some more water will drip out."

This made sense to Karen, and she nudged her nose against the faucet handle. It moved a half inch or so around, and it did indeed produce the desired effect there at the house. The drips came a little bit faster, but still not enough to provide a great thirst-quenching drink.

"It sort of worked," Poo-Poo observed.

"Yeah, sort of."

"Maybe you should move it some more," said Poo-Poo.

Karen shrugged her shoulders and said, "Sure, why not?"

She pressed her nose against the faucet again, but this time it didn't move. She pressed a little harder, and it still didn't move. She pulled her head back a couple of inches and bumped the faucet handle. It still didn't budge. "It's stuck," she declared.

"Stuck, huh?" Poo-Poo said, and backed several steps away. "We'll see about that."

Poo-Poo lowered his head, tightened his shoulder muscles, and took six quick strides forward, bashing his head directly into the faucet. Not only did it move, the faucet handle spun freely. It made four or five complete revolutions.

Staggering a bit to regain his balance, Poo-Poo joined Karen close to the spigot to observe. The water still dripped, but not a whole lot more than before—and certainly not as much as they thought it would after spinning around so many times.

"Nothing really happened," said Karen. "Strange."

Poo-Poo rubbed his head a bit on the ground to make it feel better. When he did, he noticed that the long green tube running between the spigot and the water machine had expanded. It looked as if it had filled up with something. It was a very curious thing, and Poo-Poo lifted his head to inform Karen about it.

Except he didn't get the chance.

Do you know why he didn't get the chance?

It's because he was interrupted by Mutt and Stripes.

You see, way out in the yard at that exact moment they both screamed at the top of their lungs, "WATER ATTACK!! WATER ATTACK!! WATER ATTACK!!"

The sprinkler had burst to life. It shot streams and sprays of water at full blast in every direction. Mutt and Stripes jumped up and down to get away from the watery onslaught. Every time they went one way to escape, the water machine changed its shooting direction. They ran in and out of the water sprays like maniacs. They bumped

into each other, lost their footing in the
wet grass, and generally did everything
except get away.

Stick Dog, who had not tried to nudge
himself closer and closer to the dripping
sprinkler like the others, was a safe
distance away. He had been sprayed a

couple of times at the very start but simply
backed away a few steps to be completely
out of range. He sat on his hind legs to
observe Stripes and Mutt frantically leaping

and smashing about. He found it both
fascinating and amusing that they dashed
in and out of the water sprays just like
the three little humans had done minutes
earlier.

Now, to Mutt and Stripes it seemed as if they had been caught in the torturing water sprays for an eternity. But, in truth, it was only several seconds. During those several seconds, Stick Dog noticed the pattern and rhythm of the water machine. When the time was right and there was a brief opportunity for them to escape, he called to his friends.

"Mutt, Stripes! Over here," he yelled. He watched and timed the movement of the water patterns. "Now!"

That was all they needed to hear. Blinking the wetness from their eyes, Mutt and Stripes made for the direction of Stick Dog's voice as fast as they could. They sprinted and hurtled across the lawn. They quickly reached Stick Dog, sliding and stumbling to a stop at his side—safely out of reach of the still-spraying water.

By this time, Karen and Poo-Poo had arrived as well. They had carefully circumnavigated the shooting water.

"I told you it was a water-attacking machine," panted Stripes. "That thing's a monster. Why did that happen?! Why did it just come to life like that?!"

Karen glanced at Poo-Poo. Poo-Poo looked at Karen. Stick Dog stared at them both.

Mutt continued to try to work the sock strings out from between his teeth.

"Why, Stick Dog?" Stripes asked. She was only now beginning to catch her breath. "Why did that monster come to life and attack?"

Stick Dog had a pretty good idea about what had happened. The exchanged glances between Poo-Poo and Karen only confirmed his suspicions. He didn't want Stripes to get mad at them. But Stick Dog didn't want to lie. He really didn't like lying.

"Umm," he said, trying to pause for time to think of something to say.

And that pause worked out perfectly.

That's because, at that precise moment, a loud voice bellowed out of the house that the three little humans had entered.

"Didn't I tell you kids to turn off the sprinkler when you were done?!" an older human voice yelled from the house. The dogs could all hear it booming out of the open windows.

"We did," answered a younger human voice.

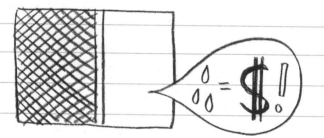

"Well, somehow it has *magically* turned itself back on and is running up the water bill," the adult yelled back. You could tell by the tone of his voice that he didn't really believe in magic. "Get back out there and turn it off."

"All right," the little human voice called. "Come on, you guys. Let's go turn it off. *Again*."

That was all Stick Dog needed to hear.

"The humans are coming," he said urgently. "We have to get out of here."

Chapter 6

IT'S TOTALLY ANNOYING

They ran as fast as they could between the house with the water-attacking machine and the one with the badminton net. There, the dogs found several large lilac bushes arranged in a circle. The open space in the center of the bushes was mainly occupied by a big green metal box. There was still, however, plenty of space for the dogs to comfortably duck for cover.

"Stick Dog?" Stripes asked a little nervously. She leaned gingerly against the metal box, not quite sure what to make of it. "What is this big green thing? Is it dangerous?"

Stick Dog had seen boxes like this one before. It was large and had a screen covering three of its sides. On the side without the screen, this one had a sticker that read "Cool Breeze AC." Stick Dog knew this type of box had a big fan inside that sometimes blew out warm air—and made the box shake and vibrate. It was not vibrating now though, and Stick Dog thought it was a safe place to hide—especially since it was surrounded by lilac bushes.

"I think it's fine," replied Stick Dog. He was secretly thankful that Stripes no longer wanted to know why the water machine came alive just a few minutes earlier. "I don't think it's dangerous."

This made Stripes feel better, and she leaned more fully against the side of the box.

"I've seen those things around in yards a lot," Karen explained. "Humans grow plants around them to conceal them, I think."

"It makes a great hiding place," Mutt commented, turning his head to check out the surroundings.

"Oh, yeah. They're really nice hiding spots," Karen confirmed. "I always mark my territory whenever I find one."

At this, Stripes jumped immediately to her feet and lost all contact with the big green metal box. "You mean I was leaning where you—" she began to exclaim.

But Karen cut her off. "No, no! Not this particular one. Just similar ones in the neighborhood is all."

"You're sure?" Stripes asked.

"I'm sure."

Stripes then relaxed and leaned against the metal box again.

After the excitement of the water-attacking machine and the race to this hiding spot, they all calmed down a good bit. This respite did little to quench their thirst on this hot, hot day, however. And it was only a few minutes before Mutt said, "I'm still thirsty."

Poo-Poo, Stripes, and Karen immediately all said, "Me too!"

Stick Dog nodded his head and looked at the sky. There was not even a hint of relief in sight. There was not a single cloud. There was not the slightest breeze. And dusk was still hours away.

"What can we do, Stick Dog?" Mutt asked.

"We came all this way," said Stick Dog. "We might as well keep looking for another drinking source. Maybe we can find some more puddles or something. But before that, let's do our best to relax here in this nice safe spot. Try not to think about being thirsty. Close your eyes and put your minds elsewhere."

Mutt, Karen, Stripes, and Poo-Poo all closed their eyes.

Stick Dog watched them.

In nine seconds, Poo-Poo said, "I'm still thirsty."

Stick Dog tried again.
"Come on, now. You can
do it. Just relax and think
of something else."

Again they all closed
their eyes as Stick Dog watched.

In seven seconds,
Stripes said, "I can't
think of anything."

"Shh," Stick Dog
encouraged. "Try a little harder."

In twelve seconds, Karen said, "I put my thoughts elsewhere, Stick Dog, like you said. So I went for an imaginary walk in the woods. And while I was walking, I had to cross the creek. And that dumb creek was full of water, and now I'm thirsty again!"

They all opened their eyes and stared at Stick Dog to await further instructions.

Stick Dog tried something else.

"Let's all concentrate on something together," he suggested. "I can hear some music off in the distance. Can you hear that? Let's all listen to it with our eyes closed."

In six seconds, Mutt said, "That's the most annoying music I've ever heard."

"Shh," said Stick Dog.

After another eight seconds, Karen added, "It's *totally* annoying."

"Shh."

After eleven seconds, Poo-Poo said, "And it's getting closer!"

They all opened their eyes again when they realized Poo-Poo was right: The music was, in fact, growing louder and louder. It was as if the music was moving toward them.

All the dogs—even Stick Dog—stood up and pointed their noses toward where the music came from. There was no doubt. The annoying music was getting nearer and nearer.

"This is kind of scaring me," Stripes whispered. The pace of her words picked up as she continued. "I've already been attacked by a water machine today. I don't want to be attacked by an annoying music machine too. Let's get out of here! I don't care how thirsty we are. Let's just go back to Stick Dog's pipe. I'll drink creek water; I don't care."

The nervousness in Stripes's voice had clearly affected the other dogs. They immediately nodded along with her idea.

"I'm sure there's a reasonable explanation," said Stick Dog calmly. As he said this, the music blared quite loudly. The volume of it, however, was now not changing at all. It was as if something had come closer and closer and closer and then stopped—and stopped nearby. Stick Dog asked, "Who wants to go check it out?"

Mutt said, "These strings in between my teeth will, unfortunately, prohibit me from investigating the music source." He quickly sat down and scrunched and unscrunched his mouth in an obvious and valiant attempt to dislodge the offending strings.

Poo-Poo answered next. "I'm a smeller, not a hearer," he said with great dignity and pride.

Stripes provided her excuse next. "I think the water-attacking machine may have temporarily damaged my hearing capabilities," she said. She then leaned her head over to the right side while tapping the left side to demonstrate that there was, indeed, water in her ear.

"No problem, Stripes," said Stick Dog.

"What?" she asked. She straightened up and held a paw to her ear.

"I said, 'No problem,'" Stick Dog repeated.

"Huh?"

"I said—" Stick Dog answered, and stopped himself. Then he said, "The water machine gave your coat a nice rinse. Your spots look great."

"Oh, thank you," Stripes answered quickly, and glanced down at herself. "Thank you very much."

Stick Dog smiled and turned to Karen. She would provide the last excuse, he knew, not to investigate that annoying music.

"Stick Dog?" she asked.

"Yes?"

"I really just don't want to go."

Stick Dog nodded his head in understanding. "I'll go," he said.

With that, he immediately wriggled through the lilac bushes to discover what was making that annoying sound.

He didn't have to go far.

Chapter 7

WHAT'S WEIRD ABOUT IT?

Stick Dog didn't even need to leave the safety of the lilac bushes. As soon as he stuck his head out, he discovered the source of that annoying music.

It was parked right on the street.

It was one of the strangest trucks Stick Dog had ever seen. And Stick Dog had seen quite a few trucks in his day. His pipe was below Highway 16, after all. And he would often sit outside it and watch the traffic—

including many trucks—go by on the big
highway above.

But he'd never seen one like this before.

It was more square in shape than usual—
most trucks were long rectangles. It had
many strange features. Stick Dog read two

words—"ICE CREAM"—on the side of
the truck.

He ducked back into the bushes to tell the
others what he saw.

"It's nothing to be afraid of," Stick Dog
began. He wanted to put everybody at ease
right away. "It's just a weird truck parked
out on the street."

"What's weird about it?" Mutt asked.

Stick Dog answered, "Just about everything. It's kind of a strange shape, it has a screened window, and it's decorated with colorful pictures. It also has a shelf that runs along its side. And the music is coming from a strange contraption on the top that looks like a big, metal mouth."

"I have to see this," said Mutt as he began to push his head through the lilac bushes. Stripes, Karen, and Poo-Poo wanted to see too.

They stared out at the truck for nearly a minute and then shimmied backward into the hiding spot.

"You're right, Stick Dog," Mutt said. "That really is a strange truck."

Everyone agreed.

Stripes asked, "What's 'ice cream'?"

Now, we need to pause here for a minute. Just for a little reminder. You remember that the dogs can all read, right? Remember how they read "Peter's Frankfurters" on the side of the cart in the second book? And how they read the address on the pizza box in the third book?

And who says dogs can't read anyway? It's possible. Maybe they just can't read out loud to us in human language. When we all go off to school during the day, maybe our dogs all reach out to the bookshelf and pick out a favorite novel or something. Then when they hear us come back, they shove the book back into its place and lie down real fast and pretend to be asleep. When we walk in the doorway, they stretch and yawn as if they've been asleep the whole time—when really they've been enjoying a mystery or a dictionary or a comic book.

Think about it. It's possible.

You know what would be really funny? What if you had a dog and that dog could read? And what if when nobody is looking, your dog picks up *this* book and opens it to *this* page and reads all *this*?

And then the dog is like, "Oh, man! We are SO busted! The humans have figured out that we can all read. It says so right here in this book!"

Now, if you ARE a dog who is reading this

right now, I just want to tell you this: Don't
worry about it. We won't let the secret out.
Please go on reading whenever you want.

It's okay. Go grab a lemon cupcake off the
kitchen counter and enjoy the rest of the
book.

Anyway, the dogs in this book can definitely
read.

"I have no idea what 'ice cream' is," Stick

Dog answered, after giving Stripes's question a moment of thought. "But I do know what ice is—it's real cold, and it turns into delicious water when it melts. It forms on the creek in the wintertime. On a day like this, ice sounds pretty good, doesn't it?"

They all nodded their heads in the blazing-hot sun.

"Let's watch this truck for a few minutes," Stick Dog suggested. "Maybe it will lead us to this 'ice cream' in some way."

Before they could even poke their heads back out of the lilac bushes to investigate further, however, the music stopped abruptly.

And that annoying music was replaced by a
sound that brought fear to their hearts.

Chapter 8

RAINBOW PUDDLES

Suddenly, they heard running footsteps everywhere around them.

The footsteps charged from the left and the right, from the back and the front. It was as

if a dozen or more humans had suddenly started running right at them.

Now, the sound of human footsteps is not very scary to you and me.

But that's only to you and me.

To five stray dogs who live on their own, don't trust humans, and are afraid of being caught by them, the sound of many human footsteps converging on their location was about as scary as it gets.

Immediately, Poo-Poo said low and hard, "Somebody has spotted us! We have to get out of here!"

"Where can we go?!" Mutt whispered

urgently. "It sounds like they're everywhere!"

Karen couldn't say anything, but she did spin around and smash her shoulder into Mutt's knee. He barely noticed in all the commotion.

"Hold still, everybody. Stay where you are," Stick Dog whispered. He leaned his head sideways a bit and listened. The footsteps seemed to be going around them and past them—some close by and some farther away. Stick Dog was pretty sure they weren't coming right at them. "I think we're safe here."

"We aren't spotted, after all," sighed Poo-Poo, utter relief in his voice.

"Speak for yourself," Stripes said, pointed at herself, and smiled.

Mutt, Poo-Poo, and Karen groaned.

Stick Dog smiled, but his attention was still focused on the footsteps. They seemed to converge and then halt in a common place some short distance away.

"I think it's safe to look now," he said.

The others, trusting Stick Dog completely, joined him in pushing their heads out through the lilac leaves to have a look.

While they did, Stripes repeated the previous conversation to herself. She smiled with great glee as she recited it again.

"Poo-Poo said: 'We aren't spotted.' Then I said: 'Speak for yourself.'" She giggled and shook her head, taking great pride in her outstanding sense of humor. "Stripes, old gal, that was a classic."

"Shh," Stick Dog whispered. "I want to see what's going on."

What was going on was some of the strangest behavior by a bunch of humans the dogs had ever seen. A group of about ten humans had gathered around that strange screen window on the side of the truck. They were mostly small humans, but there were a couple of bigger ones too. The music had stopped. The driver had parked the truck and climbed into the back of it, and a few seconds later appeared in the screen window.

That's when the really odd things started. The humans stood in a line at the window and spoke one at a time to the driver. Then the driver completely disappeared for a half minute or so. When he came back, he held a pointed brown cylinder with circles on top of it.

The entire process repeated itself for about five minutes until each human had a pointed cylinder with circles on top of it. Some hung around near the truck, leaning their elbows against the shelf. Others wandered off in different directions.

"What are those things they're holding?" Mutt asked after several minutes of observation.

"That must be 'ice cream,'" answered Stick Dog.

"It's a drink of some kind," said Poo-Poo, joining the conversation.

"A drink?" Stripes asked. "I don't think so. It looks more solid than liquid."

"No, no," Poo-Poo insisted. "It's a liquid; it has to be. See? They're lapping at it with their tongues. You only lap at things that are liquid."

Now Karen expressed her opinion. "Those circle things are liquid, all right. They're dripping every now and then. Liquids drip; solids don't. I agree with Poo-Poo."

"But just look at those circles," Mutt said. "They look solid. If they weren't solid, wouldn't they just run off the sides of those cone-shaped things? They couldn't hold their shape like that if they were liquid. I think Stripes is right. They're solid."

With two of them thinking solid and two of them thinking liquid, it was clearly going to be up to Stick Dog to break the tie. They all turned to him. He had a puzzled look on his face. To the other dogs, this was quite an unusual event. It was not very often that Stick Dog was confused about something. That was especially true when the subject was food.

"You all make perfectly good points," he said. It was difficult to tell, frankly, whether Stick Dog was puzzled by the whole solid-liquid thing— or by the fact that his four friends had all made very valid points.

OR

"So which is it?" Karen asked. "Solid or liquid?"

"Let's go find out," Stick Dog answered simply.

"Are you insane!?" Poo-Poo screamed instantly. Mutt, Karen, and Stripes all backed away from Stick Dog inside that circle of lilac bushes. "There must be a dozen humans out there!

And a big truck! And really, really annoying music!"

Stick Dog smiled. "The music *has* started playing again," he said. "And if you listen carefully, I think it's getting softer and softer. And if it's getting softer, then the truck is moving away. That probably means the humans have moved away too."

This made sense to them. They pushed their heads back through the lilac leaves to survey their surroundings again.

Do you know what they saw?

Nothing.

No humans and no truck. Everything was quiet—except for the slowly fading music.

"Let's go," said Stick Dog. He pulled himself forward through the limbs and leaves of the lilac bushes. He ran to the spot where the truck had been parked, and Poo-Poo, Mutt, Stripes, and Karen followed close behind.

The dogs looked all around for clues about

what the truck and the humans had been doing.

"There's nothing here," said Karen. She sniffed at the pavement. "The only unusual things I see are these small rainbow puddles."

"Rainbow puddles?" asked Stick Dog. He immediately came next to Karen to examine what she had found.

"Yeah, rainbow puddles," she said casually. "It's like the rain cloud that crashed into the earth earlier and was raining upside down. You know, back in that yard? Probably the same thing happened here, except a rainbow crashed into the earth and left these puddles. That's why they're all different colors and stuff."

"Well, that's certainly one explanation," said Stick Dog slowly. "But didn't we discover that the spraying water in that backyard was really from a machine?"

"A water-attacking machine," added Stripes, who, with the others, had now wandered over to investigate the colored puddles as well.

"Oh, right. A water-attacking machine. I remember now." Karen nodded and considered these puddles and their origin a little more. "So these, obviously, came from a rainbow-attacking machine then."

Stick Dog stood very still. He didn't say anything for several seconds. Ultimately, he said, "I can see why you would think that."

"Do you think it's safe to taste them?" asked Mutt.

"I think the drips from the humans' ice cream made these puddles. They were lapping at the ice cream, so we probably can too," said Stick Dog.

That was all the encouragement they needed. Immediately, Poo-Poo, Stripes, Mutt, and Karen lowered their necks and began to probe the small puddles with the tips of their tongues.

Do you remember the first time you

tasted something sweet? Probably not. You were probably too young. Maybe it was a nibble of a cupcake on your first birthday. Or maybe it was a piece of candy on Halloween. Whatever it was, I guarantee the smile that came to your face as your taste buds first awakened to something sweet was exactly the same kind of smile that came to all the dogs' faces.

Immediately, they wanted to share these wonderful, sweet flavors with their friends.

"Try this brown puddle," yelled Mutt. "It's the best, the absolute best! And guess what?! While I was taking a taste, the strings from that old gray sock came loose. They just came right out while I was tasting this amazing brown flavor! The strings are gone, and I've never tasted anything so good. I mean, this is like a miracle puddle or something! A miracle, I tell you."

"Try this yellow one," Stripes panted, before turning quickly to the brown puddle.

"Okay," Mutt said. "We'll switch. But be prepared. If you have something that's bothering you, the miracle puddle is going to make it all better!"

Karen couldn't leave her puddle, despite her friends' urgings. She was lapping at a delicious white puddle.

Poo-Poo was over a blue puddle.

He tasted it ever so carefully—the bright blue was not a typical food color, after all. He dipped the tip of his tongue in. And then he pulled it back quickly. He paused for a moment and closed his eyes to allow that little drop of blue flavor to spread in his mouth. He smiled.

Stick Dog watched all this. He had already tasted a dark-brown puddle of his own and he, like the others, had found a flavor that was utterly scrumptious. But he had noticed Poo-Poo and that strange blue puddle he was tasting. When Poo-Poo, still smiling, opened his eyes, Stick Dog asked him, "What is it? Is it good?"

"Really, really good," Poo-Poo whispered. "And really, really familiar."

"Familiar?"

Poo-Poo nodded and raised his head, staring off into the distance. Lost in thought, he swayed his head a little. "I can see circles, small circles," he said. "They're flavorful and of many different colors. They're hollow in the middle. Yellow, purple, orange, blue. Just circles. They're coated in something— something powdery."

Mutt, Stripes, and Karen had overheard all this. They knew Poo-Poo's descriptions were not to be missed. They left their puddles and came closer to listen.

"I can see a garbage can. It's tipped over," Poo-Poo continued. "A human had thrown out a cereal box. And a lot of those circles had spilled out. And I found them, Stick Dog; I found them. There must have been thirty or forty of those multicolored circles. And I ate them all. They were so sweet. A flavor I'd never tasted before. That's what this small blue puddle tastes like. I'm trying to remember the name. It was something dramatic, elegant, and beautiful. A name for the ages. A name I'd always remember."

"What is it?" asked Mutt, Stripes, and Karen all at once. "What's the name?"

Poo-Poo's eyes flashed open. "Froot Loops!" cried Poo-Poo. "That's what that blue puddle tastes like! Froot Loops! Froot Loops!! Froot Loops!!!"

"Well, I'm glad you remembered," said Stick Dog.

"Me too," Poo-Poo said as a sense of calm came over him. "That would have driven me nuts."

Stick Dog looked both ways down the street. There were no cars or humans visible, but he knew they had to hurry.

"I'd like to take our time here and explore and enjoy all these flavors," Stick Dog said quickly. "But we're way out here in the open. We'd better finish off these little puddles and fast."

There were not that many puddles; they were pretty small, and there were five dogs. So it was only a matter of twenty or thirty seconds before all the different-colored puddles were gone.

"Now what?" Mutt asked. Poo-Poo, Stripes, and Karen all turned toward Stick Dog as well.

"That's easy," he answered. "We follow the truck."

"Follow the truck!?" Stripes exclaimed. "That's impossible. It must be miles away by now! We'll never catch up to it. We're not nearly fast enough!"

Stick Dog calmly held up his front right paw—and Stripes stopped speaking.

Stick Dog pointed down the street. Perhaps only a quarter of a mile away was the strange truck with "ICE CREAM" written on its side. It was stopped like before, and there was a small crowd of humans gathered around it.

Stripes, Poo-Poo, Karen, and Mutt couldn't believe their eyes. It was the exact same truck—and not very far away at all.

Stick Dog repeated, "We follow the truck."

And that's exactly what they did.

CHAPTER 9

DRIPS ARE DRIPPY

What followed over the next hour—and the next mile—was a pattern that Stick Dog came to understand and, more important, predict. The truck stopped three times, and each time the same things happened in the exact same order.

Stick Dog wanted to make sure they had all paid attention. He was beginning to think that maybe, just maybe, he could steer his friends to a greater ice cream reward than just a few small puddles every twenty minutes. This would be, he thought, one of their toughest food-snatching missions ever.

They would deal with many, many humans.
The truck itself was large and intimidating.
And it was moving.

Stick Dog knew that lots of humans and
big, moving vehicles do not make it very
easy to grab something to eat. But he also
knew something else: he had never tasted
anything as sweet and delicious as the small
puddles left behind from those ice cream
drippings. Not only were they delicious,
they were also cold and wet—the perfect
combination on this mega-hot day.

He knew it was worth the risk.

After the truck made its third stop—and
the third bunch of colored puddles was
licked dry—Mutt, Poo-Poo, Karen, and

Stripes prepared to race after it again. They stretched their legs and gathered their energy. But Stick Dog stopped them.

"This isn't working," he said simply.

"What do you mean, Stick Dog?" asked Karen with surprise. "We're tasting some amazing flavors. And we've got it down to a pretty good routine. It seems safe and everything."

Mutt, Stripes, and Poo-Poo wagged their tails in agreement.

"We're getting some great flavors here, that's true," Stick Dog responded. "But the reward isn't worth the effort. I'm getting tired of all this chasing, and at the end, all we get are a few good laps at a few small puddles. We're just getting the tiny drippings from that ice cream. We need more than that. It's delicious—some of the best flavors I've ever tasted, to be honest. But ultimately not very satisfying."

At this, the others all came to the immediate understanding that Stick Dog was right.

"What are we going to do, Stick Dog?" asked Karen.

"We actually need to grab some of that ice cream from the truck," he answered.

"But how?" Mutt asked.

"Let's think about it a minute," said Stick Dog as he led them into the shade of a big oak tree by the side of the road. There were a few smaller trees, bushes, and mailboxes around them, and it was a fairly secure place to decide their plan of action. "We've chased and observed this ice cream truck for a while now. What have we learned so far?"

Karen spoke up first. "I like the light-brown flavor the best! That's what I've learned."

LIGHT BROWN!

At that, Stripes, Mutt, and Poo-Poo all declared their favorite colors too.

"Okay. Umm, that's good to know," Stick Dog said. "But what have we learned about the whole process? About the pattern of things? About the truck and where it goes and what the driver and the other humans do? What have we learned that will help us get some ice cream?"

Poo-Poo, Stripes, Karen, and Mutt all thought about this for a moment. They tried their best to help Stick Dog.

Mutt said, "I have some information that might be useful, Stick Dog."

"Okay, let's hear it."

"It's really hot out today," Mutt said with satisfaction in his voice.

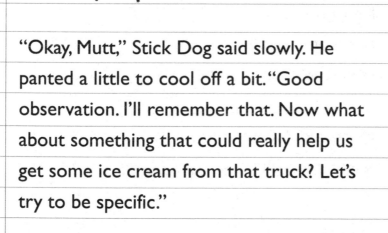

"Okay, Mutt," Stick Dog said slowly. He panted a little to cool off a bit. "Good observation. I'll remember that. Now what about something that could really help us get some ice cream from that truck? Let's try to be specific."

Karen then said, "Stick Dog, I have something important to say."

"Go ahead."

"I've changed my mind," she said. "I think I like the yellow color the best. Instead of the light brown."

YELLOW!

"Okay, Karen," said Stick Dog. He knew that the ice cream truck was getting farther and farther away—even though it was moving quite slowly. "I'll make a note of that."

Poo-Poo seemed to take this all very seriously. "I have an observation that could help," he said, and pointed to where the truck had been. "The truck is no longer there."

Stick Dog looked at the spot where Poo-Poo pointed. The truck hadn't been there for at least ten minutes. In fact, they had already raced in and licked the small, colorful ice cream puddles after the truck had moved down the street.

"Yes, it's been gone for a little while now,"
Stick Dog said.

"I just didn't want us all attacking the truck
when it's not even there. You know what
I mean?" Poo-Poo explained. He then sat
back on his hind legs and bumped his front
paws against each other five or six times.
"That would be kind of foolish, don't you
think? We'd all be banging into each other
and stuff."

Stick Dog looked back and forth a couple of times between Poo-Poo and the empty space where the truck had been. "Do you really think we would try to attack the truck when it isn't even there?"

Poo-Poo got back on all fours and sort of shuffled a few steps closer to Stick Dog. He lowered his voice to a whisper and said, "Look, Stick Dog. You and I would probably notice. We are the real brains in this group, after all. But I don't know about these other guys. You know what I mean?"

Stick Dog nodded, and Poo-Poo shuffled back to his spot.

"Do you mind if I interrupt, Stick Dog?" asked Karen. She was polite enough to

wait until Poo-Poo stopped whispering and
returned to his place.

"No. Not at all."

"It's the brown one. That's my favorite,"
she said. "My mind changed back again. Just
thought you should know."

BROWN!!

"Okay, Karen," he said. "I'm glad you told me."

"No problem. No problem at all."

Stripes spoke up next. She was a little envious that the others had come up with important observations, and she had worked very hard to come up with one of her own. It wasn't always easy to be surrounded by so many dogs with so many smart ideas. It made her try extra-hard.

"I have an observation to make too, Stick Dog."

"Okay, Stripes. What is it?"

"When I was watching that truck, I think I noticed something really important," she began. "You know how those ice cream drips made those colorful puddles?"

"Mmm-hmm."

"Well, it's about those drips," Stripes continued, but her voice slowed down. It was almost like the pressure got to her a little bit. Now her idea was kind of evaporating out of her mind. She was so concerned about coming up with a great observation. Then she came up with one. And then she got so excited about actually coming up with an idea that she forgot what it was.

"Yes? About the drips?" Stick Dog encouraged.

"Umm, I think, umm. Those drips," Stripes murmured, and waited. She really hoped that great observation would pop back into her mind. But it didn't. So she said, "They're drippy."

Stick Dog stared at Stripes, but not for very long. That's because Karen decided now would be a good time to say something again.

"Stick Dog?"

Stick Dog held up his paw. "Don't tell me," he said. "The yellowish ice cream puddle is now your favorite again, right?"

"No, Mister Furry Pants," Karen said, and smiled. She was pretty happy that Stick Dog hadn't guessed what she was going to say. "I just thought you should know that my mind *hasn't* changed since the last time. Light brown is still my favorite."

Stick Dog closed his eyes and nodded. "Okay," he whispered.

"Wait a minute, wait a minute," Karen said, and snapped her head up and looked off into the distance. Then she lowered her head to look at Stick Dog again. "Yep, that's right. Still light brown. Thought maybe my mind changed again there for a minute. But it didn't."

"Okay," Stick Dog sighed, and addressed them all. "Let's see if I got all the information from you guys that we'll need to get our paws on some ice cream. Here's what we know: Karen's favorite flavor is light brown. It's very hot out today. The ice cream truck is no longer where it was before. And the ice cream drips are drippy. Is that right? Did I forget anything?"

"Nope," answered Mutt with satisfaction. The others seemed pleased with their answers too. "That about sums it up."

"Okay, then," said Stick Dog. He paced a
bit, thinking to himself. "I have a couple of
observations that might be helpful as well."

"Don't you think the four of us have already
covered everything?" asked Poo-Poo.

"Oh yes. Yes," said Stick Dog. "I'm just going
to try to fill in a few details, that's all."

"Sounds okay to me," replied Poo-Poo matter-of-factly. He plopped down to listen, as did the others.

"There's definitely a pattern here. And maybe we can take advantage of it by knowing and predicting that pattern," Stick Dog began. He seemed to talk to himself as much as to the others. He listed the order of things the way he remembered them happening. "The driver gets into the truck and turns on the music, and the truck starts moving. It rolls along very slowly for about seven minutes."

All the running and chasing from the previous hour had worn everybody out. Poo-Poo, Stripes, Mutt, and Karen were all now down on their bellies with their chins resting on their front paws. They watched Stick Dog pace back and forth in front of them. It was sort of like watching a gold pocket watch go back and forth when someone is trying to hypnotize you.

"The humans follow the truck on their bikes on the sidewalk. Some of them just walk or run," Stick Dog continued. "The truck stops. The music stops. The driver gets out."

Poo-Poo's
eyes closed.

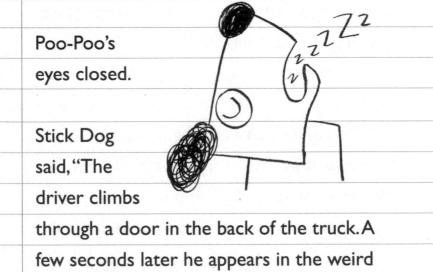

Stick Dog
said, "The
driver climbs

through a door in the back of the truck. A few seconds later he appears in the weird

screen window
to speak to the
humans who have
gathered there."

Mutt's eyes closed.

"One by one he brings each human
the ice cream circles, opens the screen
window, and hands them out. Some
humans stay by the truck and talk as they
lap at the circles. Others wander away
from the truck."

Karen's eyes closed.

"When they all
have their ice
cream, the driver
closes the window

and comes out the back. He walks around
the other side and climbs back in behind
the steering wheel."

Stripes's eyes closed.

"After he gets in, the
annoying music starts,
and the truck slowly
drives away again,"
Stick Dog concluded,
and stopped pacing. He
looked at the others—
who were all now asleep.
"Is that about it? Is that the pattern?"

Nobody answered.

Stick Dog turned away and gave a sudden
loud cough. Without turning back around,

he repeated, "Is that about it? Is that the pattern?"

COUGH!

Everybody sighed, "Mm-hmm."

"Did I forget anything?"

"Hmm-mm."

"Okay," Stick Dog said. "We're going to catch up to that truck and pass it. We're going to try to predict where it will stop next. Then we'll figure out a way to get into that truck and get the ice cream. Got it?"

"Got it," they all sighed as they rose up and stretched.

"Since we rested a little, we should be able to catch up to it pretty easily," Stick Dog commented.

"We weren't resting!" they all said quickly.

"Oh, okay. My mistake," Stick Dog said as he took off.

"I was dreaming of light-brown puddles," Karen whispered to the others before they chased after Stick Dog. "Mmm-mmm. I love the flavor light brown."

Chapter 10

DANCE PARTY

Stick Dog and his friends raced after
the truck with increased energy and
enthusiasm. They knew they were running
toward the potential of a huge and
delicious ice cream treat.

The dogs remained careful even as
they sped along. They scurried through
backyards and the edge of the forest
whenever they could—but they always
stayed on a parallel track with the street.

It was only a matter of several minutes until the dogs caught up with and passed the ice cream truck. The truck, after all, moved quite slowly—and it was now stopped again to serve several more humans some ice cream.

After running past the truck's current parking spot for a few minutes, the dogs slowed and stopped near the street again. In the far distance, they could see where the truck was still parked behind them— and they could see quite a few humans still standing in line there.

"Okay, we have a few minutes," Stick Dog said as he looked in both directions along the street. "He's going to hand out ice cream there for a little while and then drive slowly in this direction. The question is: where will he stop next?"

"Couldn't we just *make* him stop?" Karen asked.

"How would we do that, Karen?" asked Mutt.

"You know, run in front of the truck while he's driving." Karen shrugged. "He's sure to stop when he hits us. When we get hit, the one who is hurt the least could climb into the truck somehow and grab the ice cream."

Mutt considered this for a moment. "Sounds good. Do you want to just run across the street as the truck goes by or straight at it or what?"

"Oh, I think across is best. That would be more of a surprise—and increase the likelihood of being hit," answered Karen. She then turned to address Stick Dog. "Do you agree, Stick Dog? Do you think running across would be the best way to get hit by the truck?"

Stick Dog had noticed something down the street—a large open space without many houses around. But he wasn't

completely distracted—he still overheard
the conversation. He shook his head and
said, "We're not going to stop the truck by
getting hit by it."

"Why not?" asked Karen, genuinely curious.
"You don't think it will work?"

"No, I mean—" he started to say and then stopped himself. His mind was busy working out the details of a possible plan, but he knew he had to stop this idea right away. "I mean, I guess it would work. But I don't think we should get hit by the truck. I think it would hurt. A lot."

"Oh," Karen said. She considered Stick Dog's response for a few seconds. Then she added, "So, it *would* work—you just don't think it *should* work?"

"Umm. Right."

"So it's a great idea. We're just not going to use it."

Stick Dog hesitated in answering, but

ultimately said, "Right."

"I can live with that," Karen said, and nodded. "But I don't know how we're going to get into that truck if we don't make it stop."

While Stick Dog continued to think, Poo-Poo attempted to answer Karen's concerns. He said, "I chase cars and catch them all the time."

"You do?" Karen asked.

"Oh, yeah. It's easy," Poo-Poo replied. He came across as quietly confident on the subject. "You just have to know how to do it, that's all."

Mutt asked, "How do you do it, Poo-Poo?"

"You just have to pick the right car,"
Poo-Poo explained. He liked the way the
others were paying such close attention to
him.

Stripes was interested now too. She asked,
"Where do you find the right car?"

"Oh, just about anywhere. I find a lot of my
car targets at the mall down Highway 16."

Karen observed, "That makes sense. Cars
move much slower in a parking lot than
on a street. And they don't drive in long,
straight lines. They sort of go around in
circles—like I do when I'm chasing my tail."

Karen then started chasing her tail.

Poo-Poo didn't seem to notice Karen's comment. He was going on about his car-catching expertise.

"I've caught dozens of them," he continued. "I stalk around behind bumpers or tires or guardrails or whatever. Then I pick my target and pounce. I run full speed until I catch up to that car. It usually only takes a few seconds and then—BAM!—I run right into it headfirst. But you know, that doesn't bother me too much."

"You really do that, Poo-Poo?" Mutt asked.

"Sure. I really teach those things a lesson. No car gets the better of old Mr. Poo-Poo."

"Wow!" Karen panted. She was no longer chasing her tail. She hadn't caught it. "I had no idea you were such a good car chaser, Poo-Poo."

"It just comes naturally to me."

Stick Dog had been listening while also trying to figure out where the truck would stop next. He now joined the conversation.

"Poo-Poo? One question," he said.

"Yes? What is it, Stick Dog?"

"When you chase and catch these cars, are they moving or are they parked?"

"Parked, of course," Poo-Poo answered, and laughed a little to himself. "Who would chase a moving car? That's ridiculous."

While Mutt, Stripes, and Karen groaned, Stick Dog looked back and forth between the street and the parked ice cream truck. He tried to calculate how far the truck would travel once it started to move again—and tried to figure out the kind of place it might stop next. It seemed he was getting closer to a solution.

This whole thing Stick Dog is going through kind of reminds me of word problems in math. I can't stand word problems. Can you?

You know what I mean, right?

Example: You're on a train and you are 60 miles away from the train station. The train is going 20 miles per hour. How long will it take for you to get to the train station?

I had that exact question on a math quiz.

Do you know what my answer was?

I wrote: *I have no idea because I really dislike word problems, and I jumped off the train.*

Unfortunately, I didn't find out how long it took me to get to the train station. I did, however, find out exactly how long it takes me to get from math class to the principal's office.

Anyway, Stick Dog was working this all out while the others talked about stopping the truck. Stripes, it turned out, also had an idea.

"I know how to do it," she said. "See that bridge down the street about halfway to the truck?

They all looked at the bridge.

"Well, we get to the top of that bridge," continued Stripes. "When he drives that truck under the bridge, we jump onto the roof of the truck. While he's driving, we start dancing."

"Dancing?!" Poo-Poo, Karen, and Mutt asked at once.

"Dancing," Stripes confirmed. She turned sideways and shook her hips a little to demonstrate before continuing. "See, the driver will hear our paws banging away above him and wonder what in the world is going on. He'll park and get out and see this great dance party. Then he'll think, 'Hey, I've never danced on top of a truck before! That looks like fun!' So he'll climb up and start dancing too. He'll be so busy dancing and screaming and stuff that we'll be able to

jump off the truck and get all the ice cream
we want while he's still on top."

As soon as Stripes was done explaining her
idea, Mutt, Poo-Poo, and Karen began to
dance. Mutt wriggled his body from front

to back, releasing an old chewed-up tennis ball and three crayons from his fur. Poo-Poo got up on his hind legs, balanced on his toes, and put his front legs out to the side dramatically. And Karen began to turn in a circle.

Karen's dance practice didn't last too long, to be honest. That's because as soon as she started turning in that circle, she spotted her tail and began to chase it again.

She didn't catch it.

Stick Dog, meanwhile, had a great deal of satisfaction on his face. He was beginning to suspect where that truck would stop next. And the more he thought about it, the more certain he felt. He thought that maybe, just maybe, they would be able to get their paws on some ice cream.

But he knew he had to stop the dance party first.

"I just have one issue with your plan," Stick Dog said.

It was as if Stripes had anticipated Stick Dog's objection. "Is it the jumping off the bridge part?" she asked. "Because it's a pretty low bridge."

"No," Stick Dog answered.

"Is it timing the landing on the truck just right?" asked Stripes. "Because remember, it's moving pretty slowly."

"No."

"Is it keeping our balance while we're dancing and the truck is moving and going around curves and stuff?"

"No."

"Then what is it, Stick Dog?" Stripes asked. "Why can't we use my dance-party idea to stop the truck?"

"Listen," he said, and tilted his head slightly. Far down the road, the final customer had been served, and the truck had begun moving slowly toward them again. And the music had started. "I don't think we can dance to that annoying music. And even if we could, I'm sure the driver could not. He doesn't look like he has any rhythm at all."

Stripes frowned and punched her front right paw toward the ground. "Dang it!" she said. "And everything else about the plan would have worked perfectly too. It's just a darn shame."

"It sure is," said Stick Dog as he eyed the slowly approaching ice cream truck. "But right now we need to get moving. I think

I have an idea where that truck is going to stop next."

"You mean we don't have to stop it ourselves?" asked Mutt.

"No, we don't," answered Stick Dog. "Remember, it makes a lot of stops to give humans ice cream."

"Oh, that's right!" exclaimed Mutt. He and the others seemed quite relieved about this.

"Where's it going to stop next, Stick Dog?" asked Stripes.

"Come on, I'll show you," he said, and padded off along the street.

The others followed closely behind—but only after Stripes sighed and said, "I really wanted to show you guys all my nifty dance moves."

Chapter 11

POO-POO FIGURES
IT OUT

There was an open space with a big building a few minutes' run up the street. And Stick Dog led them there. It was a school with plenty of playground equipment and a huge maple tree that provided a generous area of shade.

NEAR NORTH MONTESSORI SCHOOL

Of course, it was right in the middle of summer, and school was not in session. There were only ten or twelve humans— several small ones and a few large ones— from the neighborhood scattered about the playground. Some were on a set of tall swings, the smallest humans were in a sandbox, and a few more were on a climbing dome.

Stick Dog stopped across the street from the school playground. There was a line of several mailboxes; and Karen, Stripes, Mutt, and Poo-Poo settled safely there as well. Through the mailbox posts they could see the playground clearly without being detected.

"I think the ice cream truck is going to stop here next," Stick Dog said to the others as he surveyed the entire layout of the playground. There was a large semicircular driveway that entered and exited to the street. The small humans played and climbed and swung within the driveway's semicircle.

"Why do you think the truck will stop here, Stick Dog?" Mutt asked.

"Because there are plenty of humans here who will want ice cream," he answered. He looked down the street to see how far away the ice cream truck was. "The music is getting louder. He's going to be here in just a couple of minutes. I think I know

exactly where he's going to park when he
gets here."

"Where?" Stripes asked.

"There," Stick Dog said, and pointed. "In the
shade beneath that big maple tree. I think
he will actually pull into the driveway when
he sees that shade. He'll want to stay as
cool as possible
just like us. If he
parks there, we'll
have a chance.
If he stays on
the street, we'll
just have to go
back to my pipe
and the creek.
We'll have to

be satisfied with the ice cream drips we've already had."

"If he parks there, how are we going to get in the truck and get the ice cream?" asked Mutt.

It was a difficult question to answer, because it would depend both on Stick Dog's understanding of the ice cream truck's regular routine and a great deal of luck.

"When he stops, the humans will go over to the far side of the truck by the school to get their ice cream. They will go to the screen window on that side," Stick Dog explained. "We'll be able to see that the coast is clear from here. When it is, we'll sprint across the street and the playground and find a way into that truck."

Karen, Mutt, Poo-Poo, and Stripes all looked at him.

And I bet you know why, don't you?

It's because Stick Dog usually had more precise step-by-step plans when it came to grabbing some tasty food. This time, however, there was a lot left to chance.

"That's it?" asked Stripes doubtfully. "We hope he parks in the shade? And if he does, we find a way into the truck? I mean, really? Maybe we should go back to my dance-party idea."

"No, no," Stick Dog said, and smiled. "There's more to it than that. If I can get into that truck—"

But it was too late to explain any more.
The annoying music was getting louder. The
truck was close. Very close.

They all turned to watch it. It was both
threatening and inviting. It was a big, moving
vehicle—something all the dogs knew could
be very dangerous. But they also knew that
some of the most delicious flavors they had
ever tasted were inside that truck.

"Turn into the driveway," whispered Stick
Dog as it passed by slowly. "Turn into the
driveway."

TURN.
TURN.
TURN.

The truck slowed down to a near stop.

"Oh no," said Mutt. "It's going to park in the street!"

Stripes, Poo-Poo, and Karen all moaned. After tasting all those puddles made of delicious ice cream drippings, it was terrible to think that was all the ice cream they would ever taste: a few tiny drips.

Stick Dog was still watching. He whispered, "Turn. Turn. Turn."

Then he saw something.

A small light.

A small, blinking light.

It was the ice cream truck's flashing turn signal. The truck pulled slowly into the driveway and parked smack dab in the middle of that huge shady area.

Mutt, Karen, Poo-Poo, and Stripes began to hop and yelp.

"Shh," said Stick Dog. "We have to move as soon as we can. Everybody hold still and watch."

The music stopped. The driver got out. He waved at the humans on the playground and climbed into the back of the truck. Stick Dog knew he was getting ready to give out ice cream.

Most important, every human on the
playground began walking—or running—
to the other side of the truck. The smaller
humans were the first ones out of sight;
the larger humans were the last.

Stick Dog said just one thing when the
playground was empty.

"Now!"

They looked both ways and then raced
across the street and across the playground.
They passed a swing set, a flagpole, a
climbing dome, and a sandbox on their way.
They stopped near a seesaw right next to
the truck. Panting there, the dogs quickly
considered how to reach the open window.

"Let's just stack up again," Mutt said. He
spread out his legs and lowered his head,

ready to form the base of a dog stack. "It's worked before."

Stick Dog shook his head. "It won't work," he said. "We don't have the time. And I have to be the one who goes in—that's part of the plan. And I'm too heavy to be on top."

They could all hear the happy voices of the humans on the other side as they ordered their ice cream. Karen could see their shoes when she looked underneath the truck.

"We have to hurry!" she exclaimed. "They're moving around over there. They're going to be back soon; I just know it."

"We have a minute. He doesn't serve the ice cream that fast," Stick Dog said. He jerked his head back and forth to find something—anything—that could help him get inside. "I have to get in there."

It was then that Poo-Poo said, "I always find when I'm faced with a particularly perplexing problem that it's best to sit down and think about it. When I do, often a solution will present itself."

Stick Dog looked at him. Considering the absolute urgency of the moment, he really couldn't believe what Poo-Poo had just said. He watched as Poo-Poo sat down on the end of the seesaw. It sank down, bounced

a bit, and stopped against the ground.
Poo-Poo appeared to be deep in thought
already.

In an instant, Stick Dog was by the middle
of the long seesaw board. He stared at it
from one end to the other. He saw the
curved rocking mechanism in the center.
He saw the ends move every time Poo-Poo
shifted his weight.

"Poo-Poo," Stick Dog
said. "Get off there
for a minute, please."

"Not now, Stick
Dog," Poo-Poo said.
"I'm trying to come
up with a way to get you into that truck's
open window."

Stick Dog tried to keep his cool. He knew one or more of those humans probably had their ice cream now—and he knew they would soon return to the playground to lap at those delicious colored circles.

"You've already found a solution," Stick Dog said. "But you need to move."

Poo-Poo got up, and Stick Dog quickly took his place at the end of the seesaw. He didn't sit down but stood firmly with his legs spread out as much as he could for balance. Stick Dog turned his head over his shoulder to address the others. "You guys climb on the other end of the board. Quickly!"

There was no hesitation. The others didn't know what Stick Dog was up to—but they could tell he had solved the problem.

Stripes was the first up. She jumped to the center of the seesaw and walked to the end opposite Stick Dog. Stick Dog began to rise off the ground immediately. Then Mutt climbed on and walked toward Stripes and sat right next to her. Stick Dog rose even farther into the air. With one end almost touching the ground now, Karen was able to step up onto the board easily between Stripes's legs. It was the little bit of extra weight they needed.

Stick Dog rose as high as the board would lift him—almost to the exact height of the truck's window. He crouched down a little and calculated the distance and trajectory he would need. After estimating the jumping angle necessary, Stick Dog narrowed his eyes and clenched his teeth.

And leaped.

He flew straight through the middle of that truck's window, barely brushing the fur on his back against the top of the window frame.

He was in.

The others watched in amazement. They couldn't believe that Stick Dog had actually made it into the truck.

Poo-Poo looked at Mutt, Stripes, and

Karen, who had all stepped off the seesaw now. He shrugged his shoulders and said, "I told you I'd figure it out."

Stick Dog propped himself up in the window to talk to the others.

"You guys go hide now! Fast!" He talked quickly and glanced all around to make certain no human had come back yet. "When the truck starts moving, follow it from a safe distance. I'll take it from here."

The others heard the urgency in his voice and saw the controlled panic on his face. They hid—and hid fast.

Stripes ran to the flagpole and hid behind it. Mutt ran to the climbing dome, stooped low on the ground under it, and covered one eye with a paw. Poo-Poo hid behind a swing. Karen sprinted toward the sandbox, jumped nine inches into the air, and plummeted down into the sand pile, burying herself the best she could.

Stick Dog watched his friends find their hiding places.

Unfortunately, he could see them all quite
clearly. He waved frantically at them and
pointed across the street to the mailboxes
where they had hidden before. Poo-Poo,
Mutt, Karen, and Stripes all understood
his motions instantly and raced across the
street to their previous hiding place.

Knowing they were safe, Stick Dog turned
his body around to look and listen out the
truck's windows.

He knew he was on his own now.

What he didn't know was this: he was
about to be seen by a human.

Chapter 12

WOGGY!

Stick Dog stretched out across the long bench seat in the front part of the truck. He listened for two distinct sounds.

First, he wanted to hear the screen window slide shut. He knew that would mean the driver was done serving ice cream to the other humans.

Second, he would hear the driver climb out and close the back door. That would mean, Stick Dog knew, that the driver was about to return to climb into the truck and drive away.

It was then that Stick Dog would need to put the rest of his ice cream–snatching plan into action. He nodded his head backward, flopping his ears back a bit to hear even better. He looked up and out of the passenger-side window and listened. There were fewer human voices with every minute that passed.

Finally, there was just one voice left. It was female and sounded like a large human. "I'll just take a vanilla cone for me and my doodlebug here."

"Coming right up" was the answer that Stick Dog heard.

He also heard the large female human pacing a little bit outside the truck as she waited. The steps seemed to come closer, and Stick Dog crouched down even lower. He listened and stared up out of that window.

Then a small human stared right at him through that window and yelled, "Woggy!" The little human began bouncing up and down. Stick Dog could see a larger human arm holding the tiny human.

And the tiny human pointed at him and exclaimed, "Woggy! Woggy! WOGGY!!" louder and louder.

Stick Dog instinctively held his paw up to his mouth to try to hush the tiny human.

This had an enormous impact.

It started screaming, "WOGGY! WOGGY!! WOGGY!!!" and bounced even more wildly in the big human's arms.

"Yes, yes, I know. You're a little doggy," the big female human said in a calming voice. "And the little doggy is going to get an ice cream cone, don't worry. But calm down. You're going to jump right out of my arms."

With that, the tiny human was gone.

Stick Dog panted his
relief and heard the
big female hand some
coins to the ice cream
man. There were no
more voices near the
truck. All the humans
had returned to the
playground to eat their sweet treats. Stick
Dog heard the screen window slide shut.
The truck vibrated. He guessed the man
had just stepped out from the back of the
truck. Two seconds later the back door
slammed shut.

The man was returning.

And Stick Dog knew he had to get out—
fast.

He reached out the passenger-side window
as far as he could with his front paws. For a
split second, sheer panic coursed through
his body. His paws found nothing but air.

But then, with extra stretching effort, they scratched against metal—the shelf that ran along the side. Using his front paws to balance on that shelf, Stick Dog lifted his back legs onto the lower edge of the passenger-side window. He closed his eyes, shifted his weight forward, and pushed hard with his back legs.

For the shortest instant, he didn't know if he would keep his balance or fall down to the blacktop. He leaned in toward the truck, scooted his legs forward, and got all four paws onto the shelf. He stood there for a moment to rebalance his body on the slick metal shelf.

But only for a moment.

He heard the driver's door open and felt the truck shake as the man sat down behind the steering wheel. He heard the annoying music start blaring above him. He felt the truck shimmy as the driver turned on the engine.

Stick Dog took three steps on the shelf until he was at the screen window on the side of the truck.

He pushed it open with his nose.

He squeezed himself in and fell down to the floor in the back of the truck.

Stick Dog stood up and felt the truck begin to move. He had never been in a vehicle before, and he leaned back and forth and

bumped into things until he got used to it. What he bumped into were boxes and boxes filled with cartons and cartons of ice cream.

He sat down for a moment as the ice cream truck rolled slowly out of the school driveway and onto the street.

For seventeen seconds, Stick Dog just sat

there. He had made it. He was inside the
truck. There was ice cream everywhere.

And it was wonderfully, wonderfully cold
inside.

Chapter 13

KAREN TACKLES STICK DOG

Stick Dog took pleasure in his accomplishment—and the coldness—for only a moment. He knew it was just a matter of time—about seven minutes or so—until the truck stopped again. When it did, the driver would come immediately to the back of the truck to start serving ice cream to a new bunch of humans. Stick Dog would be caught for sure if he didn't hurry.

He began to open the flaps of several of the cardboard boxes. Inside each box were six large, circular cartons of ice cream.

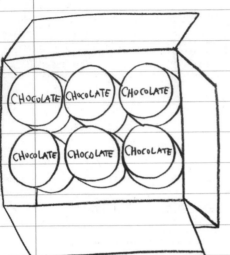

He pulled out several of the cartons. He saw words that he didn't recognize— "chocolate," "vanilla," "mint chocolate chip," "blue moon," "butter pecan," "cookie dough"—but spent absolutely no time considering them.

He pushed one of the boxes beneath the screen window and climbed on top of it. There, he bent down, grasped a circular carton by the lid with his mouth, and pulled it up. He pushed carton after carton out the open screen window. He heard them

PLOP! when they landed on the street. After the seventh or eighth ice cream carton, Stick Dog stretched forward and leaned his head out the screen window to look behind the truck.

VANILLA

He could see Mutt, Stripes, Karen, and Poo-Poo as they ran along the sidewalk. Whenever they saw a carton roll along the blacktop, one of them would check for traffic and then scoot out into the street to push it to the side with their nose.

Stick Dog retrieved a few more cartons of ice cream and pushed them out the screen window in the same manner. He had lost count, but he knew he must have pushed close to a dozen cartons out to the street. And while he had lost track of how many cartons he had pushed out, he had not lost track of the time.

That truck would stop again pretty soon.

It was time to leave. It was time to jump out.

Stick Dog climbed up on the box and pushed his head out the screen window. He looked forward down the road. He needed to find a soft landing spot—and soon.

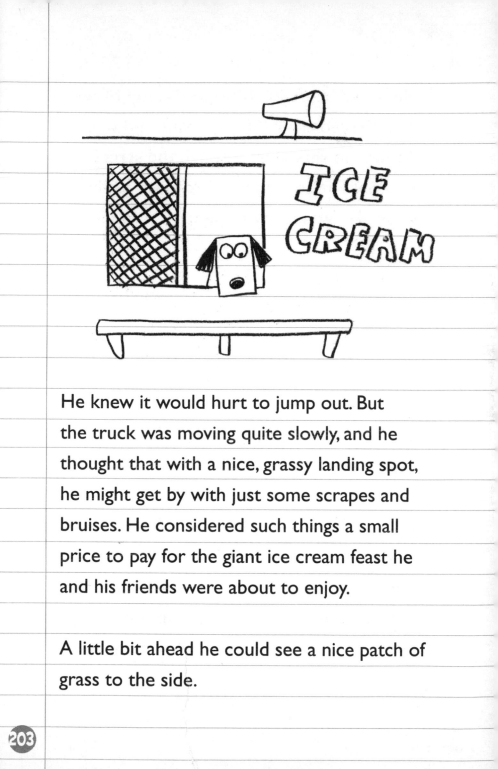

He knew it would hurt to jump out. But
the truck was moving quite slowly, and he
thought that with a nice, grassy landing spot,
he might get by with just some scrapes and
bruises. He considered such things a small
price to pay for the giant ice cream feast he
and his friends were about to enjoy.

A little bit ahead he could see a nice patch of
grass to the side.

He pulled himself fully up to the top of the box, glanced around for humans, and then pushed his shoulders through the screen window. The soft, grassy patch was getting closer. He was ready to jump.

But he didn't.

Because he couldn't.

There was a sound coming up from behind the ice cream truck on the road. It was louder than even the annoying music.

It was a sound every stray dog feared. And it was a sound that a stray dog who had just snuck into an ice cream truck, snatched several cartons of ice cream, and thrown them out the window to his friends feared more than anything in the world.

It was a police siren.

Stick Dog ducked back into the truck and jumped down to the floor. As he did so, he knocked over the box that he had climbed on.

He knew about police cars. They were fast and loud, with flashing red lights. Big humans in blue uniforms were inside them. They were called policemen. They had loud, booming voices. Most important, Stick Dog knew that policemen who drove around in the loud cars with flashing lights did not like stray dogs.

He and his friends had been chased away from garbage cans, Picasso Park, and the back of the mall a few times by these giant humans in blue uniforms.

For the first time in a long time, Stick Dog was scared.

He was caught in this enclosed space. There was no way out. Stick Dog knew he couldn't hop out the window now. The policeman was too close. He had been stealing food from the ice cream truck. The evidence was behind him down the street. And he had nowhere to go.

The ice cream truck slowed to a stop, and the music stopped playing. Stick Dog could hear the police car stop behind the ice cream truck, spitting gravel across the pavement. He heard a door slam and the heavy footsteps of a policeman approaching the vehicle. He was coming to speak to the driver.

Stick Dog knew what that policeman would say. He would say, "You have an ice cream thief in the back of your truck. I've seen ice cream cartons scattered down the street for the last half mile. I'm going to catch whoever is back there and take him away forever."

That's what the policeman was going to say.

Stick Dog listened as the policeman made his way with thundering steps to the driver's-side window. It was, indeed, a booming voice. Stick Dog could hear it easily through the open screen window even though it was on the opposite side of the truck. And he could hear the driver's softer voice as well.

"Yes, officer?" the ice cream truck driver said. "Was I doing something wrong? I certainly wasn't speeding."

"I have to tell you something," the policeman said in his deep voice.

"Yes? What's that?"

Stick Dog squeezed his eyes shut. He knew what was coming. For that instant before the policeman answered, Stick Dog thought of Poo-Poo, Stripes, Karen, and Mutt. In his mind, he could see them enjoying all that ice cream he had thrown out just minutes ago. It made him feel good to know that all his efforts had paid off for them in such a big, tasty way.

"I have to tell you," the policeman continued, "on a day as hot as this, I could really go for a chocolate cone."

Stick Dog couldn't believe his ears. He was not caught snatching the ice cream. The others either hid it fast or the policeman had just turned from a side street or something. He felt a tremendous sense of relief.

But only for a single second.

That's because a single second later the driver said, "I totally understand, officer. I'll make you one right away."

Stick Dog felt the truck move a bit as the driver got out. And he heard his door slam shut. He was coming around to open the back door to climb in and make the policeman an ice cream treat. In seconds, the back door would open, and the first thing the driver would see would be Stick Dog.

There wasn't even enough time to push the box back and scramble up to the open window. He would be trapped by the driver. And the policeman was right there to help him.

The door handle turned. The door itself cracked open, allowing a sliver of bright sunlight to enter the back of the truck. The door swung halfway open, flooding the truck with light and illuminating Stick Dog right in the middle of the back compartment. He could see the driver's hand on the edge of the door.

Then the policeman called, "Hey, you know what?"

And the driver's hand disappeared as he turned to walk back around the corner of the truck to answer, "What's that?"

It was Stick Dog's one and only chance.

And he took it.

Stick Dog quickly and quietly jumped from the back and ran down the street toward his friends. He heard the policeman's voice as he ran safely away.

"I changed my mind," he said. "Can you make that vanilla?"

Stick Dog didn't look back. He didn't know if the ice cream man saw him run down the street or not. He suspected that he probably had not. It was a good ten seconds before the driver got back inside the truck. And in those ten seconds, Stick Dog had covered an awful lot of ground.

Stick Dog did not stop running. He wanted to get as far away from that truck—and that policeman—as he could.

He only slowed and stopped when he
heard this:

"Stick Dog! Over here!"

It was Karen.
She ran out
from a group
of honeysuckle
bushes in a
yard close to
the street. She
sprinted at
him and lunged
at him and
knocked him sideways. "I knew you could
do it! I knew you could!"

Poo-Poo, Mutt, and Stripes all stuck
their heads out from that huge clump of

honeysuckle bushes. They waved and smiled.
They had ice cream all over their mouths
and faces.

"Come on! This way!" Karen exclaimed.

When Stick Dog pushed through the
honeysuckle leaves and flowers, he found
that they were in another of those super-
secure areas. There was a circle of bushes, a
big green metal box, and plenty of room for
them all.

And there were eleven cartons of cold,
cold ice cream.

The End

Tom Watson lives in Chicago with his wife, daughter, and son. He also has a dog, as you could probably guess. The dog is a Labrador-Newfoundland mix. Tom says he looks like a Labrador with a bad perm. He wanted to name the dog "Put Your Shirt On" (please don't ask why), but he was outvoted by his family. The dog's name is Shadow. Early in his career Tom worked in politics, including a stint as the chief speechwriter for the governor of Ohio. This experience helped him develop the unique storytelling narrative style of the Stick Dog books. Tom's time in politics also made him realize a very important thing: kids are way smarter than adults. And it's a lot more fun and rewarding to write stories for them than to write speeches for grown-ups.

Visit www.stickdogbooks.com for more fun stuff.